Teen Guide
to Personal
Financial Management

Teen Guide

to Personal Financial Management

Marjolijn Bijlefeld
and
Sharon K. Zoumbaris

GREENWOOD PRESS
Westport, Connecticut • London

Library of Congress Cataloging-in-Publication Data

Bijlefeld, Marjolijn, 1960–
      Teen guide to personal financial management / by Marjolijn Bijlefeld and Sharon K.
Zoumbaris.
         p. cm.
      Includes bibliographical references and index.

         1. Teenagers—Finance, Personal. I. Zoumbaris, Sharon K., 1955– II. Title.
HG179.B478   2000
332.024'055—dc21   00–020464

British Library Cataloguing in Publication Data is available.

Library of Congress Catalog Card Number: 00–020464
ISBN 978-0-313-36092-3

First published in 2000

Greenwood Press, 88 Post Road West, Westport, CT 06881
An imprint of Greenwood Publishing Group, Inc.
www.greenwood.com

Printed in the United States of America

The paper used in this book complies with the
Permanent Paper Standard issued by the National
Information Standards Organization (Z39.48–1984).

10 9 8 7 6 5 4 3

Copyright Acknowledgments

The authors and publisher gratefully acknowledge permission for use of the following material:

Excerpts from authors' interviews with J. Jermain Bodine; Joanne R. Dempsey from Illinois Council on Economic Education; Dara Duguay from Jump$tart Coalition for Personal Financial Literacy; William B. Howard, Jr.; Ross Levin; Tracey Barnes Priestly; James E. Putnam; Roger Smith; Robert Billingsley; Dr. Harvey R. Carmichael; Joan L. Spence from Virginia Council on Economic Education.

"Semester Budget Worksheet" from the College Board Web site; "The Bill Graph" from the section on Financial Aid Services; "Net Worth Worksheet" from the Credit Education Loan Program courtesy of The College Board.

"Bank USA Guideline Sheet," "Welcome to USA Inc.," "Getting Ready for USA Market Day," and "The End of USA Inc.: A Company Report" by Kim Sigler.

Appendix C: "State Resources" courtesy of National Council on Economic Education.

Excerpts from *Genuine Progress Indicator: 1998 Update—Executive Summary* by Jonathan Rowe and Mark Anielski. Reprinted with permission, copyright 1999, Redefining Progress.

Appendix E: "66 Ways to Save Money" courtesy of Consumer Literacy Consortium.

"Buy a Car" by Karlys Wells. Courtesy of Kyle Yamnitz; available at www.Lesson PlansPage.com.

"What is Stock, or, Who Owns McDonalds?" courtesy of Securities Industry Foundation.

Every reasonable effort has been made to trace the owners of copyright materials in this book, but in some instances this has proven impossible. The authors and publisher will be glad to receive information leading to more complete acknowledgments in subsequent printings of the book and in the meantime extend their apologies for any omissions.

Contents

Contents ix

1

Introduction

On June 8, 1999, Tricia Johnson stood before a crowd gathered at a press conference. She told the audience that a year earlier, she had received a telephone call from police, saying her daughter, 18-year-old Mitzi Pool, a student at the University of Central Oklahoma, had hung herself with a bedsheet. Spread out on her bed were bills from her three credit cards totaling more than $2,500. Mitzi's pay from her part-time job was about $65 a week, her mother said.

Earlier in the evening, before Mitzi's anxiety gave way to the worst despondency, she had called her mother and told her she was in over her head. Her mother recalls trying to reassure her sobbing daughter, telling her that they'd find a way to work it out.

Mitzi's mother was joined on the press podium by Jane O'Donnell, mother of Sean Moyer, who committed suicide in 1998. His parents knew he had gotten one credit card when he was a freshman in college, but without their knowledge, he had gotten a total of 12 credit cards and ran up a $10,000 debt. In her statement, O'Donnell said:

A week before he killed himself Sean and I had a long talk about his debts and about his future. He told me he had no idea how to get out of his financial mess and didn't see much of a future for himself. He had wanted to go to law school but didn't think he could get a loan to pay tuition because he owed so much on his cards.

His father and I were appalled that he had gotten into so much debt but we also didn't have an extra $10,000 to pay his bills. He thought he was a failure at 22. I will never know the exact reason Sean killed himself—he didn't leave a note—but I have no doubt that his credit card debt played a significant part in his decision.

Mitzi's mother echoed those sentiments. After the shock of her daughter's suicide wore off, she said she was angry.

But I didn't know who to be more angry at: Mitzi or the credit card companies. I thought I had taught my daughter the value of money and responsibility. [When she was] 16 I co-signed a department store credit card for Mitzi with a $200 limit. She did so well with that. But her good credit gave her access to others, without my consent. So then I was angry at the credit card companies for issuing these cards. . . . The credit card companies target these young adults just like the tobacco industries. They lure them in and then they have them hooked. Hooked for a long time. These debts can tear a family up.

These women joined the Consumer Federation of America as it released a 90-page study by Georgetown University sociologist Robert Manning on student credit card debt. Manning's study suggested that far more students are in financial trouble with credit card debt than previously thought. For example, the study found that about 70% of undergraduates at four-year colleges have at least one credit card. "Revolvers"—those who carry debt from one billing cycle to the next—carry debts on these cards that average more than $2,000, with one-fifth carrying debts of more than $10,000. A number have also refinanced additional debt with student loans or private debt consolidation loans. The study, "Credit Cards on Campus: Costs and Consequences of Student Debt," was based on more than 300 interviews and more than 400 responses to a detailed questionnaire completed by students at Georgetown University, American University, and the University of Maryland.

The report argues that credit card issuers aggressively target this young market. Over the past decade, students obtained their first credit card at a younger age. In 1994, 66% of college students with at least one card received their first card before entering college or during their freshman year; in 1998, 81% had received their first card by the end of their freshman year.

According to the press release announcing the study, "Many colleges and universities not only permit aggressive credit card marketing on campus; they actually benefit financially from this marketing. Credit card issuers pay institutions for sponsorship of school programs, for support of student activities, for rental of on-campus solicitation tables, and for exclusive marketing agreements such as college 'affinity' credit cards. On the other hand, few issuers or institutions support effective financial education of undergraduates beginning with freshman orientation."

O'Donnell expressed her outrage at the ease with which students can obtain credit cards and that their ability to pay seems to have little bearing on the decision. "You can't attend a college event without seeing credit card booths giving students gifts for signing up. The University of Oklahoma's Web page allows a student to sign up without asking how much money they make. They do ask, however, how many of the student's other credit cards they want to transfer to the new card. There simply have to be some limits set on credit card companies before more students end up in bankruptcy or dead," she said.

The results of such large debts are varied. Students from wealthier families are often bailed out by their parents. But students whose parents can't afford to help have to work more hours at their jobs. As a result, they may have to cut back on their course load or, even worse, drop out of school. The press release quoted an unnamed University of Indiana administrator who said in 1998, "We lose more students to credit card debt than to academic failure."

Such disastrous financial footing early on has implications for years afterward. The study noted that many of these students are having trouble getting good jobs because employers are reviewing credit reports. A seriously bad credit report might eliminate an applicant from consideration, especially for a position that involves financial oversight.

Why is this happening? Some are quick to point an accusatory finger at credit card issuers for taking advantage of what they say is a vulnerable market segment. Others say that parents or teachers need to take greater responsibility in educating young people about financial management. Still others blame the young people themselves for giving in to temptation so easily. The problem is likely due to a combination of these factors. It is difficult for young people to be on their guard about financial matters if they do not have a fundamental understanding of the principles involved. And, overall, that seems to be lacking.

According to a June 1998 survey of young people, conducted by Yankelovich Partners, Inc., 55% consider themselves more spenders than savers. And while 57% expect to be wealthier than their parents, only 18% expect to work harder than their parents. Seventy-four percent said they would work just as hard, and 8% said not as hard.

Yankelovich interviewed nearly 1,300 students aged 12 to 21 for the Phoenix Home Life Mutual Insurance Company and its Fiscal Fitness Survey, an annual look at how financially savvy young people are. The survey was conducted primarily in households in which at least one parent earned $40,000 a year.

There was a certain amount of optimism in the survey responses. College students expected an average annual starting salary of $36,000, with 18% responding that they expected to make $50,000 or more in their first job—which the majority expected they would find within three months of graduation. Yet responses also showed that materialistic goals are very important. Sixty percent of the students agreed that having enough money is important to their happiness, and fully 35 percent said that "being able to buy what you want" is very important to achieve as an adult, up from 31% in 1996. Twenty percent said having nice clothes is very important, and 15% said having a million dollars is very important.

The students also seemed to have practical goals, with a whopping 92% believing young people should save for the future. Charity giving, retirement funding, and debt-free living also were considered very important to more young people in this survey than in previous years' responses.

However, while their stated goals might be practical, the road toward achieving them could be bumpy. Only 23% said they are very good at managing money; 64% said they were pretty good at it, and 13% said they were either not too good or not good at all. And of those students who hold credit cards, 21% said their parents pay the entire bill. There was actually a decrease in the number of students who said they paid their own credit card bills.

Perhaps of greatest concern was the limited knowledge these young people had about basic financial terms. The study found that 53% of the college students had a credit card for personal use, but 24% couldn't define "buying on credit." Even more alarming, 33% had no understanding of the term "mortgage," and 50% had no understanding of Social Security. Compound interest was not understood as a concept by 82% of the students surveyed; mutual funds stumped 79%.

Another 1999 surveyed mirrored those results. The study, conducted by the American Savings Education Council (ASEC), the Employee Benefit Research Institute, and Mathew Greenwald & Associates, surveyed 1,000 students aged 16–22 and found that most think their understanding of financial matters is deeper than it truly is. Fully 67% responded that they understood money matters fairly well, and 15% said they understood the basics very well. A smaller percentage responded that they were doing a very good job (18%) and a good job (38%) of managing their money. "The survey findings show that many of today's students are making money and saving money," said Don Blandin, president of ASEC, in a press release announcing the study. "At the same time, many appear to have a misconception of the level of their financial understanding, which can hurt them financially in the future."

For example, among those who feel they do a very good job of managing their money, 27% do not think saving regularly is a very high priority. Only 23% said they make a budget and stick to it.

Where are students getting their financial education? An overwhelming 94% said that their parents provide financial counsel. Many also responded that they turn to other relatives or teachers or professors, and 50% said their advice comes from their friends.

Of those surveyed only 21% of high school and college students have taken a course on personal finance in school; the other 79% have not.

"That isn't for lack of opportunity: 62 percent of students say their current school or a prior school they attended has offered a personal finance or financial education course, but only 34% of students who were offered a course on personal finance actually took the class," according to the press release.

And those who did take the classes didn't necessarily take the lessons to heart. There was no significant difference between the money management habits of those students who took classes on personal finance and those who did not.

Certainly, most states do have some mandates in economic education. James Madison University in Virginia periodically surveys members of the National Association of Economic Educators to gather the following information: whether or not the state has a mandate (state standards requiring the teaching of economics at some point in grades K–12), a course (a required course in economics at some point in the K–12 curriculum), testing (required by the state to measure the students' knowledge of economics); and consequences (if there is some penalty, such as loss of accreditation, to the school or system if grades are low, or some reward for high student performance). (See Table 1.1.)

Why is it important that students learn about money management and put the theories into practice? Because more students and adults are finding themselves in financial trouble. The pressure to spend is high. And most young people are getting some kind of income, so the ability to spend is also high.

The ASEC study found that 41% of students worked full time (35 or more hours per week) during the summer; only 6% didn't work at all. Of those surveyed, 39% received an allowance or some kind of performance-based stipend from their parents.

Only those students earning $5,000 a year or more were likely to invest their savings in certificates of deposit, stocks, or mutual funds. Of student savers, 80% had a savings account and 57% had a checking account. Thirty-three percent of students had a credit card for which they were responsible, and nearly 30% of students with credit cards rolled over credit card debt each month. Yet optimism remains high. On November 23, 1999, the *Wall Street Journal* reported that in an online poll by the accounting and consulting firm KPMG LLP, 42% of 1,743 college students expected salaries of at least $50,000 per year in a first job.

But the reality doesn't necessarily mirror this rosy outlook. The rate of personal bankruptcy filings continues to rise. And young people are susceptible to poor financial management for several reasons: peer and marketing pressure to spend is high, and many young people have had little real experience in handling money. Suddenly, they find themselves

Teen Guide to Personal Financial Management

6

Table 1.1
1999 Economics Education Mandates, K–12

State	Mandate	Course	Testing	Consequences
Alabama	Yes	Yes	Yes	Yes
Alaska	No	No	—	—
Arizona	No	No	No	No
Arkansas	No	No	No	No
California	Yes	Yes	Yes	Yes
Colorado	Yes	No	Yes	No
Connecticut	Yes	No	—	—
Delaware	Yes	No	Yes	Yes
Florida	Yes	Yes	Yes	Yes
Georgia	Yes	Yes	Yes	Yes
Hawaii	Yes	No	No	No
Idaho	Yes	Yes	No	No
Illinois	Yes	No	Yes	Yes
Indiana	Yes	No	No	No
Iowa	Yes	No	No	No
Kansas	Yes	No	Yes	Yes
Kentucky	Yes	No	Yes	Yes
Louisiana	Yes	Yes	Yes	Yes
Maine	Yes	No	Yes	No
Maryland	Yes	No	Yes	Yes
Massachusetts	Yes	No	Yes	Yes
Michigan	Yes	No	Yes	Yes
Minnesota	Yes	No	Yes	No
Mississippi	No	No	—	—
Missouri	Yes	No	Yes	No
Montana	No	No	—	—
Nebraska	No	No	No	No
Nevada	Yes	No	—	—
New Hampshire	Yes	Yes	—	—
New Jersey	No	No	—	—
New Mexico	No	No	—	—
New York	Yes	Yes	—	—
North Carolina	Yes	Yes	Yes	Yes
North Dakota	No	No	No	No
Ohio	Yes	No	Yes	No
Oklahoma	Yes	No	—	—
Oregon	Yes	No	No	No
Pennsylvania	No	No	No	No
Rhode Island	No	No	No	No
South Carolina	Yes	Yes	—	—
South Dakota	No	No	No	No
Tennessee	Yes	Yes	—	—
Texas	Yes	Yes	Yes	Yes

Table 1.1 (*continued*)

State	Mandate	Course	Testing	Consequences
Utah	Yes	No	—	—
Vermont	No	No	—	—
Virginia	Yes	No	Yes	Yes
Washington	Yes	No	Yes	No
West Virginia	Yes	Yes	—	—
Wisconsin	Yes	No	Yes	Yes
Wyoming	Yes	No	—	—

earning salaries, having neither the knowledge nor the discipline to create a budget.

One of the reasons that parents and schools aren't spending more time on teaching young people about money is that it is complicated and can be an emotionally charged topic. An Internet search on "financial management" can yield leads to thousands of sites that offer advice. The same is true for magazines and newspapers that offer financial advice. Much of the information is tremendously useful—if you don't feel intimidated by the depth. In the following chapters, you can get a base of knowledge that makes it easier to follow financial, economic, and social news that affects your money and how you manage it.

Look at the table of contents as if it were a menu. Do you need to know the basics—how to balance a checking account, or why it's important to save, or how to apply for a credit card? You'll find it in Chapter 3. If you feel you know that much, but want to learn about retirement plans and initial public offerings on the stock market, or if you want to know what the big fuss is over day trading, skip to Chapter 4. Want to know what schools are doing to teach economic education? Try Chapter 2. Students and teachers can also turn to Appendix D for sample lessons on economic education. Try them yourself, or use them in a class.

If you want to know more about a particular topic, an extensive listing of Web sites is offered in Appendix B. These sites provide a wealth of information and links to other sites of interest. They are divided by category for easy use.

Chapter 7 talks about consumerism and the high cost of keeping up with peers. Young people are targeted by advertisers on television, in magazine ads, and even in school. The message is that spending is cool. It's little wonder that the rate at which Americans save is dropping lower. In Chapter 8, financial counselors and others share their tips for developing healthy money management habits. A minister discusses why couples should talk about money matters before getting married, financial consultants share years of expertise with helping people professionally manage assets, and a family counselor talks about the intense pressure of a consumer society.

Certified financial planner William B. Howard, Jr., of Memphis, Tennessee noted that if young people start saving 10–15% of their income early, it becomes much easier to continue the habit. In most people's early working years, expenses are fairly low. You might be sharing a house or an apartment with friends, for example, rather than paying a mortgage. But once you've made a habit of tucking away a percentage of your weekly check, the chances are much greater you'll continue doing that even when your salary increases. So, obviously, your savings increase. And any cushion of savings makes it less frightening to take on debt. Debt is not a bad thing, he said. "It's how you manage it," he said.

Roger T. Smith, a Sacramento certified financial planner, said his experience has shown him that the world is divided into two types of people: savers and spenders. On rare occasions, he's seen spenders become savers. The major reason for saving is to be prepared for what Smith calls "Oh my God" reasons: the car engine blows out or other unexpected major expenses crop up. He advises his clients, high-income professionals, to have at least 10% of their annual income as a cash reserve. "In a young adult or kid's case, they don't have as many expenses so there's no reason they can't save 25%. You don't know what will come up, and without money, you can't get there from here."

Ross Levin, a Minneapolis certified financial planner, said that, in one way, money is like sex: parents often don't like to talk to their kids about it. "Find an adult who doesn't have hangups about money. The message needs to be that it's OK to talk about money. We need to break the taboo that it's something we can't discuss. If a young person starts showing an interest in money and interviewing others, the parents will become interested in what they're learning. Their hands will almost be forced to participate." He also added these words of encouragement: "There are few permanent mistakes you can make around money. The biggest mistake is not exploring it to a level with which you're comfortable."

Jim Putman, a certified financial planner in Appleton, Wisconsin graphically pointed out the advantage young people have in terms of time and compounding interest. He detailed what happens to a saver who tucks away just $2,000 a year for 10 years, starting at age 18. That's a total of $20,000. At age 65, that account earning 10% interest, is worth $1.3 million dollars. He compared that to another saver who didn't start saving until age 45. To get to that same $1.3 million nest egg, the second person had to put away $18,650 per year for 20 years. The second person had to invest $373,000 to end up with the same amount of money. So think about that: 10 years of dedicated savings now means much less worry later. Because the amount invested in those early years is smaller, it's more manageable. The 45-year-old investor probably has a mortgage and may even have children's college educations to plan or pay for. Putman's message is to take full advantage of the time and opportunity to save early.

Tracey Barnes Priestley, a family education consultant, said money is at the root of many family problems. It's not the dollars and cents that people fight about. Instead, "money represents so many things to people within the context of their relationships. It's love, power, control, independence, security and ambition." Because money is so many things to people, Barnes Priestley noted, it is being used to fill in more and more gaps in our personal lives. Advertising, the media, and even guilt felt by some working parents all contribute to spending without consideration of actual value.

Barnes Priestley advises the people she works with to look realistically at how they use money to meet psychological needs. "Ask yourself what money is doing for you." She suggests keeping a journal. "I call it mapping your spending habits. Write down what you buy, how you feel afterwards and how you feel a few days later about that purchase."

J. J. Bodine, a Stratham, New Hampshire, minister, said conflicts over money often foreshadow deeper conflicts in a marriage. That's why he spends time in premarital counseling sessions talking about money and how it's handled. "Young people need to recognize the symbolic and real value of money in our culture and the ease with which secrecy about finances can submerge a marriage," he said. He has them work on a joint budget—something many young people haven't even done on their own, much less with someone else's money. He also encourages them to think about the future—particularly children and who is going to work and how they'll manage that. In his experience counseling parishioners, he's found that when the first child comes along, financial conflicts suddenly bubble to the surface. Bodine hopes that simply by letting young people know that money management is a struggle for everyone at some point, it will allow them to get help before it submarines a marriage. "It's one thing to say love conquers all, but these are issues every couple needs to work at."

Rob Billingsley, a Fredericksburg, Virginia, attorney and financial advisor, believes that goal setting is the single most important step in money management. "The same sorts of things that enable you to become successful in a career and other parts of your life are transferable to the financial arena and vice versa," said Billingsley. The sooner young people develop a mind-set to defer gratification today to achieve something better tomorrow or down the road, the better. "Most people have a tendency to go through life like going down the river in a raft. We tend to bounce from rock to rock," he said. That's reacting. But goal setting is proactive.

When you set goals, whether it's a new bike or car, a college education, a house, or some financial stability when children are born, you have to know how you can achieve them. That requires an understanding of the magic of compounding interest, budgeting, and saving and investing. All of these principles and more are explained in the following pages.

2

What Students Learn and Don't Learn in School

Losing money hurts, and making it can leave you feeling like a million bucks. Most young people don't realize the extent of those feelings until they are making serious money. Yet the real ups and downs of dollars made, lost, spent, and saved come alive in Kim Sigler's seventh grade class at Gayle Middle School in Stafford County, Virginia. Sigler created Bank USA and USA Inc. when she realized her students needed to understand what bankruptcy meant and what it felt like. What she designed was a tangible teaching tool to bring home the lessons on financial mistakes and responsibilities. (See Appendix D for Sigler's Bank USA and related lesson plans.) "In these two programs students clearly see what the terms really mean in a real sense. They discover the rules of supply and demand on a firsthand basis, especially on stock market day. They may also experience how it feels to lose their money and to have nowhere to turn for help," she said.

Although the students are initially surprised and sometimes upset at how strictly she runs the program, she wants to wake them up to the fact that banks, credit card companies, and employers aren't going to treat them any differently out in the real world. "Reality is a big part of this learning experience, and even though we are not using real money, because it's their money it becomes important to the students. The kids who get into financial trouble pretend they aren't upset if their companies go bankrupt, but believe me, they are very upset and they learn a great deal more from the experience, luckily without the real ramifications of bankruptcy."

Through Bank USA, Sigler gives each student wages for the previous week's attendance at $10 per day. Students can take up to two paid sick days each month. A guideline sheet and all transaction sheets are kept in the students' math notebooks. Out of the money they receive, each individual must pay $15 per week to rent a desk and locker and $10 weekly for electricity and water, using up half of a full week's wages. Anyone who reports to class without necessary supplies can purchase them, at exorbitant prices like $5 for a pencil or three sheets of notebook paper. Checks and deposit slips are introduced with each individual account, and they are kept on file for the entire nine-week program, as each student balances his or her own account on Monday morning. Students who get into financial trouble may also face late fees for rent or utilities, another reality checkpoint.

Once the majority of students are comfortable with their accounts, usually after the second week, Sigler starts USA Inc. In that program she allows the students to group themselves into teams. With $200 in a start-up account, they create companies which must produce a product to sell. As the program moves forward students can move money from their personal accounts into their companies if they wish to, but, again, the paper trail is accurate and strict. These two programs allow the students to really learn income versus expenses; how stock prices can increase dramatically for a popular company; what happens when friends negotiate about money; and how credit can solve as well as create problems. Sigler reminds the students that all these concepts and ideas are waiting for them down the road and that the lessons learned in her class can help them avoid mistakes in the future.

Sigler, who team taught the program with two other seventh grade instructors, said that the bulk of the work for both Bank USA and USA Inc. is in the preparation. That preparation includes the paperwork for the individual student bank accounts; the materials, often donated by parents, used to create the products in USA Inc.; the actual company reports to chart student assets, expenses, and final account balances when the program finishes; and the stock certificates issued when the companies go public with their stock. She likened her role as teacher to that of an accountant who doesn't tell someone how to spend their money but who sees it coming and going, can chart its ebb and flow, and can point out financial lessons. But Sigler remains adamant. She does not bail students out, and their successes as well as their failures are based on their own financial decisions.

Sigler developed and refined this program by looking at Virginia's Standards of Learning and following the curriculum guidelines. She then brought those definitions and concepts to life in her classroom. Programs like Sigler's rely on a strong alliance among the teachers, students, and parents, an alliance she and other educators believe is the real key to successful personal finance literacy for today's youth.

The search for hands-on, simulated activities and curriculum materials for teachers need not be difficult. There are other organizations that create the same kinds of realistic programs for personal finance education. These national and state organizations have a wealth of materials ready and waiting for educators, according to Dara Duguay, executive director of the Jump$tart Coalition for Personal Financial Literacy. "There is no lack of wonderful curriculum materials for teaching personal finance literacy, but those materials are sitting on the shelf because teachers don't know about them and because personal finance literacy has no real place in the school's curriculum" Duguay said. The Jump$tart Clearinghouse of Educational Materials contains some 250 items created by a variety of organizations and individuals.

Duguay said that without knowledge of these educational materials teachers often miss the opportunity to use programs that provide real hands-on learning. The Jump$tart Clearinghouse also includes industry publications which, like all other materials, must pass an evaluation process to be included. Anything not overtly commercial is considered in the interest of including a variety of choices. Examples of free corporate-sponsored programs include:

1. Visa's "Choices and Decisions" curriculum
2. MasterCard International's "Kids, Cash, Plastic and You"
3. "The Stock Market Game," distributed to schools by the securities industry

In a move to aid the national effort to improve personal financial literacy among young adult, the Jump$tart Coalition brought together a wide range of organizations, including federal agencies, universities, national nonprofit associations, and sponsors of education programs. They formed a partnership with a headquarters in Washington, D.C., and state coalitions in some 12 states. Jump$tart first convened in December 1995, and their mission includes evaluation of financial literacy of young adults; development, dissemination, and encouragement of the use of guidelines for grades K–12; and the promotion of the teaching of personal finance.

Just how far behind in personal finance education are we as a nation? In countries like Japan, personal finance curriculum is mandatory, yet according to Duguay there is no national mandate for personal finance in this country, and personal finance curricula vary widely in usage from state to state. There needs to be a national dialogue on this problem, which Duguay wants to see in the form of a White House summit on financial literacy. According to Duguay, the U.S. Department of Education takes its cues from the White House, and so if the push for improvement comes from the President, that could spur the Department of Education to get involved.

GUIDELINES AND BENCHMARKS

Along with a national clearinghouse of information and curriculum materials, Jump$tart also developed a set of educator guidelines after seeking input from elementary and secondary schoolteachers and educators from across the country. The four key areas in the guidelines are (1) income, (2) money management, (3) savings and investment, and (4) spending. Each area specifies skills and concepts that students should be taught before graduation from high school. The benchmarks correlate with the guidelines and show the skills and knowledge that students should possess at various grade levels.

For example, in terms of money management, the coalition maintains that students should be able to set up and evaluate short- and long-term financial goals and plans concerning income, spending, and saving. Students should be able to develop, analyze, and revise a budget and perform basic financial operations, such as using a checking or savings account. For savings and investing, the guidelines maintain that students should be able to compare the advantages and disadvantages of saving now and saving later and be able to explain the importance of various saving and investment strategies. They should be able to explain how taxes, government policy and regulations, and inflation might impact savings and investment decisions.

Additionally, students should be able to explain how the risk level of the borrower affects the price of credit, how payment performance determines credit history, and why credit records are maintained and accessed. Students should be able to identify sources of income and analyze how personal choices, education, and other factors affect future income. The guidelines and benchmarks are available from the coalition for educators to use when structuring and planning personal finance curricula.

According to Duguay, Jump$tart is also working to educate legislators about the importance of personal financial literacy for today's students. "It used to be that many life skills, from banking to budgeting money, were introduced to students in the old home economics classes, which were required. But those courses are now elective, and except for some vocational education classes, most students are not learning these necessary concepts."

But Duguay gives some states high marks in their efforts to bring better economics education and personal finance literacy into their curriculums. In her view, states doing well in requiring personal finance include Illinois, Kansas, Idaho, Michigan, Florida, Mississippi, Pennsylvania, and Virginia. Students in those states must take courses that include instruction in personal finance. These courses, which must be completed before graduation, may include consumer economics, economics, family and consumer science, or other subjects.

A model for state mandates may be Illinois, where to graduate every high school senior must complete a one-semester state-mandated course that covers comparison shopping, advertising, consumer fraud, how to complain, plus managing income. Joanne R. Dempsey, president of the Illinois Council on Economic Education (ICEE), sees that mandate being met in a multitude of ways across the state, in part because of funding realities. "This course ended up in different areas of the curriculum from math to home economics to business education because funding was available at the time in different places. The challenge now facing Illinois is how to raise public awareness of the need for improved personal finance education. Toward that goal the ICEE has joined with the National Council on Economic Education (NCEE) in a five-year campaign aimed at increasing that awareness. But Dempsey also agreed with Duguay and the Jump$tart Coalition that "personal finance education needs to become a national priority," she said.

Illinois currently meets the national voluntary standards for economic education set by the NCEE. Dempsey notes that the ICEE also focuses its resources on providing teacher training so that the state's educators can develop the knowledge and skills to teach personal finance from kindergarten through 12th grade.

Another state to receive high marks, according to Duguay, is Virginia, which "has been very effective with integrating personal finance literacy into all levels from kindergarten to 12th grade." In 1998, Virginia added personal living and finance objectives in middle and high school math classes. Another reason Virginia is doing well, according to Duguay, can be attributed to the efforts of Virginia Council on Economic Education (VCEE). Harvey R. Carmichael, a history and social science specialist with the Virginia Department of Education, agreed, calling the VCEE a valuable partner. Virginia's most recent changes in its Standards of Learning (SOLs) changes strongly supported by the VCEE, have meant overall improvement in economics education. The old standards called for children to receive a half unit of economics tied in with a government course. Now the economic instruction is woven throughout kindergarten to 12th grade. Carmichael notes that the VCEE also assists the state effort by helping train classroom teachers to adapt to these new standards and to keep pace with the changes in personal finance education. The council is strongly networked across the state and is a major source for staff development for the state's teachers.

According to Carmichael, Virginia's new standards incorporate more economic theory than before. Teaching theory is a tall order for educators when many youngsters don't have a chance to experience the basics. Joan L. Spence, former president of the VCEE, observed that it's difficult for teachers to find the time to teach these concepts in a way that shows students what they mean in a real sense. Spence said that simulated activities are the most effective teaching method for personal finance and that some of the best examples of those economic reality activities can be found in the state's vocational education programs.

Carmichael agrees with Spence that some of the state's vocational instruction were geared more toward how to handle money.

College-bound students under the new SOLs may have received minimal practical instruction in personal finance. It was assumed students needed to know economic theory so they can understand how problems and issues related to the world economy will impact their lives. And they all need to know how to responsibly handle credit cards and budget money. We need to bridge the gap between academic instruction and vocational education for students. If we continue to isolate the two, some students will reap the benefits of practical instruction while others may not be as well prepared, Carmichael said.

One encouraging development is staff development for teachers. Carmichael applauded Virginia's 1998 General Assembly, which budgeted $25.1 million to help pay the cost of training teachers in all areas of the curriculum, including economics. The purchase of networked copies of the CD-ROM *Virtual Economics* for all Virginia classrooms is another step in the right direction. The National Council on Economic Education, which is the major source of teacher training and materials for grades kindergarten through grade 12 in this country, developed the *Virtual Economics* CD-ROM.

A nonprofit partnership of leaders in education, business, and labor, the NCEE is working to help youngsters learn to think, to choose, and to function in a changing global economy. Founded in 1949, the NCEE also provides a nationwide network of state councils including the ICEE and VCEE and over 260 university-based centers under a program called the Economics America Schools Program. (See Appendix C for a listing of state councils on economic education.)

The Economics America Program works to develop national and state content standards in economics education and to assist in the development of national, state, and local standards-based curricula. Since being launched in 1964 as the Developmental Economics Education Program (DEEP), the program has researched, published, and evaluated classroom-tested materials. Initially an experimental program in just three school districts, the NCEE program has now grown to include an enrollment of approximately 1,600 school districts, or about 40% of the country's student population.

STANDARDS

The NCEE has also published national voluntary standards for economics education. The 20 standards established by the NCEE deal with content areas ranging from scarcity and consumers to natural resources, productivity, interest rates, monetary policy, distribution of income, monopolies, and macroeconomic indicators. Along with theses standards the NCEE has published benchmarks to gauge student understanding of these subjects. For example, the first standard covers scarcity, choice, goods and services, and natural resources, among other concepts. Fourth grade students illustrate their understanding in activities that include creating a collage representing goods they or their families consume. Students can also identify purchases they have made and explain why they had to make a choice when making the purchase. Another standard deals with the role and function of money. To meet that standard high school seniors are expected to be able to demonstrate their knowledge of various loan types as well as their understanding of what causes a country's money supply to expand or contract.

Commitment to economics instruction and to teacher education is the framework for the Economics America Program. School districts that enroll in the program must promise to provide nonpartisan economics instruction. They must also work in partnership with the program to identify needed curriculum changes and must provide in-service courses or workshops for their instructors. The training is often co-sponsored by the participating school district, college and university centers for economic education, and the Council on Economic Education in their state.

Spence noted that the staff development for teachers serves a dual purpose assisting educators in the classroom and also in their personal lives with updated information on how to handle investments, credit, budgets, and other financial matters. Like everyone else, teachers are hard pressed to keep pace with the rapidly changing face of finance. And if teachers are challenged by the confusing array of financial choices, many parents are having an even tougher time. "We are concerned that adults, especially in single parent homes, are too overwhelmed with their day to day realities and with the complexities of personal finance to find the time to teach their own children. So many children receive no information or instruction at home. And that means their sources of information are largely what they learn in school, what they learn from friends, and what they learn from television and the movies," Spence said.

ADDITIONAL READING

Barbanel, Linda. *Piggy Bank to Credit Card: Teach Your Child the Financial Facts of Life.* New York: Crown, 1994.

Continuing the Commitment: Essential Components of a Successful Education System. Washington, D.C.: Business Roundtable, Education Public Policy Agenda, May 1995.

Edgar, Susan H. "Kids and Credit." *Mortgage Banking* 58, no. 9 (June 1998): 58.

"Future Debtors of America." *Consumer Reports* 62, no. 12 (December 1997): 16–19.

"Giving Kids a Jump-Start on Finances." *Christian Science Monitor*, November 10, 1997, B3.

Making Standards Matter: A Fifty-State Progress Report on Efforts to Raise Academic Standards. Washington, DC: American Federation of Teachers, Educational Issues Department, 1995.

Pearl, Jayne. *Kids and Money: Giving Them the Savvy to Succeed Financially.* Princeton, NJ: Bloomberg Press, 1999.

Searls, Michael J. *Kids and Money: A Hands-On Parent's Guide.* Englewood, CO: Summit Financial Products, 1996.

"Teaching Finance Smarts." *Christian Science Monitor*, December 1, 1997, 16.

3

The Basics

It really can be summed up in the most elementary equation: if your expenses are less than your income, the difference represents potential savings and investments. The more you can save, the better your financial foundation. If your expenses start creeping ahead of income, the result is debt. The deeper you get into debt, the more difficult it is to get out. When expenses start to catch up to or exceed income, there are two options: increase income or reduce expenses. The first can be done by working more hours, getting a better paying job, or even adding another part-time job. But finding the time to do a job search or working additional hours can be difficult. It's typically easier to tighten the belt and find ways to economize.

But isn't all that financial worry down the road? Why learn about money management now? Many young people have little more income than what comes in through a part-time job, and things like retirement and home mortgages seem like worries for future decades.

Yet understanding the basics early means that young people will be much better prepared to meet the financial challenges that lie ahead. Plus, young people have one huge asset older savers don't have: time.

When it comes to saving, time truly becomes money. That's because of compounding interest—interest earned on deposited money and interest earned earlier. Interest is the money a savings institution or investment pays account holders to keep their money there. And the longer a young person keeps money in an interest-bearing account, the longer the investment continues to pay interest on interest earned earlier. That's what compounded interest is—it's cumulative and it can add up pretty quickly. Here's how it works.

Invest $100 per month in an investment that yields 6% interest compounded monthly. Do this for 30 years and the investment will be worth $100,451.50. But you will have deposited only $36,000 of that money; the other $64,451.50 comes from compounded interest. While that's impressive, here's what happens in the next 10 years. The $100,000 account will be worth $199,149.06, nearly doubling in value. People who wait until they're 35 to start saving typically don't have the luxury of waiting 40 years for savings and interest to compound.

Here's another example. Let's say three people each decide to invest $1,000 a year for 10 years in an account bearing 8% interest. After 10 years of deposits, each lets the account sit until retirement at age 65. At the end of 10 years, everyone's account value is $14,486.56. However, one person opened the account at 18, the other at 28, and the third at 38. Those years make an enormous difference.

The person who started saving at age 38 has an account at age 65 worth $53,600. The one who started saving at age 28 has an account worth $115,719. But the one who started at age 18, whose money had been gathering compound interest for 37 years, has a balance of $249,828.

That's why financial planners emphasize that the earlier young people start saving, the better off they'll be. Those who regularly put money aside in some interest-bearing account reap the rewards of years of accrued savings. The higher the interest, the faster that amount of money will build up.

But there's more. While time certainly helps build the nest egg, there are other reasons to start saving early. Most important, it helps people get into the lifelong habit of spending within their limits. People who save a certain percentage of their pay are typically budgeting their money well. People who live hand to mouth, spending as much, or even more, than their income, will find their debts escalating.

That can happen fairly easily. As young adults obtain credit cards, either directly or through their parents, there's the temptation and the simplicity of spending now and paying later. For those who use credit cards as a convenience and who pay the bill in its entirety each month, credit cards can be useful money management tools. But for those who use the credit cards on unplanned and unnecessary purchases, a credit card can become a real budget blower. And credit cards come at a price—the rate of interest paid on the outstanding balance.

Interest works two ways, depending on whether you are the borrower or the lender. In effect, when you open a savings account at a bank or credit union you're lending money to that institution. That's why you receive interest payments on the deposited funds. Credit card holders, on the other hand, are borrowing money from the institution that issued the credit card. That's why they pay interest charges on the amount borrowed.

Table 3.1
APR and APY Compared

Frequency of Interest Compounding	Stated Interest Rate	Actual Annual Percentage Yield (APY)
Yearly	5.0%	5.00%
Semi-annually (6 months)	5.0%	5.06%
Quarterly	5.0%	5.10%
Monthly	5.0%	5.12%
Daily	5.0%	5.20%

Source: Wisconsin Association of Bankers.

CALCULATING INTEREST ON SAVINGS

To calculate how much interest an investment will earn, two numbers count: the annual percentage rate (APR) and the annual percentage yield (APY). The second is the actual amount of interest you'll earn if you keep your account in place for a year. The two numbers are different only if interest is compounded more than once a year.

Some variations on what 5% APR can actually yield are shown in Table 3.1.

The higher the APY, the faster interest is accumulated. For example, it would take 14 years for a $1,000 investment to double at 5% interest compounded twice a year. If the interest rate were 9%, it would only take 7 years and 11 months for the investment to double in value. At an interest rate of 12%, it would take 5 years and 11 months.

WHERE TO PUT YOUR MONEY

All of these projections are based on someone taking their money out of the piggy bank and finding some place to invest it. Banks and credit unions offer a number of savings mechanisms. Many people also choose to put some savings in stocks, but financial planners suggest first creating a cushion of readily available money.

Most people opt for either a bank or credit union, most often one near where they live or work simply for the convenience. But mailing in deposits, or having direct deposit, through which funds are electronically transferred from an employer straight to the employee's account, makes it possible to bank just about anywhere.

What's the difference between a bank or savings and loan institution (S&L) and a credit union? The ownership. Banks and S&Ls are for-profit institutions; credit unions are not for profit, owned by the people who use it. The savings vehicles are similar, although they have different names. All allow account holders, or members in the case of a credit union, to deposit money and get loans.

How safe is your money in a bank, savings and loan, or credit union? In many cases, savings are insured. For example, the Federal Deposit Insurance Corporation (FDIC) is a federal agency that insures many bank deposits in most banks and savings and loans up to $100,000. The agency was created by Congress in 1933 after the financial chaos that resulted from the Great Depression of the late 1920s and early 1930s. More than 9,000 banks closed between the October 1929 stock market crash and March 1933, when President Franklin Delano Roosevelt took office. The intent of the FDIC was to provide a federal government guarantee of deposits so that customers' funds, within certain limits, would be safe and available to them on demand. Since the program began, not one depositor has lost a cent of insured funds as a result of a failure.

But what's insured? Typically, accounts of up to $100,000 in savings and checking deposits, money market accounts, and certificates of deposit (CDs) are insured. Many institutions also offer investment accounts or provide information to customers on noninsured deposits. Some banks allow their customers to be contacted by outside agents selling investments which are not insured.

Deposits in credit unions are also insured up to the $100,000 federal limit through the National Credit Union Share Insurance Fund (NCU-SIF). This federal fund was created by Congress in 1970 and is administered by the National Credit Union Administration.

Selecting the institution for depositing money goes hand in hand with selecting the account. There are different kinds of accounts, each with different features. The simplest choice is between checking, savings, and debit accounts, although one account holder can hold several accounts. Generally, each of these accounts allows the depositor or investor quick access to cash—either by writing checks against the balance or by withdrawing the cash.

Many financial institutions are also part of a network offering customers access to money through automated teller machines (ATMs). When a customer opens an account, the bank provides a plastic card with a magnetic stripe on it. The customer is issued (or chooses) a personal identification number (PIN). ATM card holders should always keep this number secret because it's all that is needed to gain access to the money in the account.

ATMs are extremely convenient because they give customers access to their money in the evenings and on weekends when bank lobbies are closed. But customers may pay for this convenience. Most banks charge an ATM transaction fee. It might only be $0.50, but if a customer uses the ATM four times a week, that's $8 a month in transaction fees. And the charge is often significantly higher if the ATM card is used at another bank's ATM.

In fact, U.S. Public Interest Research Group released a report in April 1999 saying that banks are "double dipping" when it comes to ATM fees. More than 9 out of 10 banks add a surcharge for nonbank customers using their ATM services. In fact, 93% of the 336 banks surveyed add such a fee. A year before, the number was only 71%. What's unfair, says the consumer group, is that more than 97% of banks already charge their customers a "foreign" or "off-us" fee of $1.20 for using another bank's ATM. When that $1.20 "off-us" fee is added to the average surcharge of $1.37, that means consumers are paying $2.57 per ATM transaction at machines not owned by their own banks.

Another way to access one's money is by using debit cards (sometimes called check cards), which are becoming increasingly popular. When a merchant swipes the customer's debit card through a magnetic reader, the money for the transaction is electronically transferred from the customer's checking account to the merchant's checking account. Debit cards are popular because, unlike credit cards, users aren't borrowing money. Whereas merchants might be hesitant to accept an out-of-area check from a customer, they don't have the same hesitation with debit cards.

TRACK YOUR CHECKING ACCOUNT

A savings account typically allows a certain number of withdrawals per quarter or other designated period without a charge. After those allotted withdrawals, the institution might charge a fee to access the money. Checking accounts allow the holder to write checks. Using a checking account requires basic addition and subtraction skills, but is not tremendously complicated. It does, however, require diligence in noting all checks written as well as deposits and withdrawals made. Unless one keeps track of the amount of money in the account, it is possible—even likely—that the account holder will "bounce" a check, meaning that there are insufficient funds in the account to cover the amount of a check. Bouncing checks becomes a costly error. The bank assesses a fine, typically from $15 to $20 per bounced check, and often the business to which the check was written charges the customer, also.

The following examples show how easy it can be to overlook the small details that make the difference between keeping enough funds in the account or bouncing a check.

The Missing Entry

Bill was in the grocery store. A friend was waiting out in the car while Bill ran in for a few items. In a hurry, he scrawled out a check for $32.

He noted that he had $50 in the account. It was tight, but he knew he could cover this check. Satisfied with that, he grabbed his bags and ran out to the car. Problem: he forgot to write the transaction down in his check register. Later that night, he ordered a pizza and wrote out a $20 check to the delivery man. He entered that check into the account and subtracted it from his total, leaving him with $30 in the account. Of course, his real balance now is minus $2, so an unpleasant surprise awaits. One of those two checks is going to bounce. Even though Bill spent only $2 more than what he had in the account, the bank will charge him an overdraft fee—typically around $20. In some cases, the bank will cover the check to the merchant, meaning you won't be hit by two bounced check charges.

Certainly, entering the grocery store check in his register would have allowed Bill to see that there weren't enough funds to cover the pizza. But good record keeping could have avoided the problem, even if that entry was missed. Check registers, the place where users track their check writing, have spaces for the check number, the date, the person or business to which the check was written, and the amount. Had Bill recorded check numbers and double checked them against checks as he was writing them, he would have seen that there was a check entry missing. Checks are numbered in ascending order, so it's a simple safeguard. Bill would have noticed that he jumped from check 2017 to 2019. He would have stopped to wonder what happened to check 2018 and probably could have reconstructed the grocery store event. That would have allowed him to immediately deposit money into the checking account to cover the checks written or to find another way to pay for the pizza.

The Float Game

Sue has just finished paying all her bills for the month. She has $30 left in her checking account and a $75 check from her parents waiting to be deposited. Unexpectedly, some old friends stop by. Happy to see them, and eager to show off her independence, Sue orders out dinner for the gang. She writes a check for $42 to the eatery. She knows that total is more than what she has left in the account, but she figures she'll go to the bank first thing in the morning and deposit her parents' check. In return for the dinner treat, her friends take her out and they stay out late. Sue wakes up 15 minutes before an important class the next morning and runs out the door. She spends most of the day in the library, and when she gets home she's just too tired to do the banking errand. By the following day, she's completely forgotten about the check. She deposits it the third day after she's overdrawn her account. Chances are Sue will get burned by a bounced check fee if all the other checks she's written have been turned into a bank by then. Funds from deposited checks are often not immediately available as cash, meaning that the check Sue's parents sent her might not be credited to her account for a few more days. Hedging one's bets about how long it takes checks to arrive and be deposited can result in overdrafts. There's little room for error, and certainly no room for the kind of forgetfulness Sue had. She meant well by wanting to deposit the check the next morning. But banks don't credit you for good intentions.

Good Money after Bad

Shelley and Alison rent an apartment together. Shelley's name is the only one on the lease, so she sends the landlord the monthly rent check. One day before the rent is due, Alison gives Shelley a check for her half. "I get paid later today, so please wait until tomorrow to deposit this," Alison says. Shelley does wait and deposits the check in the morning. At the same time, she mails off the rent check, counting on Alison's check to pay the total. However, Alison forgot to deposit her check, so her check to Shelley bounced. As a result, Shelley's check to the landlord bounced, because without Alison's contribution, she didn't have enough in the account to cover the rent.

Problems like this, as well as simple mathematical errors, are common reasons that account holders find themselves staring in disbelief at overdraft notices the bank sends out. Diligent record keeping, and double checking the math, can help avoid most of the problems. Using a computer software program that keeps track of spending is also helpful. Software programs make it easy to recalculate the balance if there's a change, and they make it easy to reconcile the account at the end of every month.

Banks send out a statement once a month to checking account holders. This statement reflects deposits made and checks cleared during the month. It also reflects any charges, such as check printing fees, overdraft charges, or ATM fees. By comparing these totals against the checkbook, the account holder can see if everything matches. Reconciling an account monthly, especially if it's done with computer software, only takes a few minutes and can provide assurance that your record keeping is good, or can help detect errors before they result in bounced checks.

Checking accounts are easy to use, and personal checks are accepted as payment for many kinds of transactions. Merchants may ask for one or two forms of identification before accepting a check. While this may seem like an inconvenience to the user, the merchant is doing so because chasing after shoppers who have bounced a check costs them time and money.

Table 3.2
Types of Bank Accounts

Type of account	Will I earn interest?	May I write checks?	Are there withdrawal limits?	Are fees likely?
Regular checking	No	Yes	No	Yes
Interest checking (NOW)	Yes	Yes	No	Yes
Money Market Deposit Account (MMDA)	Yes, usually higher than NOW or savings	Yes, only 3 per month	Yes, 6 transfers per month	Yes
Savings	Yes	No	Same as MMDA	Yes
Certificate of Deposit (CD)	Yes, usually higher than MMDA	No	Yes, usually no withdrawals of principal until date of maturity	Yes, if you withdraw principal funds before date of maturity

Source: Federal Reserve Bank.

QUESTIONS TO ASK

To help account holders determine what kind of account to open, the Federal Reserve Bank has outlined the features of different types of accounts (Table 3.2). Before opening an account, there's more to consider than the APY. The Federal Reserve Bank suggests comparing interest rates, but also considering these features:

• Can the institution change the rate after you open the account?

• Are interest rates different, depending on the account balance? If so, how is the interest calculated? An example of tiered rates is that the institution might pay a 5% interest rate on balances up to $5,000 and 5.5% on balances above $5,000. Let's say you deposit $8,000. Some institutions might pay 5.5% percent only on the remaining $3,000. Check the APY disclosure statement to determine if there is one interest rate or ranges of interest rates.

• What is the minimum balance required before an account starts to earn interest?

• When is interest paid—for example, when a check is deposited, or when the institution actually receives the funds from the check?

Earning the highest interest is great, but not if it's associated with the highest fees. Look at the fee structure that the institution has created. The Federal Reserve Bank suggests finding the answers to these questions:

• Will you pay a flat monthly fee?
• Will you pay a fee if the balance in your account drops below a specified amount?
• Is there a charge for each deposit and withdrawal you make?
• If you can use ATMs (automated teller machines) to make deposits and withdrawals on your account, is there a charge for this service? Does it matter whether the transaction takes place at an ATM owned by the institution?
• Is there a check writing fee?
• Are fees reduced or waived if you agree to directly deposit your paycheck?
• What is the fee if you request the institution to stop payment on a check you have written?
• What is the charge for writing a check that bounces (a check returned for insufficient funds)?

And what happens if you deposit a check written by another person, and it bounces? Are you charged a fee?

CREDIT CARDS: POTENTIAL BUDGET BLOWERS

Aside from a checkbook, many young adults feel that a credit card is the symbol of financial independence. Establishing good credit is an important financial building block, and credit cards can offer that. But to the undisciplined or impulsive, credit cards can be a step toward serious financial trouble.

In the "pros" column, credit cards are extremely convenient. They can be used almost anywhere for almost anything. Many grocery stores accept credit cards, as do hotels, gas stations, and most restaurants and merchants. For someone planning a vacation, a credit card can mean tremendous flexibility. There's no worrying about how much cash to bring for food, hotels, and gas. Many credit cards even allow holders to withdraw cash advances at ATMs.

In the "cons" column, credit cards are extremely convenient. That's right. A credit card's greatest virtue should also be its biggest concern. Let's look at two vacation-bound young persons as an example. Each calculated they could spend about $200 on this trip.

Sue is leaving with $45 in cash in her pocket. She has a credit card with a balance of $150. She's spent the last five months aggressively paying off her large balance so she could have some breathing room on this vacation. Sue is driving to the beach to visit friends. She estimates she'll spend one night in a hotel each way, but five nights are free. Before she leaves, she gasses up, using the credit card: $15. Hotel: $42, plus she charged dinner ($18) and breakfast to her room ($8). Another tank of gas: $15. Sue arrives at her friends' house with $40 in cash and is feeling very proud of her economizing. That night, she takes the group out for dinner. It's not a fancy place, but the bill for food, drinks, and tip for the party of three comes to $58. Her friends are working during her stay, so she's on her own to explore the town. She finds some gift shops and charges about $75 in gifts for herself and souvenirs for other friends—t-shirts, hats, salt water taffy—nothing too expensive. Then she finds a glorious shell wind chime. It's $32, but what the heck. It's vacation. Two rolls of film at the souvenir stand: $14. Lunch at the little restaurants on the boardwalk totaled $47 for four days. Midweek she goes to the grocery store and spends $60 on steaks, snack food, and drinks. Sue feels like she deserves this break, so she doesn't mind paying $9 for a chocolate three-layer cake for dessert. She's a little dismayed when she sees the total, but it's too late by then. Sue leaves two days later and takes out a $30 cash advance for spending money for the ride home. She charges another $68 in a hotel and another $30 at gas stations. Total cost: $464. She blew her budget by more than $250 and now she has this total tacked on to the $150 balance she already had. And she has about $15 in cash remaining.

Now let's look at Bill. He's making the same trip and is looking forward to the break just as much. But Bill is a planner. He has calculated how much he plans to spend and has brought along $200 in cash and traveler's checks to cover those expenses. He carries a credit card as a backup, but has promised himself he'll only use it in an emergency, such as if the car breaks down. Bill did some research before starting on the trip and made reservations at a hotel charging $29 a night. He packed a cooler with food, so dinner was a salad at a fast food place: $4. He ate breakfast at a nearby diner: $4, including tip. His gas expenses also totaled $30. Before he arrived at his friend's house, he stopped in at a nearby grocery store and bought fresh vegetables and other pizza fixings, some soda, and some beer. He planned on treating his friends that night, too. But the total for his treat—homemade pizza and salad, drinks, no tip—was $16. While his friends were working, Bill did some sightseeing. He went to museums; two were free and one charged $8 admission. He would stop by a bagel shop for a sandwich. His lunch costs for four days totaled $8.50. He brought film from home. Instead of buying his friends gifts, he'd comb the beach for driftwood or shells. He'd buy postcards and put them in simple wooden frames, bringing his total cost for souvenirs to $25. His trip home—gas, hotel, food—cost the same as the trip to the beach: $67. Bill's trip cost him $191.50. He had brought his budgeted $200 in cash and had managed it carefully. He had gotten a little nervous about the dwindling cash toward the end, so he charged the hotel room. He came home with money to spare and a $29 balance on his credit card, which he would pay off as soon as the bill arrived.

Sue, however, was staring at a credit card balance of more than $600. She could have economized, but she didn't plan. Instead of calculating costs and setting up a budget, she figured she'd be able to discipline herself enough to stick to her $200. Indeed, she bought low-cost souvenirs and figured that her only splurge was the wind chime. But when the bill came and she saw the charges from restaurants, grocery stores, and hotel, she saw that she overspent repeatedly.

Just because a bank or other credit card issuer sends someone an invitation to apply for a credit card doesn't necessarily mean that the person automatically receives the card. Credit card issuers will want to ensure that the applicant is a good credit risk. People who are trying to reestablish good credit can often obtain a credit card, but these cards often carry a much higher interest rate. A credit card issuer will ask an applicant about employment and annual income and will also run a credit check. Many lenders will voluntarily submit credit information on their loan holders to one of three national credit bureaus, Equifax, Experian, and Trans Union. (See Appendix B.) These bureaus serve as huge repositories of individuals' credit histories. This is not limited to credit cards. Banks or auto finance companies that have issued a car loan, for example, or department stores that issue credit cards also submit their information.

There are three categories of loan agreements, but lenders in each category will be most eager to lend money to someone with good credit. Credit is extended to a borrower either through a revolving agreement, a charge agreement, or an installment agreement. In a revolving agreement, the holder pays some or all of the outstanding balance each month. Whatever remains is rolled over to the next bill. Most credit cards, department store cards, and gas cards are revolving agreements. In a charge agreement, the holder promises to pay the full balance each month. This agreement does not involve interest payments because no balance is carried forward. American Express cards are probably the best known in this category. In an installment agreement, the borrower agrees to pay a specific amount each month until the debt is repaid. This is traditionally the way auto loans and furniture and appliance sales are financed.

HOW DOES YOUR CREDIT SCORE?

In a recent publication the FDIC explained how banks and other lenders use automated "credit scoring" systems to determine how good or bad a risk a person is. The better a person's credit score, the more favorable the terms of a loan or credit card.

One way lenders quickly evaluate thousands (and sometimes millions) of loan applications is by using automated "credit scoring." Even if you have no plans to apply for a new loan soon, we think you should know about credit scoring. Why?

Because the next time you do want a mortgage, car loan, credit card or other type of loan, your credit score could affect the interest rate you are charged. It could determine the repayment terms and other conditions of the loan. Your credit score could even play a role in whether you are approved for the loan. To be on the winning side of this scoring system, it helps to know the basics.

What Is Credit Scoring?

Credit scoring is a tool that's designed to enhance a lender's ability to determine the likelihood that a consumer will repay a loan. It's based in part on credit scoring "models," which are computerized systems that look at a variety of factors (sometimes hundreds) relating to many consumers' credit histories and personal information, such as age, income and level of outstanding debt.

Scoring systems collect this data to try to predict a consumer's willingness and ability to pay future debts. Credit scoring systems usually produce a numerical score—a credit score. Lenders use these scores as tools to help decide if a loan should be made and to set repayment terms.

If a Credit Score Is Low

A credit score in the lower ranges doesn't automatically disqualify you from getting a loan. But it may prompt the lender to review your qualifications more carefully before deciding whether to approve or deny the loan. Or, a low credit score may result in a higher interest rate or more stringent repayment terms than those offered to other consumers.

If a lender's scoring system is properly designed, tested and monitored, it should give a faster and more impartial evaluation of creditworthiness than a loan officer could have made on his or her own.

A credit score, however, can be an imperfect way to try to predict whether someone will default on a loan. Among the reasons: the information that was reported to the company that developed the scoring model (perhaps a credit bureau) may be inaccurate or the statistical assumptions behind the program may be unsound.

Credit scores generally are not released to consumers. But under the Fair Credit Reporting Act, if you are rejected for a loan because of inaccurate information in a credit report, you have a right to get a free copy of that credit report and to have mistakes corrected. Catching and correcting any mistakes may have a positive effect on your credit score and could improve the chances that your loan will be approved.

Improving Your Score

Just like building your own credit history takes time, it also takes time to significantly improve your credit score . . . and your chances of getting a loan at favorable terms. According to a consumer brochure published by the Federal Trade Commission (FTC), you can boost a low credit score by "concentrating on paying your bills on time, paying down outstanding balances, and not taking on new debt." ("What's the Score on Your Credit?", *FDIC Consumer News* [Summer 1999])

It makes sense if you are applying for a loan or a new credit card to ensure that your credit history report is accurate. This can be done by contacting each of the major credit bureaus and asking them for a copy of the file. In fact, issuers that deny a person a credit card must supply the name, address, and telephone number of the credit bureau that produced negative information. You can contact the company within 60 days and receive a free copy of the credit report. If there's a mistake, contact the creditor and work it out. If a credit history shows one delinquent bill among a variety of good credit transactions, you should try to work it out immediately. Perhaps that bill got lost in the shuffle of moving, or old roommates didn't forward that piece of mail. Once the outstanding balance is paid, make sure the blemish is corrected on the credit report. If the credit report shows multiple incidents of delinquent payment or nonpayment, you will have to start paying much closer attention to your financial dealings. It will take time—and an excellent payment record—for creditors to conclude that you have really changed your ways. Negative comments stay on the creditor's file for seven years. A bankruptcy filing can stay on a credit history for 10 years.

For young people who have not yet established credit, it's better to start small. Apply for a gas credit card or a department store credit card. Use it sparingly and pay off the entire balance each time the bill arrives. Ask the issuer if it reports to one of the credit repositories so that there will be a record of your credit and good payment history.

Another way to establish good credit is to ask someone with a good credit history to become a co-signer. For example, a student going to college may ask one of her parents to become her co-signer. This way, the student who makes regular payments establishes good credit and the card issuer takes on little risk because the co-signer is responsible for the payments if the student doesn't make them. Such nonpayment can obviously lead to resentment and strained relationships.

If there is no relative or friend able to serve as co-signer, and no other way to establish credit, you can ask for a secured credit card. The issuer will require that you put some money in an account, and any purchases or transactions charged on the credit card come out of this reserve. It's more limiting because you can only spend a portion of the money and because the interest rates on these cards are generally higher. But by using this card smartly—making small purchases and promptly paying off the balance—and by making sure that these transactions are reported to credit repositories, you can improve your credit risk and soon apply for more advantageous credit cards.

The terms of credit cards for people with no credit history can be unattractive. For example, one recent credit card offer sent by a major national bank to someone with no credit history at all offered a $500 limit in unsecured credit, with a 23.99% APR and a one-time processing fee of $89 and an annual fee of $59 billed on the first statement. There was no grace period on purchases and a 5% transaction fee for cash advances. While accounts are reviewed every three months to determine whether the credit line is increased, the card issuer noted that it might levy a fee to increase the credit line. During this same period, people with good credit ratings were receiving offers with APRs in the single digits or low teens and no associated fees. Going with a major national credit card can be an expensive way to establish credit. Gasoline and department store credit cards, on the other hand, often require no fees and help the account holder establish some credit history.

Establishing good credit is useful for more than applying for credit cards, of course. People with the best credit receive the best terms on auto loans, home loans, and other major loans. Some employers check credit history before hiring an employee, and many landlords will check someone's credit history before renting a house or apartment to them.

Once you have decided to obtain a credit card, don't sign on the first offer received. Fees, charges, and benefits vary greatly among credit card issuers. Here's what to look for.

Annual Percentage Rate (APR): Just as banks and credit unions pay interest to bankers or investors, credit card holders pay interest to credit card issuers. The APR is stated as a yearly interest rate. It's also important to note the "periodic rate"—the rate the issuer applies to any outstanding balance to figure the finance charge for each billing period. The finance charge is the amount of interest charged to the bill each month. A zero balance, of course, doesn't accrue any interest charge. The lower the interest rate, the better.

Grace Period: This is the period between the day a credit card holder purchased something and the day the credit card company begins charging interest. If a card has a grace period of nearly a month, the credit card holder can avoid paying any interest if balances are paid off in full each month. Some credit card companies will allow a grace period for new purchases, even if the old balance isn't paid. In other words, the holder still pays the finance charge on the outstanding balance, but interest isn't calculated on purchases made that month. Others provide a grace period only for zero balance accounts. In that case, if there is an outstanding balance and new purchases are made that month, the following bill will reflect finance charges on the old balance and the new purchases. And some credit card companies provide no grace period, meaning that interest is charged on each transaction beginning the day it was made. The longer the grace period, the better.

Annual Fees: Some issuers charge no annual fee, but many credit card companies charge an annual fee, typically ranging from $15 to $55.

Credit Limit: The applicant's credit history and current income will help determine the credit limit—the amount the issuer will allow the holder to charge. It might be less than what is offered in an invitation letter. For young people just starting to establish credit, the limit can be fairly low. However, credit card companies will often increase the limit as the holder demonstrates good payment habits. As a customer service, a card issuer might agree to raise the credit limit in an emergency or at the request of the holder.

Other Charges: Some credit card issuers charge a flat fee, whether the card is used that month or not. Others charge transaction fees if the card is used to obtain a cash advance, if the payment is late, or if the holder has exceeded the credit limit.

For those who do not pay off their balance in full each month—for example someone who is using the credit card to finance a major purchase—the APR becomes the most important—and potentially costly—part of the puzzle. Look again at the earlier example of Sue and Bill. Bill pays no interest for his vacation because he had zero balance on his credit card and pays off the $29 charge as soon as the bill arrives. His credit card issuer allows a grace period, so his bill will reflect no finance charges.

Sue had an outstanding balance of $150 and added $464 during the trip, leaving her to pay off more than $600. If she does so only by paying the minimum balance due, say $40 a month, it would take her about a year and a half. All the while, she's paying an 18.5% annual percentage rate. What should be of greater concern is that Sue hasn't shown a solid understanding of her finances. Chances are that during the time she's paying off this balance, she will continue to put other charges on her account, deepening the financial hole she's in.

Credit card issuers make their money through the interest they charge. Typically, the issuer will allow a holder to pay a "minimum monthly payment," a small percentage of the outstanding balance. As long as those monthly payments are made, the credit card issuer is willing to let the person keep paying off the debt in small chunks. That's because the issuer will continue to collect interest. For example, someone with a

$2,000 balance could pay the minimum monthly payments and extend the debt for about 11 years. In that time, the interest charged to that $2,000 purchase would be $1,934, nearly double the amount.

What's worse is that debt tends to snowball. If someone is only making minimum payments, it's probably because he or she cannot afford any more. And then the temptation to use the credit card for other purchases becomes even greater. The outstanding balance grows; the finance charges grow. When it gets to the point that minimum monthly payments are only covering finance charges and not actually paying down any debt, the credit card holder is in serious financial trouble.

That apparently happens fairly regularly. Young people seem to be particularly susceptible to the lures of a credit card. In "Credit Cards on Campus: Costs and Consequences of Student Debt" (June 1999), Robert Manning noted that it would be helpful if credit card issuers and college administrators took more responsibility to see that college students, often taking those tentative steps toward financial independence, didn't end up deep in credit card debt. His report suggested that issuers limit the total revolving credit extended to individual students to no more than 20% of their incomes. Other recommendations were that college administrators should not accept subsidies from issuers, should severely restrict credit card marketing on campus, and should insist that issuers provide more financial education for students, particularly during freshman orientation.

A CREDIT CARD REVIEW: TWELVE COMMON ERRORS

If you didn't read the previous sections on credit cards, read this. Perhaps you didn't need to learn about how credit companies work, how to apply for cards, or how to use them wisely. But the following section details the 12 most common errors that people make with their credit cards. Consider it a quick review, courtesy of the FDIC.

Choosing a Card

Choosing a card for the wrong reasons. About two-thirds of card-holding Americans carry a balance on their card each month and pay interest on that debt. Yet many of these same people get an offer for a card with no annual fee and they jump at the chance, without considering whether the interest rate is high. They could pay far more in interest charges than what they save on annual fees.

Then there are people who choose a card primarily to get free airplane tickets, bonus points toward trips or cars, cash rebates, the logo of a favorite organization or sports team on the card, or other "rewards." They can end up paying more in fees or interest than the value of their "freebies." This doesn't include cases in which people buy items they might not otherwise buy just to rack up more points or miles on their card.

In general, if you expect to pay your credit card bill in full each month, your best bet is a card with no annual fee and the kinds of rebates or rewards you expect to use the most. If you don't expect to pay your card balance most months, go for a card with a low interest rate and the right mix of rebates or rewards to justify any fees.

Misunderstanding card offers. It's easy to assume too much or read too little when sorting through solicitations. At first glance, every offer may look like a good deal. But there are differences and potential dangers, depending on how you plan to use your card.

Interest rates. A low interest rate prominently featured in a mailing or advertisement actually may be a short-term "teaser" rate that, as noted in the fine print, may increase dramatically after six months or so. That low introductory rate also may only apply to balances you transfer to your card from other loans or cards you have, and not to any new purchases you put on the card. Be aware that an interest rate advertised as "fixed" still can be changed with advance notice to card holders. And if your card company does raise your rate for any reason, that new rate usually will apply to any outstanding balance plus new purchases.

Interest calculations. Consumers who routinely carry a balance on their credit card should pay closer attention to how their interest is calculated. Perhaps the most common and the most advantageous method for consumers is the "average daily balance" approach, where you'd have a 15 to 30-day "grace period" to pay before facing charges on the daily average for that period. However, a few cards have much costlier calculation methods, including the "two-cycle" system. Under that method, if you pay in full one month but only pay part of the bill the next month, you'll be charged interest for both months instead of just one.

"Pre-approved" offers. This doesn't mean you're guaranteed a card. It means that a "pre-screening" indicates you may meet the income, employment, and other criteria the card company might want in a customer. You still must apply for the card and await the results of a credit check. Also, you're not guaranteed the credit limit stated in your offer.

Before you sign up for a credit card, carefully review the solicitation and the application. By law, key terms must be disclosed; they're usually described in a separate box somewhere on the application form. If after reviewing these documents you don't understand something, call the card issuer and ask for an explanation.

Not shopping around for the best deal. It's a big mistake to assume that interest rates, credit limits, grace periods, and other card features are pretty much the same no matter which card you choose.

"The fact of the matter is that rates and terms may vary widely," says Alan Cox, a consumer affairs specialist in the FDIC's Division of Compliance and Consumer Affairs in Washington. "Because card issuers are private businesses, they set their own standards and fees according to the marketplace and internal marketing strategies." Even within one bank you can find several different types of rates and terms being offered on credit cards.

You can shop for good deals nationwide, for free, by checking the listings of cards and toll-free phone numbers that appear regularly in major consumer and financial publications. Also, twice a year, the Federal Reserve Board collects and publishes the interest rates and other terms being offered by many card issuers. The Fed makes this information and general shopping tips available in a booklet called "Shop: The Card You Pick Can Save You Money." It's available by mail (Federal Reserve Board, Publication Services, Washington, DC 20551) or on the Fed's Internet site.

You also can purchase lists of low-rate or no-fee cards regularly compiled by groups that closely follow the credit card industry. They include the nonprofit Bankcard Holders of America (524 Branch Avenue, Salem, VA 24153; phone 540–389–5445), which currently charges $4 for its report, and private publishers such as CardTrak (P.O. Box 1700, Frederick, MD 21702; phone 800–344–7714), which charges $5.

Having too many credit cards. There are good reasons to have more than one card, especially if your credit limit isn't high enough on one card to suit your needs. You don't want to be traveling and discover you can't charge a hotel room, car rental, or airline ticket because you'd exceed your credit limit. Even so, most experts agree that two or three general-purpose cards and a few (if any) cards issued by stores or oil companies should be enough for the average family.

What's wrong with too many cards? One, they make overspending too tempting. And two, they become part of your credit history. Your record will show the number of cards you own, the total amount you're eligible to borrow on your cards, the number of times you've applied for cards, plus your rejections. This can haunt you the next time you apply for a loan you really need—perhaps a mortgage or a car loan.

"Even if you don't owe a dime on those cards now, the possibility that you could borrow up to your credit limit in the future could make a lender question whether you'd be able to meet all your financial obligations," says Lisa Kimball, supervisor of the Minneapolis office of the FDIC's Division of Compliance and Consumer Affairs.

Using a Card

Getting too deep in debt. Each year millions of people drown in debt—from mortgages, home equity loans, auto loans, credit cards, and other borrowings. Many people bring on their own troubles—they can't control their spending or manage their finances wisely. But many others are responsible people who became overwhelmed by expenses or reduced income triggered by a serious illness, a job loss, or some other unforeseen event.

If you've got a serious debt problem, there may be corrective steps you can take involving your credit cards. For example, you can reduce your expenses by paying off the balance on your highest-rate loans first—usually your credit cards—even if you have higher balances on other loans. Also, you can pay for future purchases using a debit card, which deducts funds directly from your bank account.

There also are reliable credit counselors you can turn to for help at little or no cost. Unfortunately, there also are scams masquerading as "credit repair clinics" and other companies that charge big fees for unfulfilled promises or services you can perform on your own.

Running up fees and penalties that could easily have been avoided. Pay your credit card bill late—even by one day—and you may face interest charges on the outstanding balance plus your purchases. Pay with a check that bounces or exceeds your credit limit, and you could pay $20 to $30 in penalties. Become a habitual offender and your card company could significantly raise the interest rate on your card. These problems can be avoided simply by keeping better financial records and being aware of your card's fees explained in the fine print. And make sure your payment arrives at the card company by the due date; having it postmarked by that date won't suffice.

Many consumers also use their credit cards to get quick cash at an automated teller machine (ATM) or teller window, or they use one of the blank checks or "convenience checks" that card companies send to customers. In many cases these "cash advances" carry sizable up-front fees—often 2% of the amount advanced and not less than $2—a higher interest rate than regular card charges, and no grace period before interest begins accumulating. You may be better off writing a check, using a debit card, or charging purchases rather than trying to pay in cash.

Skipping a payment or paying less than you can afford. It's tempting, especially during the holiday shopping season, to take advantage of an offer from your card company to skip a payment or two. You also might like the idea of paying back only the minimum required each month or even reducing your minimum payment. But these aren't really good deals, especially if you can afford to pay off all or much of your card balance.

When you pay only the minimum on your credit card bill, you're simply taking more time to pay off your debt. That means more money in interest charges—perhaps thousands of dollars and a debt that takes 10 or 20 years longer to pay than necessary. Your card company also may begin to see you as more of a risk and decide to substantially increase your interest rate.

Not closely reviewing the notices sent by your card company. Card issuers are required to give you notice (typically at least 15 days) before increasing your interest rate, lowering your credit limit, adding fees and penalties, reducing or eliminating your grace period, or cutting back on bonus programs. But if you don't monitor your monthly billings or other mailings from your card company, you could end up paying more for a credit card that offers you less—and not even realize it.

So, to avoid paying a higher interest rate than you expected, to avoid penalties for actions that in the past were allowed, or to make sure you still get the services and bonuses you want, read that junk mail! This also gives you the opportunity to negotiate a better deal from your existing card company or to shop around for a new card.

Not correcting errors in your monthly billings. Many people don't check their monthly statements for overbillings. And even those consumers who do spot a problem don't resolve it the right way. For example, in the case of a simple overcharge, the Fair Credit Billing Act allows you to withhold payment on a disputed amount until the situation is resolved. But to be fully protected, you must report the problem to your card company in writing within 60 days of the postmark of the bill.

"A phone call—even numerous phone calls—may not be sufficient," warns the FDIC's Lisa Kimball. "I've seen several cases where people ended up responsible for fraudulent charges because they only notified the card issuer over the telephone."

If there's a problem with your monthly bill, immediately call your card company's toll-free number to report the matter. In addition, Alan Cox of the FDIC suggests that you follow up with a note that includes your name and account number, and details why the charge is incorrect. Send your note to the address designated on the bill for handling errors; do not send it in the same envelope with your payment. If you don't get an answer or acknowledgment within 30 days, follow up in writing using certified mail for proof of arrival. Keep a copy of all correspondence for your records. And be aware that you're still expected to pay the portion of your bill that is not in dispute.

Not catching errors in your credit report. Credit reports are compiled by private credit bureaus for use by lenders, employers, and others who have a legitimate need to know about your credit history and reliability. Chances are your credit reports describe how much you charge each month on your credit cards, whether you have problems paying your loans back, and whether you've filed for bankruptcy in the last 10 years.

Unfortunately, the people who supply and collect data for credit reports sometimes make mistakes, resulting in wrong or obsolete information being in your credit reports. That's why it's a good idea to review your credit reports periodically to get any errors corrected as soon as possible. First, call the three major credit bureaus and find out how to request their reports about you. You can find other credit bureaus in your phone book under "credit bureaus" or "credit reporting." Sometimes your copy is free, but if not, the most you can be charged is $8. If you spot any errors, the Fair Credit Reporting Act sets procedures and timetables for getting them corrected.

Not taking precautions against lost or stolen cards. Under federal law, if your credit card or card number is used by a thief, the most you're liable for is $50 per card. If you contact your card company before any unauthorized charges are made, you owe nothing. Still, credit card fraud is a national problem and one reason interest rates are higher on credit cards than on other types of loans. Here are some tips for fighting fraud.

First, never give your card number, confidential PIN (personal identification number), or similar personal information over the telephone unless you originate the call to someone you know is legitimate. Always save your receipts to compare to the monthly card statement, then destroy them. As for new card applications and blank "convenience checks" you receive in the mail and don't intend to use, destroy them immediately.

Second, immediately notify your card company if your card is lost or stolen, or if you spot something fishy in your monthly billing. If you've been a victim of fraud, contact the National Fraud Information Center (phone 800–876–7060, or on the Internet). The NFIC is a project of the National Consumers League in Washington, and it reports suspected frauds to the appropriate law enforcement agencies. More suggestions appear in the winter 1994 issue of *FDIC Consumer News* in a story called "Protect Your Plastic," available from the FDIC's Public Information Center.

Closing out a card for the wrong reasons, or in the wrong way. Many consumers try to cut costs by transferring the balance on one card to a new card offering a super-low introductory interest rate, but some later find out they're paying about the same money or more. That can happen if you don't pay down the transferred balance before the low rate expires—usually within six months— or if the transferred balance is subject to hefty cash advance fees or other charges. So, look before you leap from one card to another.

If you don't use a card anymore, cancel it out. Why? As previously noted, too many cards on your credit record could prompt a lender to reject your application for a mortgage or some other loan. Also, even if you don't find the card of much value, a thief who takes it from your home or wallet can use it fast!

Once you decide to cancel a card, take the following precautions. First, send a letter to the card issuer stating that you have decided to stop the card. This clarifies, for your credit records, that the card was closed by you and not by the card issuer because of any problems you may have created. Also, cut up your old card and dispose of it in such a way that a thief rummaging through your trash can't piece it together and get your account number and expiration date— it's all he needs to go on a shopping spree over the phone.

Final Thoughts

Given the intense competition in the card industry and the profits to be made, you might be surprised at how far a bank or other card company will go to sign you up or keep you as a customer. So if you're not happy with your card's interest rate, credit limit, or other terms, or if you just don't like the way a problem is being resolved, try to work things out with the card company directly.

If you can't resolve a complaint on your own, consider contacting the government for help. There may be a consumer protection law or regulation that these offices can enforce or provide information about.

Remember, a credit card can be one of your most important possessions. With more than 6,000 banks and companies now offering credit cards, chances are you'll find at least one or two cards to your liking! ("Lessons from the School of Card Knocks," FDIC Consumer News [Winter 1996/1997])

INCOME AND TAXES: UNITED THEY STAND

Previous discussions have focused on basic methods of saving and spending money. Of course, none of that can happen until some money starts to flow in—income. And any discussion on income has to touch on income taxes—the method this country uses to pay for a wide variety of government programs and services. Taxes pay for public roads, public schools, universities, and colleges, and public assistance programs such as welfare and Women, Infants and Children (WIC) payments. Taxes fund the military, the National Park Service, and acquisition of new park lands. The federal government functions because of taxes collected from American workers and businesses. On the state and local level, Americans can particularly see their tax dollars at work in services such as potholes being filled, garbage being collected, and airports being built.

American workers cannot direct where their tax dollars go. In other words, no one can say, "I'm only paying 80% of my tax bill this year because I don't approve of the military action overseas." That's not an option. It is the job of federal, local, and state legislators to determine where and how taxes are spent. Americans do have some input into tax issues, as evidenced by relatively frequent updates in tax laws.

But the Internal Revenue Service (IRS) makes it clear that it expects workers to pay their taxes on time. For most workers, taxes are deducted directly from their paychecks. When employees start a new job, they fill out an Employee's Withholding Allowance Certificate or Form W-4. (See Appendix E for a sample form.) This IRS form determines how much of the paycheck will be withheld for federal income taxes. An employer uses the number of allowances claimed, together with income earned and marital status, to determine how much income to withhold. An employer also has the opportunity to withhold more than the recommended amount, because the employee might owe taxes for other reasons—another part time job, or a tip-based job, for which taxes withheld won't be enough to cover the tax liability. The idea is that it is easier to withhold small amounts on a per-paycheck basis than to pay larger amounts when taxes are due quarterly.

The IRS recently offered the following examples on its Web site showing what taxes are withheld from paychecks. It created two teens: a music store clerk who receives an hourly wage and a pizza delivery person receiving a wage plus tips.

The music clerk works a cash register at the store, from 10 A.M. to 5 P.M., five days a week. At $8 an hour, her earnings are $280 per week.

Here's what happens to that $280 paycheck. For federal taxes, $26 is withheld (based on one exemption); her state taxes withheld are another $5.08, and local taxes equal $1.23. Social Security tax is $17.36 and Medicare tax is $4.06. That brings her total deductions to $53.73. Her net pay, or take-home pay, is $226.27.

The pizza delivery guy works from 5 P.M. to 10 P.M. five days a week. He's earning $5.25 per hour plus tips. His weekly paycheck is $131.25 and his tips total an additional $150. Tips are taxable and must be reported as income. So his total earnings for the week in this example equal $281.25. On weeks that his tip total is lower, his overall earnings are lower; on weeks when it's higher, his earnings and therefore his tax liability are higher.

Since his weekly total is almost exactly the same as the music clerk's, his deductions are almost the same as well. Federal tax withholding is $26, state taxes are $5.25, local taxes are $1.28, Social Security taxes are $17.46, and Medicare tax is $4.08. His total deductions are $54.07, leaving him with $227.18 in take-home pay.

Workers who have income from tips are supposed to track the total of that income and report it on their annual tax return. In fact, it is frequently reported on Form W-2. All employers send out these W-2 forms every January (or sometimes sooner) to every employee who worked for the business during the previous year. (See Appendix F for a sample.) The form is a statement of the employee's earnings in wages, tips, and other compensation. It also shows how much money was deducted from the employee's paychecks for federal, state, Social Security, and Medicare taxes and how much money the employee put into a tax-deferred 401(K) savings plan. These are very important forms, and a copy must be filed with federal and state taxes. When they arrive in the mail, store them in a safe place where they can easily be found when it's time to complete the tax return.

April 15 is a date ingrained in most Americans' minds. It's the date tax returns are due to be filed for the previous year. Many young people can use a simplified version of the tax return called Form 1040EZ. Single taxpayers and married taxpayers without children or other dependents who have earned less than $50,000 and have interest income of less than $400 can use the EZ form. Before filing a tax return, make a copy of it and save it. Many counselors suggest holding onto tax returns and critical supporting documents forever. Lenders of large sums, such as mortgages, often ask to see several years' worth of tax returns to determine whether an applicant is a good risk for a large loan. And should questions about a tax return ever arise, it's much easier to pull a copy out of storage than to try to recreate the year's filings.

For taxpayers who fall outside the parameters for filing the EZ form, Form 1040 is the one to use. These forms and instruction books can be found in libraries, post offices, government office buildings, and even online beginning early each year.

The more complicated one's income stream, the more complex the filing. People who buy and sell stocks and earn more than $400 in taxable interest income, people who earn money as independent contractors or are self-employed, and people who use home office deductions or own rental property are required to file special forms and keep evidence of these deductions.

ARE TAXES FAIR?

That's a question that legislators and economists regularly ask. The better the national economy and the bigger the federal budget surplus, the more some people ask why the IRS continues to collect taxes at the same rate. Many organizations, states, communities, and legislators revisit this question regularly.

In September 1999, the Washington, D.C. based Tax Foundation published "The Price of Civilized Society." (The titled was inspired by Justice

Oliver Wendell Holmes, Jr., who said in 1904, "Taxes are what we pay for civilized society.") Tax Foundation economist Patrick Fleenor, who authored the report, projected that in 1999, Americans would spend more money per capita on taxes than on food, clothing, and shelter combined. The price of civilized society tallied up to $10,298 for every man, woman, and child in the country. The report allocated major per capita spending in 1999 as follows:

Taxes: $10,298—$7,026 of which is federal taxes alone.

Food: $2,693

Clothing: $1,404

Shelter: $5,833

Health and Medical Care: $3,829

Transportation: $2,568

Recreation: $1,922

The Tax Foundation is also known for its annual announcement of Tax Freedom Day, a way to illustrate how much of your budget goes to pay for taxes. By projecting an average tax rate and calculating federal, state, and local taxes, economists figure out how long employees need to work to pay off their tax debt. In 1999, the Tax Foundation economists calculated an average 35.7% tax rate, meaning that national Tax Freedom Day fell on May 11. The average worker would have to work 131 days to pay his or her annual tax share; 89 days would be needed to pay federal tax, and 42 days to pay state and local taxes. Said another way, until May 11, employees worked to pay off their tax debt; for the rest of the year, the money was theirs.

Tax Freedom Day falls on a different day each year, and there is a difference among the states, too, as tax burdens differ. In 1999, residents of Washington, D.C., had the highest tax burden in the country. Their Tax Freedom Day wasn't until May 23. The five states with the highest tax burden in 1999 were, respectively, Connecticut, New York, Minnesota, Wisconsin, and New Jersey. Residents of Alabama, Arkansas, and West Virginia, states with the lowest tax burden, could celebrate their Tax Freedom Day on April 30.

INSURANCE: THE PRICE OF PROTECTION

Calamities cost big money. So people buy insurance to limit their financial risk in case of an unforeseen event. You have car insurance even if you drive an old jalopy so you don't have to pay out of pocket for the damage you might do to someone else's car. You have health insurance so that an accident that puts you in the hospital for three days doesn't also send you to the poor house. Mortgagers require homeowner's insurance to protect their investment as well as yours.

Buying the different insurance products is done fairly easily and can even be done over the phone or the Internet. They all have the same variable elements—a premium and a deductible and added on services. The higher the deductible, the amount you'll have to pay before the insurance company will start kicking in when you file a claim, the lower the premium—the amount you pay monthly or at some other regular interval.

It's also important to recognize how many life insurance agents are paid. Often, it's by commission, meaning they earn a percentage of the policy sold. In other words, the more coverage you purchase, the higher their commission. That's not to say all insurance agents are out to sell you more insurance than you need, but it does suggest that purchasers of insurance should ask lots of questions, understand completely the policy they're purchasing, and shop around.

Another factor to keep in mind when shopping for insurance is the stability of the insurance company issuing the policy. There are several insurance rating services, such as Moody's and Best's, which regularly review and update their characterization of the financial health and stability of insurance companies. After all, when an accident occurs or disaster strikes, you want to make sure the company has the assets to pay. The following kinds of insurance are available to cover financial losses that could occur from damage to your car or home or serious injury or death.

Auto Insurance

Drivers are required to have their own auto insurance or be covered by another's policy. Auto insurance can cover a variety of claims, including roadside assistance, towing, collision, injury, and death. Review auto policies regularly and make adjustments when needed. For example, the policy purchased for a new car might include collision coverage for repairs to your own car. However, it might be worth dropping this coverage, or increasing the deductible, for older cars.

Homeowner's Insurance

A homeowner's policy protects the homeowner (and the mortgage holder) from damages caused by natural disasters, fire, theft, and other factors. Typically mortgage holders require, at the minimum, insurance coverage for the full value of the loan amount. Homeowners who live in flood-prone areas, or areas where natural disasters strike fairly rou-

tinely, purchase additional coverage for those circumstances. Homeowner's insurance also covers private property in the home.

Renter's Insurance

Renters who have considerable private property—computers, jewelry,
and electronic equipment, for example—can purchase renter's insurance.
This insurance allows the renter to file claims for those covered items in
case of theft, fire, or disaster. Renter's personal property is not covered
by the landlord's homeowner's insurance.

Health Insurance

Purchasing health insurance is one of the more complicated insurance
decisions. Often employers offer health insurance, also called major medical, as an employee benefit. How these plans are offered varies widely.
Some employers pick up the entire premium for the employee; others
contribute part of the premium. Employees may need to pay for additional coverage for family members, and some employers offer "cafeteria
plans" that allow employees to select the services that best suit their
needs. Other employers may contract with a number of health insurers
or plans, from which employees can select the plan that best suits their
needs. Typically, the human resources department will explain to a new
employee what the coverage terms and options are.

Health insurance is a major benefit that employers provide. And it's
expensive. That's why some smaller employers don't provide it. Purchasing individual health insurance is possible. Do some online research,
ask co-workers if they belong to any purchasing groups, or check in with
some local insurance agents to find out what the options are.

Young people who have finished their schooling but haven't yet found
a job that provides health benefits might find themselves facing a period
of being uninsured. Take action before that happens. There are several
options:

• Short-term insurance. Many insurers offer special policies for people who need
  health insurance for a short period, usually between 30 days and 12 months.
• Continue student coverage. This must be arranged before the student graduates
  from college.
• COBRA. This federal law—Consolidated Omnibus Budget Reconciliation Act
  of 1985, provides guaranteed rights to stay on a former employer's health plan
  under most circumstances. If the young person has an illness or condition that
  would make him or her uninsurable if health insurance coverage lapsed, parents should contact the health insurance carrier or human resources department

that has covered the student while he or she was still in school. It might be possible to continue coverage for at least 18 months through COBRA.

It may be tempting for the self-employed or part-time employee to skip the cost of self-insuring, but the consequences can be severe. A bill for a day or two in the hospital can get into the thousands of dollars quickly. In contrast, healthy young people, especially those who don't smoke or are not involved in high risk activities, typically can get adequate insurance for relatively low rates.

Health care coverage is and continues to be a key social issue. How much should the federal government do to make sure Americans have health coverage? Legislators tried to tackle some of those issues in the late 1990s. In 1997, Congress approved medical savings accounts (MSAs) into which self-employed or other uninsured workers could deposit a percentage of their high-deductible health insurance premiums. The idea was to stimulate savings for medical expenses by offering this as a pretax option. The money invested in the MSA would not be subject to federal income tax. And the insured would benefit by having this pool of money to draw from for paying medical expenses. As long as disbursements from these MSAs are used for medical expenses, they will not be taxed. The MSA legislation was temporary. Congress agreed that it would test the concept of MSAs until 2000. However, if the analysis proves positive, the concept might be continued or reintroduced in a similar form.

The federal government also passed the Health Insurance Portability and Accountability Act (HIPAA) in 1996. One of the ideas behind this law was to ensure that people with serious or chronic conditions could continue to get health coverage. HIPAA allows states to tackle how this will be accomplished. Some states have guaranteed-issue policies, meaning that these patients in high risk categories are guaranteed coverage, but at much higher premiums. In order to qualify for HIPAA coverage, certain conditions have to be met. Essentially, an individual with an illness or serious health condition should not let coverage lapse. Someone leaving an employer-provided health plan can continue to purchase insurance through that employer for 18 months. This is known as COBRA.

Disability Insurance

Disability insurance provides income should a person become disabled for a limited period or for the duration of a lifetime. Typically, self-employed professionals consider disability insurance a necessity. Imagine a surgeon who is blinded in an accident. Traditional health insurance will cover any life-saving procedures, rehabilitation, and prosthetic devices. But it seems unlikely that the surgeon will be able to return to surgery. Perhaps the injury is to one eye only, so the physician will be able to continue to practice medicine, but in a lower-paying capacity. Whether the disability is short-term or permanent, disability insurance would provide a stream of income.

Life Insurance

Again, life insurance is a benefit that is sometimes provided by employers. What kind of life insurance—and how much—you need depends on the circumstances at the time you're purchasing it. If others—for example, a spouse and children—rely on your income, life insurance would provide some of that lost income should you die. Other people use life insurance as a part of their estate planning, to ensure that beneficiaries of the estate have the cash on hand to pay taxes and other outstanding bills without having to sell assets. Because beneficiaries of life insurance policies do not owe federal income tax on the proceeds, life insurance policies play a predictable role in financial planning of estates.

Before meeting with an insurance agent, try to calculate how much insurance you need to carry. Insurers typically suggest a rule of thumb that a recommended policy should equal five to seven times a person's annual gross income. But for a young, unmarried professional with employer-sponsored life insurance that figure seems large. On the other hand, for a young married person with children who is the sole or primary income earner, a policy of that size would provide a needed safety net for the surviving family.

Some calculations to keep in mind are how much money the people who rely on your income would need to cover your expenses for illness, burial, and taxes. Also calculate how much time it would take a spouse, for example, to find a better paying job. Most people would dread the thought of a spouse who has been home with young children having to find a job right away to avoid financial devastation. That's precisely what life insurance is for. It can provide at least interim support and potentially much more: money to seed college funds or the spouse's retirement.

The amount of the policy is only one consideration. There are different kinds of life insurance policies, including term, whole life, and universal or adjustable life.

Term insurance

Term insurance provides protection for a specific number of years, generally between 10 and 20 years. The policy pays out to your beneficiaries only if you die during the term. Some term policies can be renewed when the term expires. But term policies generally carry no cash value when they expire. (It's like auto insurance that way. Even if you don't file any claims that year, you don't get your premiums refunded.) Why consider term insurance? Premiums are typically lower than for permanent insurance, at least initially. The premiums increase as you grow older. If you plan on holding the policy less than 10 years, term is almost always the way to go.

Here's an example of someone who could benefit from term insurance. Let's say our policy holder is a young accountant. She's the primary income earner while her husband is developing a carpentry business that he runs out of the home. Right now, he's working around their four-year-old twins' preschool hours and on weekends. The couple has decided that his schedule has the greater flexibility, so he'll be the primary caretaker of the children while they're young. She selects a term policy for 20 years because it has low premiums now and would provide for her husband and children during these years when he is building his business and the children are in school. They're three years into a 15-year mortgage, so the insurance benefit would help her family keep the house should she die. She's actively contributing to her retirement account and believes that if they stay with the modest spending habits they've developed, they'll have plenty of money on hand for college education and retirement when the 20-year term is up. Because the premiums are initially lower for term policies than for permanent policies, disciplined savers could probably earn more by taking out a term policy and putting the difference in another investment vehicle. But for people who don't make saving a habit, permanent policies could be an advantage.

Permanent life insurance

There are several different kinds of permanent policies: whole life, universal life and variable. What they have in common is that they provide lifelong protection, and most have a cash value, some amount of money accrued in the account that you can use later. But this is clearly a longer term policy. The amount of cash value builds slowly in the early years.

The greatest advantage of permanent insurance is that protection is guaranteed, so long as the policy holder pays the necessary premiums. In other words, once you have a policy, it's yours. In contrast, someone with a term policy could develop an illness or medical condition during the term that would make it difficult or expensive to get another type of insurance when the term expires.

A second advantage of these types of policies is that they have cash value, all or some of which can be surrendered (traded in, essentially) or borrowed against. The cash value can also be converted into an annuity, another kind of insurance product that provides an income for a specific amount of time.

Whole life or ordinary life   This is the most common form of permanent life insurance and typically requires that premium amounts remain constant over the life of the policy.

Adjustable life   After your initial payment, this policy allows you to pay premiums at any time, in virtually any amount, subject to certain minimums and maximums. You also can reduce or increase the amount of the death benefit more easily than under a traditional whole life policy. To increase your death benefit, you usually will be required to furnish the insurance company with evidence of your continued good health.

Universal life   This policy is a variation of whole life. In a universal policy, the "term" portion—the pure insurance part of the policy—is separated from the investment portion. The investment portion is invested in money market funds and therefore could grow faster than whole life policies, in which investments are made in bonds and mortgages.

Variable life   This policy passes some risk on to the policy holder because it is based on the performance of a portfolio of investments. As with other kinds of investments, the policy holder can allocate the premiums among a variety of investments such as stocks, bonds, or some combination thereof. The advantage to a variable life policy is that good investment performance yields higher cash value and death benefits. Poor performance, on the other hand, reduces both.

There are universal life and whole life versions of variable life. And annuities are also available in variable policies. While variable policies have the greatest chance of fast growth, they also carry risk. In other words, it is possible to lose some or all of the money invested.

That's why it is important to take your time in making insurance decisions. Do not allow an agent to pressure you into making a decision on the spot. Research the company and the specific insurance product you're purchasing. Ask if there is a review period. Some insurance companies will allow you about 10 days to review the policy; if you cancel the policy within that time, you may be entitled to a refund of some or all of your initial payment.

When the policy arrives, review it thoroughly. Make sure there are no surprises, errors, or missing information. And think hard before buying another policy to replace the one you have. Sometimes you may be approached with a great offer on a new policy, but calculate in the costs of surrendering your existing policy before moving ahead.

ADDITIONAL READING

The Federal Trade Commission (FTC) provides the following free booklets on credit: "How to Dispute Credit Report Errors," "Fair Credit

Reporting" and "Credit Scoring." For these and other FTC consumer publications, write the Consumer Response Center, Federal Trade Commission, Washington, DC 20580, call (877) FTC–HELP (382–4357), or check out these publications at www.ftc.gov. Also look at Patrick Fleenor, "The Price of Civilized Society" (Washington, DC: Tax Foundation, 1999).

ADDITIONAL RESOURCES

A. M. Best's insurance reports. Life-Health United States, published by A. M. Best Company.

Local insurance agent.

National Insurance Consumer Helpline (NICH): 1 (800) 942–4242. NICH is a toll-free consumer information telephone service sponsored by insurance industry trade associations.

Moody's bank and finance manual, published by Financial Information services, a division of Financial Communications Company Inc.

4

Saving and Investing

Young savers often see the reward of their actions. Their money grows. At intervals, they see statements showing how much interest their savings have earned. And many people also decide that letting money sit in a savings bank passbook account, with a low single digit interest rate, is not the kind of growth they'd like to see. That's when it's time to start looking at other options.

CERTIFICATES OF DEPOSIT (CDs)

Banks sell certificates of deposit that earn a higher rate of interest than ordinary savings accounts. The account holder, in return, agrees to keep the money in the bank for a certain amount of time, typically ranging from six months to five years. Generally, the longer the term, the higher the interest rate. The CD "matures" when the time is up. Account holders can withdraw the money before the maturity date, but a penalty is applied. CDs are generally insured by the U.S. government for up to $100,000.

SAVINGS BONDS

Another savings vehicle is U.S. Savings Bonds. They are popular and easy. Some of the features savings bond investors particularly like are that they are as safe and secure as the U.S. Treasury. Series EE bonds are purchased at half of their face value. In other words, a $50 bond costs the buyer $25. Bonds are issued in denominations ranging from $50 to $10,000. The interest rate determines when a bond reaches maturity. For example, a bond earning an average of 5% would reach face value in just over 14 years, while a bond earning an average of 6% would reach face value in 12 years. If, for some reason, interest rates aren't high enough so that a bond has reached face value at 17 years, the U.S. Treasury will increase the bond value to redemption value at that time. If bonds are lost, stolen, or destroyed, they can be replaced.

The interest earned on Series EE bonds is exempt from state and local taxes, and federal income tax is deferred until the bonds are cashed in, or until they stop earning interest after 30 years. Interest is accrued monthly, and the rate of interest is determined on the first of May and the first of November of every year. The rate of interest is 90% of the average of the five-year Treasury note and bond yields for the six months prior to the date the new rate is announced.

Another tool offered by the Treasury Department are inflation-index bonds. With these bonds, the Treasury guarantees a real return to the investor. In times of high inflation, the return on a bond could be negated by the inflation. But with inflation-indexed bonds, the Treasury is taking the inflation risk and adjusting principal and interest payments to the changes in the inflation rate.

Some people use savings bonds as a college funding tool. Lower- and middle-income investors might qualify for special tax benefits, which would allow them to exclude all or part of the interest earned from income taxes if the bonds are used to pay for college. Some investors also like savings bonds as part of their retirement funding because savings bonds earn interest for 30 years.

Series EE bonds can be cashed any time after six months, but most investors hold onto them longer. Bonds cashed in before five years are subject to a three-month interest penalty. For example, if one were to cash a bond after holding it two years, one would receive 21 months' worth of interest, not 24 months' worth. After holding the bond for five years, there is no penalty.

There are some other restrictions. U.S. Savings Bonds are only available to residents of the United States or its territories or American citizens living abroad. They can be purchased by residents of Canada or Mexico who work in the United States and have a Social Security number. There is a limit of $15,000 purchase price of bonds per year, per person. Bonds can be owned individually, co-owned with another person, or registered to a beneficiary. The owner may then cash the bond during his or her lifetime, but a surviving beneficiary becomes the sole owner after the first owner dies.

The bond earns interest from the U.S. Treasury. That's why a bond can be sold for $25, for example, and still say $50 on the bond itself. Bond owners can choose to pay tax on interest annually or defer that payment until the bond is cashed or reaches final maturity 30 years after it was issued. Interest stops accruing after 30 years. However, Series EE bond owners can exchange mature bonds within a year after final maturity for Series HH bonds and defer taxes for an additional 20 years, the life of HH bonds, or until those bonds are cashed. Because the holder can choose when to cash in bonds, he or she can often select a time during which the taxes will be lowest.

In fact, one way some lower- and middle-income Americans can avoid taxes on the interest earned on Series EE bonds is to use them to pay for postsecondary (college, university, or qualified technical school) education. There are a number of conditions, but generally, if the bonds are redeemed in the year the owner is paying for tuition and required fees, not including room, board, or book expenses, the bond owner may exclude interest on these bonds from income for federal income tax. The income limits to which this exemption applies are adjusted annually. A critical requirement is that the savings bond be held in the parent's name.

Savings bond owners should keep track of their bonds. Notably, they should keep complete records on the bonds, including their serial numbers, face amounts, issue dates, redemption dates, and total proceeds received. If bond owners hope to qualify for the postsecondary education income tax exemption, they should also keep records on the expenses paid for college tuition and the dates they were paid.

There's some nifty free software available that helps savings bond holders determine the value of their bonds. It can be downloaded from the Web site: http://www.savingsbonds.gov.

Savings bonds are among the safest investments because the government guarantees they will reach their face value. But 17 years is a long time to wait for an investment to double in value, especially when the news reports talk about one of the strongest runs on the stock market. The time it takes money to double is known as the "Rule of 72." Divide 72 by the interest rate an investment is earning and the result is roughly the number of years it should take for money to double. Remember most investments don't earn a consistent amount of interest—rates fluctuate. But here's an example. A $1,000 investment earning 18% interest would be worth $2,000 in about four years (72 divided by 18). On the other hand, it would take more than 10 years for a $1,000 investment earning 7% interest to double in value (72 divided by 7).

THE STOCK MARKET

So why doesn't everyone put their money in high-growth stocks? Because stock performance is not predictable. These kinds of investments carry the potential of much higher rewards, but they also carry more risk. In fact, typically reward and risk go hand in hand. Aggressive investments aim for the highest return. These are often investments in new technologies. If the company is a hit, the rewards are big. If the company collapses, so does its stock value. Since investments in stock are not insured by the FDIC, you face the possibility of losing even the principal—the amount you've invested.

Many investors, either alone or with the help of a financial counselor, undergo a risk assessment. Simply put, this exercise helps you decide how much risk you're willing to take with your money. Investors should do this exercise regularly because one's risk tolerance changes. For example, someone opening a college fund for a toddler can risk the higher volatility and higher potential gain from an aggressive investment. Chances are good that over 15 or so years, the account can weather any downturns and still come out ahead. But the 63-year-old couple facing retirement in two years probably doesn't want to take too many chances that a sudden downturn will leave them with a fraction of their retirement savings.

But how does money earn high rates of return? Investors turn to the stock market—most often the New York Stock Exchange (NYSE), the American Stock Exchange, or the Nasdaq. At the end of November 1998, 3,104 companies had stock listed on the NYSE. It is on Wall Street that investors buy and sell stock in companies, but of course, you don't have to physically be there. Stocks are shares in the company, purchased or sold at the price at which they are trading that day. When companies do well, their stock value increases. When companies do poorly, the stock value drops. But that doesn't necessarily mean it's time to ditch the stock. Many investors believe that if the company is operated by competent business people and makes a good product, the stock will continue to be profitable.

Companies sell stocks because it brings them money. Here's one example of how it works. A small company has been making widgets for the local community. These widgets are of fine quality, and demand is increasing. In order for the company to grow, it needs an infusion of money to buy additional equipment, hire more workers, and expand its distribution network. It might do some of this with a business loan. For the next five years, the company becomes the predominant widget maker in a five-state area. And still the demand grows. The company then develops plans to "go public" with an initial public offering (IPO) of its stock. This is a complex process during which time the company must file financial reports with the Securities and Exchange Commission, the federal agency created to act as watchdog over publicly held companies. When the SEC approves, the company holds its IPO and can sell up to a specified number of shares of stock.

The result is that the company gets access to more cash than it could have gained through loans, and believers in the company's product gain a chance to share in its success. If the widget maker does well, the shareholders see the value of their stock increase and may receive periodic dividends. If it does poorly because of mismanagement or if a competitor comes out with a widget that's far superior, the stock price will drop and investors could lose money.

That's why advisors counsel that money allocated for investments should be money you don't need right away. Most experts suggest keeping a cushion of at least three to six months of living expenses in a savings or checking account. But beyond that, people turn to investments such as bonds, stocks, mutual funds, real estate, and commodities such as silver and gold.

One way to protect against the risk of one investment going sour is to spread your money among different types of investments. That's where the risk assessment comes in handy. Let's say a person decides she is willing to take a high risk with about 40% of her capital. Another 40% will go into medium-risk investments—those that have shown moderate growth at a steady pace. And the final 20% is kept in safe, liquid investments, such as CDs. Now she can seek investments that match her tolerance for risk.

MUTUAL FUNDS

Investors can diversify by selecting a wide variety of individual stocks and bonds or can obtain built-in diversification by purchasing shares in stock mutual funds. Mutual funds are operated by professionals who pool individuals' investments. With the pooled money, managers can buy stocks and investors own a portion of the various stocks. Before investing in a mutual fund, an investor should read the prospectus, a description of the fund that includes which stocks comprise the fund. Investors can select mutual funds that match their investment ideals. For example, there are "green" fund companies that select ecologically friendly companies, or funds in which the companies meet a set of social criteria—such as a commitment to hiring women and minorities, or investing in developing companies.

Investors buy shares of a mutual fund, and those shares rise or fall as the values of the stocks and bonds held by the fund rise and fall. Many funds charge an up-front fee for buying or selling shares of the fund. Called loads, these fees help pay administrative expenses. However, there are some low-load and even no-load mutual funds, so compare the costs along with the performance and makeup of the funds.

BONDS

Some companies also issue bonds, which give investors more of a guarantee than stocks. "More of a guarantee does not mean risk-free, however. You purchase the bond, and the company agrees to pay you back your initial investment plus interest. Even if the company is very profitable, however, the interest rate doesn't go up. If the company does poorly, both stock and bond holders are likely to lose money. But the companies are obligated to pay bond holders before stockholders, if any money remains after liquidation.

Buying a bond means you are lending money to a government, municipality, corporation, or federal agency. Among the types of bonds you can choose from are U.S. government securities, municipal bonds, corporate bonds, mortgage and asset-backed securities, federal agency securities, and foreign government bonds.

Bonds typically have a predictable stream of payments and repayment of principal, so many people invest in bonds to preserve and increase their capital or to receive dependable interest income.

INVESTING: WITH AN ADVISOR OR FLYING SOLO?

Investing can be a hairy experience. Have you seen those images of businessmen flinging themselves from windows when the stock market crashed in October 1929? For many people, the stakes are big, Misjudging the timing or what a stock is going to do can cost thousands of dollars, and a few wrong choices can devastate your life savings.

Even so, many people are investing in the stock market. And the Internet has made that even easier. There are now online brokerage services that allow investors to buy and sell stocks electronically. That option has become more popular with hands-on investors who study companies and their stock performance before they invest.

But many other investors don't have the time or interest to scour a company's financial reports trying to gauge what's promising and what's not. Those investors are more likely to benefit from investment options such as mutual funds, where the choices are limited to the funds rather than to the individual companies issuing stock, or by using an investment professional.

There is no shortage of people willing to give investment advice. As the stock market becomes more familiar to more people, the number of individuals who can report on a terrific year with a certain stock is likely to increase. While investment advice from colleagues might provide a great tip, that's not the kind of advice brokers, investment advisors, or accountants typically provide. Financial and investment advisors are more likely to develop a complete financial plan, analyzing each of the financial goals you have and creating a strategy for how to meet them.

Before hiring an advisor, find out how they are paid. Fee-only advisors charge a fee for their professional services but receive no commissions from the choices you make. Often, these fees are higher than what a commission advisor may charge, but depending on how much and how often you buy and sell stock, the final charge will vary. Others may charge a management fee, often a percentage of the assets they are managing for you. It is appropriate to ask advisors what services they will provide, the total cost, and how they are paid.

Another way to get investment advice is through brokers. Brokers typically work for large firms, many of which have researchers who spend their days analyzing specific markets and companies. An investor who wants to try to make money in the IPO market, for example, can go to a broker who works for a company that follows IPOs specifically. The same is true for an investor who believes the financial future belongs to high tech companies. Some brokerages follow the technology field more closely than others.

Brokers are typically paid on commissions. Discount brokerages, as the name implies, typically charge lower commissions, but might not provide the same level of guidance as they do at full-service brokerages.

The SEC suggests asking the following questions during an interview with an investment professional:

What training and experience do you have?

How long have you been in business?

What is your investment philosophy? Do you take a lot of risks or are you more concerned about the safety of my money?

Describe your typical client. Can you provide me with references, the names of people who have invested with you for a long time?

How do you get paid? By commission? Amount of assets you manage? Another method? Do you get paid more for selling your own firm's products?

How much will it cost me in total to do business with you?

As part of your decision to purchase stocks, you have to determine what kind of investor you are. Are you jumpy? Do you think you'll want to sell if the stock dips in value? Selling too fast can result in losses— not only do you have to pay commissions, but you may have panicked during a momentary downturn. On the other hand, you can't be too sanguine about a stock that is performing poorly. At some point, it might be worth selling at a loss, particularly if you fear that the stock will continue plummeting.

On most evening news broadcasts, you'll hear an announcer say that trading on Wall Street was up or down in heavy or light trading. But what happens on Wall Street overall might not necessarily be an indication of what happened with your particular stocks. Sometimes news reports—such as changes in the unemployment rate, consumer spending levels, trade deficits, financial trouble in international markets—affect stock prices as investors and analysts anticipate what they mean. But there are an increasing number of investors who continue to tuck money into retirement plans, for example, who worry little about the day-to-day goings on at the stock exchange. These investors feel they are in the market for the long haul and can accept the fluctuations. In fact, some investors like to look for bargain stocks after a quick drop in stock prices.

It's easy to find out how your stocks or mutual funds are performing. Many publicly held companies or mutual fund companies have their own Internet sites which have links to investor information. Through the Internet, investors can check on the current price of stocks or see graphs of recent performance. This information is also available in business sections of newspapers. Most newspapers run a weekly synopsis of New York Stock Exchange, Nasdaq, and mutual fund prices. These reports typically include charts showing the movement of stocks over the week in the Dow Jones Industrial Average, Nasdaq, NYSE, and Standard & Poor's 500. Follow the column heading for the NYSE to find the following: a 52-week high and low trading price, the stock's name, abbreviated; any dividend; the yield; the price to earnings ratio (PE); volume of trading; the week's high and low trading values; the "last" or closing price at the end of the previous business day; and the change, the increase or decrease from the prior day's closing value.

Just as important as how individual stocks or funds are performing is how one's overall portfolio is performing. Let's go back to the investor who decided that her risk tolerance was for 40% aggressive risk, 40% moderate risk, and 20% low risk. To achieve that, she allocated half of her 401(k) contribution to an aggressive growth fund and half to a more moderate fund. She's also continuing to put money into CDs on her own. When she receives a quarterly report from the investment management company, she sees that her aggressive growth stock has done so well that it now accounts for 64% of her portfolio. That represents more risk than she was interested in. She now has to decide whether she wants to reconsider her risk tolerance level or whether she wants to switch some of the assets in that fast-growing fund into the more moderate plan.

DAY TRADING: XTREME INVESTING?

Day trading made the headlines in the summer of 1999, not because of anything that happened in the financial markets but because of grisly murders. In July, Mark Barton walked into two Atlanta, Georgia, day trading firms and shot and killed nine people, injuring a dozen more. Clearly, Barton's troubles went beyond financial losses—he had also murdered his wife and two children—but the incident spawned a series of stories around the country about the high stakes and high stress of day trading.

However, even before this incident, day trading and the inherent dangers of the get-rich-quick lure had appeared on the radar screen of politicians and regulators. Day trading is a relatively new phenomenon by which traders hold their stocks for only minutes or hours. They buy and sell stocks based solely on the numbers, not on the more traditional methods of determining the value, business plan, and stability of the company itself. Day trading is characterized by a fast and furious pace. For example, the slogan for the group Day Traders USA, based in Orange County, California, is "Where long term investing is holding a stock over the weekend."

Day trading is not the same as online trading. Most online brokerages allow investors to order a stock electronically. Those transactions are not immediate.

Day traders can potentially make—or lose—huge amounts of money. Split-second timing can make a difference of thousands of dollars:

Day trading is not yet huge—and it might never be. SEC Chairman Arthur Levitt testified before a Senate subcommittee on September 16, 1999, saying, "This new trading phenomenon, while well-publicized, is relatively limited in its reach, with the number of day traders estimated to be less than 7,000. By comparison, there are close to 80 million individuals that own stock and more than 5 million investors using the Internet for brokerage services."

Still, the SEC and others find the practice worrisome. Senator Susan M. Collins (R-ME), chair of the Senate subcommittee conducting the hearings, cited these examples of day traders' disastrous decisions: "[A] 28 year-old bank employee in California left his job and borrowed $40,000 from credit cards to become a day trader, only to lose all of his money day trading within two months. The young man is now deeply in debt and living with his parents. In Chicago, a waiter with no investment experience became a day trader and lost an inheritance of more than $200,000. The waiter told the Subcommittee staff that many people with whom he day traded knew as little about investing as he did. In Boston, an elderly man with severe health problems lost about $250,000 of his wife's savings in just a few hours at a day trading firm," she said during the hearings.

Levitt also testified that day and explained how day trading evolved:

The practice of marketing day trading on a retail basis appears to have started about three years ago when advances in computer software allowed individuals to have direct links to the securities markets in a way previously available only to registered professionals. Because the level of individual trading activity varies across a wide spectrum, it is difficult to clearly define "day trading" or "day trader." On one end of the spectrum lie investors who trade occasionally—sometimes on-line—and hold their investments for the longer term. Moving along the spectrum, an increasing number of individuals use their on-line accounts both to invest longer term and to trade short term on momentum or small changes in the price of a stock. On the far end of the spectrum are so-called "day traders," who exclusively buy and sell stock rapidly throughout the day trying to make money on short-term market moves.

A fundamental distinction between a day trader and a more traditional retail investor who manages investments on-line is the kind of broker-dealer through which he or she trades. The typical broker-dealer the Commission identifies as a day-trading firm advertises the day-trading services it offers along with the benefits of day trading, and solicits individuals to become full-time day traders. Most day-trading firms also teach individuals to engage in strategies based on rapid-fire buying and selling of price-sensitive stocks and then encourage these individuals to use this strategy on an ongoing basis. For a fee, some firms—or their affiliates—provide training on how to make money trading on small price movements. Day-trading firms also frequently provide their traders with proprietary software and systems that analyze and chart activity in particular stocks. Typically, day-trading firms offer these services at on-site trading facilities, rather than through Internet web sites. On-line firms, by contrast, merely offer an electronic order entry service to their customers and do not encourage the use of any particular trading strategy.

A second distinction between traditional brokerage and day-trading firms is that day-trading firms provide individuals with "real time" links to the major stock markets and the Nasdaq. These linkages give individuals substantial market information not readily available to the average retail investor and provide direct entry to the firms' order processing systems. This direct access to market-operated order execution systems allows these individuals to send their orders to a particular market or market maker. Through these systems, day traders can receive a trade execution within seconds.

Although broker-dealers are not required to identify themselves as "day-trading firms," 62 broker-dealers, with 287 branch offices, were recently characterized as day-trading firms by the North American Securities Administrators Association ("NASAA"). The Commission estimates that the number of day-trading firms, in fact, exceeds 100.

Most day-trading firms require investors to open accounts with the firm and to use the assets in their own accounts to trade. These firms register with the SEC and are members of the National Association of Securities Dealers (NASD). But some day-trading firms are organized differently. For example, the firm may establish itself as a limited liability company and then sell interests to those wishing to day trade. Since these traders are part owners, they are not considered customers and can therefore tap into the firm's funds. In effect, they are risking money that they might not be able to repay.

The SEC and others are concerned that day trading can appeal to inexperienced investors who don't fully understand the risks. Senator Collins noted that an adult education program brochure sent to her by a constituent offered a $5 class on "Day Trading for Beginners." "The very fact that adult education programs in small communities like Gardiner might be teaching day trading strategies reflects the increasing pervasiveness of the day trading phenomenon and the degree to which it is being presented to ordinary investors as just another bona fide investing strategy. As an interesting side note, this particular course was canceled after the tragic shooting by an Atlanta day trader."

Day-trading firms, noted Levitt, contribute to the lure of day trading by exaggerating the potential benefits and downplaying the potential risks. "The Commission staff recently reviewed the risk and related disclosures on web sites of more than 20 day-trading firms. Many of these sites had little or no risk disclosure, and some contained statements that were not fulsome about, or even downplayed the risks associated with, day trading. Nevertheless, half of the web sites had considerable disclosure about those risks," according to his testimony.

Plus there's the concern that day traders are more likely to engage in riskier trading activity, such as short selling and buying on margin. Short selling is selling stock you don't actually own. To sell short, an investor identifies a stock he thinks is dropping in value. Then he borrow shares of the stock from a broker and sells them on the market. If the stock price does indeed drop, the investor can buy the stocks at the lower value and return them to the broker. Let's say a $10 stock is dropping. The trader borrows the stock when the value is $9 and sells it immediately. By the end of the day, the stock has dropped to $7. That means the trader made $2 off each share he borrowed, then bought back later at a lower price. If it works, it's profitable. But sometimes this borrowed stock doesn't drop in value. Let's say the stock in this example started to climb again. By the end of the day, it settled back in at $10 a share. Now the trader has lost $1 for every share he's borrowed.

Another risky trading strategy is buying on margin. Again, the trader is borrowing from the broker, although this time he's borrowing money, not stock. To trade, investors have to set up a margin account with a brokerage, essentially a credit line. The trader can then borrow from this credit line to purchase stocks. If the stocks increase in value, the trader has made more money because he was able to buy more stocks. He can then repay the credit line. But if the stock value falls, the broker can issue a margin call, a demand that the trader either put more money into the margin account or sell the stocks at a loss and pay back the margin account first.

Other observers say that reports about day trading have been sensationalized and that the practice has actually helped all investors. The Electronic Traders Association (ETA) released a following statement on September 16, the day of the Senate subcommittee hearing:

Day trading is not gambling. The majority of those who day trade after training do not lose money. The individuals who day trade represent the democratization of securities trading. They neither seek nor need the protection of regulators. Their lack of complaints in itself speaks volumes.

More importantly, day trading provides great benefits to the economy and to small investors everywhere. . . . If it were not for day traders, the technology of the securities industry would not have advanced to its present level.

James H. Lee, chairman/president of the ETA, issued a press statement on February 4, 1999, noting that the organization had developed a model disclosure statement for day-trading firms to use with clients. He also "cautioned individuals interested in becoming day traders to be aware of the following facts.

- Successful day trading requires skill, extraordinary discipline, and hard work. The securities markets are very competitive and most investors are not suited for day trading. Successful day traders must regard trading as a career, like many others, that will require them to be in the office, and at their terminals each and every day before the market opens and until after the market closes.
- Most persons that begin day trading careers sustain losses or produce only marginal profits during the initial three to five months of trading. Successful day trading requires talent, discipline and experience. Individuals that are not willing to sustain losses while gaining trading experience should not engage in day trading.
- Only risk capital that the individual does not need for retirement or current income should be used to fund day trading activity. Most ETA member firms offer comprehensive training classes focused on utilizing order entry and decision support software systems and teaching investors how to minimize their risks. No training course can guarantee success as each trading decision is ultimately made by the individual. Moreover, individuals should be prepared to lose all of their risk capital if they are not successful.
- Individuals that are not highly disciplined should avoid day trading."

The SEC has also issued recommendations for online investing:

- Set your price limits on fast-moving stocks: market orders vs. limit orders.

To avoid buying or selling a stock at a price higher or lower than you wanted, you need to place a limit order rather than a market order. A limit order is an order to buy or sell a security at a specific price. A buy limit order can only be executed at the limit price or lower, and a sell limit order can only be executed at the limit price or higher. When you place a market order, you can't control the price at which your order will be filled.

For example, if you want to buy the stock of a "hot" IPO that was initially offered at $9, but don't want to end up paying more than $20 for the stock, you can place a limit order to buy the stock at any price up to $20. By entering a limit order rather than a market order, you will not be caught buying the stock at $90 and then suffering immediate losses as the stock drops later in the day or the weeks ahead.

Remember that your limit order may never be executed because the market price may quickly surpass your limit before your order can be filled. But by using a limit order you also protect yourself from buying the stock at too high a price.

• Know your options for placing a trade if you are unable to access your account online.

Most online trading firms offer alternatives for placing trades. These alternatives may include touch-tone telephone trades, faxing your order, or doing it the low-tech way—talking to a broker over the phone. Make sure you know whether using these different options may increase your costs. And remember, if you experience delays getting online, you may experience similar delays when you turn to one of these alternatives.

• If you place an order, don't assume it didn't go through.

Some investors have mistakenly assumed that their orders have not been executed and place another order. They end up either owning twice as much stock as they could afford or wanted, or, with sell orders, selling stock they do not own. Talk with your firm about how you should handle a situation where you are unsure if your original order was executed.

• If you cancel an order, make sure the cancellation worked before placing another trade.

When you cancel an online trade, it is important to make sure that your original transaction was not executed. Although you may receive an electronic receipt for the cancellation, don't assume that that means the trade was canceled. Orders can only be canceled if they have not been executed. Ask your firm about how you should check to see if a cancellation order actually worked.

• If you trade on margin, your broker can sell your securities without giving you a margin call.

Now is the time to reread your margin agreement and pay attention to the fine print. If your account has fallen below the firm's maintenance margin requirement, your broker has the legal right to sell your securities at any time without consulting you first.

Some investors have been rudely surprised that "margin calls" are a courtesy, not a requirement. Brokers are not required to make margin calls to their customers.

Even when your broker offers you time to put more cash or securities into your account to meet a margin call, the broker can act without waiting for you to meet the call. In a rapidly declining market your broker can sell your entire margin account at a substantial loss to you, because the securities in the account have declined in value.

• No regulations require a trade to be executed within a certain time.

There are no Securities and Exchange Commission regulations that require a trade to be executed within a set period of time. But if firms advertise their speed of execution, they must not exaggerate or fail to tell investors about the possibility of significant delays.

Whether or not federal regulations on day trading increase, the burden falls on the investor to make smart choices up front. Ask questions of the day trading firm just the same as you would with a traditional brokerage firm or a financial advisor.

The SEC advises investors to always check with the SEC and the state's securities regulator to ensure the following:

Is the investment registered with securities regulators?

Have investors complained about the investment in the past?

Have the people who own or manage the investment been in trouble in the past?

Is the person selling me this investment licensed in my state?

Has that person been in trouble with the SEC, my state, or other investors in the past?

INVESTING FOR RETIREMENT

To make their money work the hardest for them, many people turn to the stock market. It typically provides the greatest return. During the 1990s, for example, investors saw average annual returns of nearly 20%. That's far better than bond returns or the interest rate offered on CDs or savings accounts.

Of course, overall stock market performance doesn't mean that every stock gained 20% a year. Some did far better—and others performed disastrously. That's part of the risk of investing.

Thanks to the 401(k), there are probably thousands more investors today than there were a few decades ago. The 401(k) is a retirement savings account, an employee benefit offered by many employers. If your employer offers one, take advantage of it. There are three excellent reasons for doing so. First, it's a painless way to develop a savings habit; employers typically withhold the 401(k) contribution and invest it for you. Second, contributions to 401(k) and other tax-deferred investments reduce your tax payments right now. Third, employers often make contributions to employees' 401(k) accounts. So your money grows even faster.

Aside from health concerns, the most important factor affecting retirement planning is financial and revolves around the question, "Will my retirement income be enough for me to live comfortably and without concern?" Generally retirement income for most people comes from the same sources: employer pension or retirement plans; retirement savings accounts such as 401(k) or 403(b) plans; Social Security benefits; and personal savings and earnings. When planning, it's important to understand the impact of life expectancies and inflation on retirement budgets. Obviously one of the biggest retirement worries for seniors is that their money won't keep pace with inflation. Added to concerns about health care costs and coupled with increasing life expectancies, the need for retirement planning and saving has never been greater.

When the United States government under President Franklin D. Roosevelt created the Social Security program in 1935, it designed a retirement plan intended to provide a living income for people over the age of 65. In the early days it succeeded, as over a dozen workers contributed to the program for each person drawing benefits. Unfortunately, recent figures show that about three workers support each recipient. As the baby boomers reach retirement age the number of workers supporting each Social Security recipient will shrink again, creating major concerns about the future of the Social Security program.

The Social Security Administration wants people to know that they shouldn't count on Social Security for the sum total of their retirement income. Older Americans today typically receive about 41% of their income from Social Security; the rest is from pensions, annuities, salaries, and income from assets.

While the future of Social Security seems uncertain, pension plans for employees have changed dramatically in recent decades, a shift that may work to the advantage of those who plan early for retirement.

The largest change for Americans is the concept of being a shareholder nation. Many people now believe that what they will have in retirement will come from what they reap as investors, not as workers. This is in direct contrast to traditional pensions, which are now becoming an endangered species. Gone are the days when employees spent their entire working life with the same company and retired on a benefit plan designed as a fixed monthly income. That retirement income was not adjusted for inflation and was generally based on the person's final salary and the number of years they worked for the company. Now, enter the new retirement plan being used by private business, the 401(k), where investment decisions are up to the worker, not the employer.

With the enactment of section 401(k) of the Revenue Act of 1978, employees now decide if and how much to contribute to retirement savings. Individuals also choose among investments and bear the risks or rewards of those decisions while their savings grow tax-free. This shift in responsibility offers advantages for the well-informed investor. But it also increases the risk for those employees who manage their benefits poorly, an increasingly likely circumstance as typical 401(k) plans continue to provide more choices. A typical plan in 1984 offered just three choices. Plans in 1998 offered up to 10 investment options.

Let's say you earn $25,000 a year. You decide you're going to put 12% into your 401(k) fund. At the end of the first year, you'll have $3,000 in your retirement plan—and your federal income taxes will be calculated on $22,000, instead of $25,000. This is pretax money you're investing. Not many investment opportunities allow that. Plus the earnings grow tax-deferred. That means you don't pay taxes until you withdraw the money, presumably when you're older and your income bracket might be lower than during your peak earning years.

It's a pretty good deal, but it gets even better. In most cases employers will match a portion of the worker's contribution, typically 50 cents for every dollar, up to a certain percentage. For example, you make your $3,000 contribution for the year, and your plan calls for your employer to match half your contribution. The employer contribution would be $1,500. Now your retirement fund is suddenly worth $4,500 at the end of the first year. However, you may not get all the employer's part of the contribution if you leave your job. When you become "vested," the employer contributions are yours to keep. Ask your employer what the vesting criteria are. Some employers gradually increase the percentage. In other words, you could be 50% vested after two years, 75% vested after three years, and fully vested after four. That means that if you left after three years, you would get to keep 75% of the employer's contributions to your 401(k). Other employers may choose to vest their employees all at once. For example, for the first four years, none of the employer's contributions would be yours to keep if you changed jobs. After that, you would be fully vested. Your own contributions are completely yours, of course, and are portable, so you can "roll over" your 401(k) into a similar plan with another employer or on your own when you change jobs. That's not possible with traditional pension plans.

For people not covered by a pension plan, an Individual Retirement Account (IRA) is a personal retirement fund that can be set up by an individual. Under current law, you can contribute up to $2,000 a year, which may be tax-deductible, partially tax-deductible, or non-tax-deductible depending on the plan and individual or family income. There are a variety of IRAs, and they can be set up at a bank or other financial institutions, with a mutual fund or life insurance company, or through your stockbroker. But all must meet IRS code requirements whether they are individual retirement accounts, annuities, or part of a Simplified Employee Pension (SEP). Although contributions cannot exceed $2,000 per year, rollover contributions and employer contributions can be more than that amount. The account must be for your exclusive benefit or for the benefit of your beneficiaries, and the money in the account cannot be used to buy a life insurance policy, nor can it be combined with other property except in a common trust fund or common investment fund. With an IRA, distribution must start by April 1 of the year following the year in which you reach age 70 1/2, except in the case of a Roth IRA, to which you can continue contributing indefinitely. Simplified Employee Pension plans (SEPs) were authorized in 1978 by the federal government. A SEP is a written arrangement that allows nongovernment employers with 25 or fewer employees to make deductible contributions to a traditional IRA set up for each of those individuals and to benefit from appropriate tax deductions.

Financial planners suggest several areas to consider in retirement planning. First and foremost is the financial aspect of income and expenses. Those financial issues also involve the management or disposition of assets at death, ideally with the least possible tax cost. Wills and trusts are an important financial aspect to consider. Another area of importance is the legal arena, dealing with questions about property ownership, bankruptcy, and other business matters. Physical and mental health involves planning and purchasing appropriate health insurance. To cover gaps in health insurance coverage, more and more people are turning to long-term nursing home care and custodial home health care insurance policies.

Another variation is the SEP-IRA, or Simplified Employee Pension. It is set up and administered just like an IRA and is a good choice for self-employed workers. Individuals can contribute up to 15% of earned income up to a maximum.

In 1998 a new wrinkle was added to the IRA concept. That was the year that Roth IRAs became available. Unlike 401(k) or IRA contributions, contributions to a Roth IRA are not tax deductible. In other words, if you earn $25,000 and deposit $2,000 in a Roth IRA, you'll still have to pay taxes on $25,000 of salary. The advantage to the Roth IRA comes at the other end. Although you pay full income taxes, the earnings are compounded tax free. Withdrawals from the account are not taxed if you're over 59 1/2, if you are using the money to buy a first home, or if you become disabled. The Roth IRA seems well suited to young people, who can benefit the most from the compounded, tax-deferred growth in the IRA.

POP QUIZ: SAVING AND INVESTING

For those who feel they know enough about saving and investing, consider this a pop quiz. If the answers surprise you, go back and read more in the previous section. For those who have read the previous sections, try the quiz as a review. It's from the Facts on Saving and Investing Campaign, launched in 1998 by a national partnership of government agencies, securities regulators, financial industry associations, educators, and consumer organizations.

1. If you buy a company's stock,

    A. you own a part of the company.

    B. you have lent money to the company.

    C. you are liable for the company's debts.

    D. the company will return your original investment to you with interest.

    E. don't know.

2. If you buy a company's bond,

    A. you own a part of the company.

    B. you have lent money to the company.

    C. you are liable for the company's debts.

    D. you can help manage the company.

    E. don't know.

3. Over the past 70 years the type of investment that has earned the most money, or the highest rate of return, for investors has been

    A. stocks.

    B. corporate bonds.

    C. savings accounts.

    D. don't know.

4. If you buy the stock of a new company,

    A. you cannot lose money.

    B. you can lose all the money you used to buy the stock.

    C. you can lose only a portion of the money used to buy the stock.

    D. don't know.

5. Monique owns a wide variety of stocks, bonds, and mutual funds to lessen her risk of losing money. This is called

   A. saving.

   B. compounding.

   C. diversifying.

   D. don't know.

6. Carlos has saved some cash and faces these choices. What would be the best thing for him to do?

   A. put it in his savings account.

   B. invest in a mutual fund.

   C. buy a U.S. Savings bond.

   D. pay off the balance on his credit card that charges 18% interest.

   E. don't know.

7. Maria wants to have $100,000 in 20 years. The sooner she starts to save, the less she'll need to save because

   A. the stock market will go up.

   B. interest rates will go up.

   C. interest on her savings will start compounding.

   D. don't know.

8. Jennifer wants to take some of her savings and invest in a mutual fund because mutual funds are

   A. guaranteed to earn more than savings accounts.

   B. risk free.

   C. managed by experts at picking investments.

   D. don't know.

9. Bob is 22 years old and wants to start saving now for his retirement in 43 years. Of these choices, where should Bob put most of his money now for this long-term goal?

   A. a savings account at the bank.

   B. a checking account at the bank.

   C. a mutual fund that invests in stocks.

   D. the stock of one company.

   E. don't know.

10. Federal and state laws protect investors by requiring companies to

   A. show profits before they can sell stock.

   B. give investors important information.

C. pay dividends.

D. repay investors who have lost money.

E. don't know.

Answers

1. If you buy a company's stock,

    A. you own a part of the company.

    When you own stock, you own a part of the company. There are no guarantees of profits, or even that you will get your original investment back, but you might make money in two ways. First, the price of the stock can rise if the company does well and other investors want to buy the stock. If a stock's price rises from $10 to $12, the $2 increase is called a capital gain or appreciation. Second, a company sometimes pays out a part of its profits to stockholders—that's called a dividend. If the company doesn't do well, or falls out of favor with investors, your stock can fall in price, and the company can stop paying dividends, or make them smaller.

2. If you buy a company's bond,

    B. you have lent money to the company.

    When you buy a bond, you are lending money to the company. The company promises to pay you interest and to return your money on a date in the future. This promise generally makes bonds safer than stocks, but bonds can be risky. To assess how risky a bond is you can check the bond's credit rating. Unlike stockholders, bond holders know how much money they will make, unless the company goes out of business. If the company goes out of business, bond holders may lose money, but if there is any money left in the company, they will get it before stockholders.

3. Over the past 70 years, the type of investment that has earned the most money, or the highest rate of return, for investors has been

    A. stocks.

    If you had invested $1 in the stocks of large companies in 1925 and you reinvested all dividends, your dollar would be worth $2,350 at the end of 1998. If the same dollar had been invested in corporate bonds, it would be worth $61, and if it had been invested in U.S. Treasury bills, it would be worth $15. (This information came from Ibbotson Associates, Inc.)

4. If you buy the stock of a new company,

    B. you can lose all the money you used to buy the stock.

    One of the riskiest investments is buying stock in a new company. New companies go out of business more often than companies that have been in business for a long time. If you buy stock in small, new companies, you could lose it all. Or the company could turn out to be a success. You'll have to do your homework and learn as much as you can about small companies before you invest. If you decide to buy stock in a new or small company, only invest money that you can afford to lose.

5. Monique owns a wide variety of stocks, bonds, and mutual funds to lessen her risk of losing money. This is called

C. diversifying.

One of the most important ways to lessen the risk of losing money when you invest is to diversify your investments. It's common sense—don't put all your eggs in one basket. If you buy a mixture of different types of stocks, bonds, or mutual funds, your entire savings will not be wiped out if one of your investments fails. Since no one can accurately predict how our economy or one company will do, diversification helps you to protect your savings.

6. Carlos has saved some cash and faces these choices. What would be the best thing for him to do?

D. pay off the balance on his credit card that charges 18% interest.

Most advisers suggest that before you start to invest, you should save cash for emergencies and pay down any debt you have. If Carlos has money in a savings account or buys a U.S. savings bond, he'll earn 3 to 5% on his savings. Mutual funds are not guaranteed, and they may earn or lose money. But if Carlos pays off his credit card, it's like earning 18% because that's how much he's paying now to maintain the balance. If you owe money on your credit cards, you save money if you pay off the balance in full or as quickly as possible.

7. Maria wants to have $100,000 in 20 years. The sooner she starts to save, the less she'll need to save because

C. interest on her savings will start compounding.

When you leave the interest in your account or reinvest the money you earn on your investments, the money you earn starts to earn money too. Over time, the magic of compounding works, allowing your money to grow with dramatic results. The more time you have to save, the less money you need to save because of compounding. And the longer you wait to start saving, the more you have to spend to reach your goal. For example, let's assume that Maria's savings grow by 5% a year. If she starts to save $243 a month now, it will cost her $58,320 to have $100,000 in 20 years. If she waits 10 years to start saving, she will have to save $644 a month for 10 years, and it will cost her $77,280 to reach $100,000 in 20 years.

8. Jennifer wants to take some of her savings and invest in a mutual fund because mutual funds are

C. managed by experts at picking investments.

A diversified mutual fund invests in a wide variety of stocks, bonds, or other securities. The manager of the fund makes decisions about which stocks or bonds to buy, based on the objective of the fund. When you buy shares of a mutual fund, you share in the profits and losses of the portfolio, and pay your share of the expenses.

9. Bob is 22 years old and wants to start saving now for his retirement in 43 years. Of these choices, where should Bob put most of his money now for this long-term goal?

    C. a mutual fund that invests in stocks.

       As you read in the answer to question three, over the long term, stocks have earned more money than any other investment. Since Bob doesn't need his money for a long time, he can afford to take on the risk of investing in stocks. Even if the stocks in his fund go up and down in value, chances are his savings will grow in value over the long term. He lessens the risk of losing money by choosing a diversified mutual fund rather than the stock of one company.

10. Federal and state laws protect investors by requiring companies to

    B. give investors important information.

       Most businesses that raise money from the public must register with the SEC or the states and publicly report important information about their businesses on a regular basis. Federal and state laws protect you by requiring that the people who seek your investment dollars must tell you the truth about their businesses, and the people who sell securities must be licensed and treat you fairly and honestly, putting your interests first.

ADDITIONAL READING

General Reading on Saving and Investing

Bertrand, Marsha. *A Woman's Guide to Savvy Investing.* New York: American Management Association, 1998.

Clements, Jonathan. "The Education of a Financial Columnist." *Wall Street Journal*, November 17, 1998, C1.

Groz, Marc M. *Forbes Guide to the Markets.* New York: John Wiley & Sons, 1999.

Hallman, G. Victor, and Jerry S. Rosenbloom. *Personal Financial Planning.* New York: McGraw-Hill, 1993.

Kazanjian, Kirk. *Wall Street's Picks for 1999.* Chicago: Dearborn Financial Publications, 1999.

Kobliner, Beth. *Get a Financial Life: Personal Finance in Your Twenties and Thirties.* New York: Simon and Schuster, 1996.

Lewis, Michael. *The Money Culture.* New York: W. W. Norton, 1991.

Maloni, Kelly, Ben Greenman, and Kristen Miller. *Net Money: Your Guide to the Personal Finance Revolution on the Information Superhighway.* New York: Random House Electronic Publishing, 1995.

Morris, Kenneth M, and Virginia B. Morris. *The Wall Street Journal Guide to Understanding Money and Investing.* New York: Lightbulb Press and Dow Jones & Co., 1998.

Westheimer, Julius. *Generations of Wealth: Time-Tested Rules for Worry-Free Investing.* Baltimore: Bancroft Press, 1997.

Williamson, Gordon K. *Smart Guide to Making Wise Investments.* New York: John Wiley & Sons, 1998.

Reading on Retirement

Garner, Robert J., Young Ernst, William J. Arnone, Glen Pape, and Bob Garner. *Ernst & Young's Retirement Planning Guide: Take Care of Your Finances Now . . . and They'll Take Care of You Later.* New York: John Wiley & Sons, 1997.

Haynes, Marion E. *The Best of Retirement Planning.* Menlo Park, CA: Crisp Publications, 1995.

Kaplan, Lawrence J. *Retiring Right: Planning for a Successful Retirement.* Garden City Park, NY: Avery Publishing Group, 1996.

Landis, Andy. *Social Security: The Inside Story.* Bellevue, WA: Mount Vernon Press, 1993.

O'Shaughnessy, James. *How to Retire Rich.* New York: Broadway Books, 1998.

Robertson, A. Haeworth. *Social Security: What Every Taxpayer Should Know.* Washington, DC: Retirement Policy Institute, 1992.

Smith, Anne Kates. "Road to Riches." *U.S. News & World Report* 26, no. 25 (June 28, 1999). 66–74.

FOR ADDITIONAL INFORMATION ON INVESTING

NASAA—State Regulators
10 G Street, N.W.
Washington, D.C.
Toll-free: (888) 84-NASAA
Web site: www.nasaa.org

Securities and Exchange Commission (SEC)
450 Fifth Street, N.W.
Washington, D.C. 20549
Toll-free: (800) SEC-0330
Web site: www.sec.gov

5

The Cost of College

The first, last, and best advice for anyone when it comes to financing a college education is to start early. The sooner students and parents save money the better. But it's never too late. Even if you are in your senior year of high school, with hard work you and your parents can pull together a combination of savings, loans, scholarships and grants, and work-study programs to finance that college education.

The annual national survey of college costs prepared by the College Board for the year 1998–99 shows that college tuition and fees rose 4%. But financial aid from federal, state, and institutional sources was available to students at a record level: more than $60 billion, an increase of 6% over the previous year, after adjusting for inflation. However, according to the College Board, much of the increase was in the form of loans rather than grants.

Financing tuition is the biggest cost you will face, but it is not the only cost. Money will also be needed for fees, room and board, books, supplies, transportation, and other miscellaneous expenses from clothing to eating out. Personal preferences can often be budget breakers, especially for freshmen students. For example, many students expect to come home once or twice a year yet find they make the trip once or twice a semester. On campus, if students who pay for a dorm meal plan find the food unappealing and begin eating out or ordering pizza often, they can quickly double their food expenses. When estimating expenses, it is important to be realistic and honest with yourself.

According to the College Entrance Examination Board, the average cost of private college tuition and fees in 1999 was about $13,664. Public college or university tuition averaged about $3,111 for in-state students (and typically about $5,000 more for out-of-state students). In addition, room and board, books and supplies, transportation, and personal expenses tacked another $7,000–$8,000 onto the annual bill, bringing the total to about $21,424 for private school and $10,069 for public schools.

Keep in mind that there are many types of schools, and each comes with a different price tag. Public and private institutions have different tuition rates. Although private institutions traditionally charge the same tuition price for in-state and out-of-state students, their costs tend to be higher than those of public colleges.

Public institutions receive portions of their budgets from federal, state, or local governments, and they charge students who are residents of that state lower tuition than nonresident students.

Other factors affecting college costs include size, location, and academic programs. In the United States the most accessible form of higher education for students is the community college. Typically these regional institutions provide an associate degree at the end of a two-year program and can be a stepping stone for students to continue their education at a four-year institution. Community colleges are usually funded by appropriations from state and local governments, although a few have foundations or endownment funds. The majority of financial aid funds at the community college level come from federal and state grants and job and loan programs.

Liberal arts colleges, state-supported and private, focus on the education of undergraduate students and are smaller than universities. Although they differ greatly from one institution to another, they generally expose students to a broad base of courses in humanities, social sciences, and sciences. The private colleges tend to be higher priced but may also be able to provide more generous aid packages than their state-supported counterparts, where tuition rates are lower.

Universities are larger and include a liberal arts college as well as a variety of professional colleges and graduate programs. This varies depending on the individual institution. They offer a greater range of academic choices, with both professors and graduate students teaching classes. Professors at major universities are involved in research, which adds to the academic prestige of the institution. Financial aid often comes from federal and state grants and job and loan programs and is available through the university's office of financial aid.

Private research universities include some of the most selective institutions in the country, among them Harvard University (Massachusetts), Princeton University (New Jersey), the Massachusetts Institute of Technology, and Columbia University (New York). These universities are often well endowed and have strong financial aid programs.

Technical institutes and professional schools are most attractive to students who have made a clear career decision because these schools emphasize preparation for that specific career.

Once you have decided where to go you need to see the projected costs in black and white. The Semester Budget Worksheet (College Entrance Examination Board) will help you estimate expenses for a semester while also projecting income for the same period. Remember, be as realistic as possible and talk to friends or relatives who have been to college to get an honest picture of your needs.

SEMESTER BUDGET WORKSHEET

Estimated Expenses for Semester
Tuition $_____
Fees_____
Books/Supplies_____
Rent/Housing_____
Board/Meals_____
Phone/Utilities_____
Clothing_____
Laundry/Dry Cleaning_____
Transportation (carfare, gas, parking, insurance, etc.)_____
Medical/Dental_____
Recreation_____
Personal Expenses_____
Savings_____
Child Care_____
Credit Card Debt_____
Other_____
TOTAL SEMESTER EXPENSES $_____
Projected Income for Semester
Money from Parents $_____
Money from Savings_____
Work/Study_____
Other Work_____
Scholarships_____
Grants_____
Loans_____
Public Benefits
(Social Security, Veterans Admin., etc.)_____
Spouse's Wages_____

Other_____

TOTAL SEMESTER INCOME $_____

Note: If your total semester expenses exceed your total semester income, carefully review your spending habits and look for areas where you can economize.

The next question becomes how best to finance those costs. It's never too late to save, but there are things you and your parents can do if college starts in less than a year. First, adults who think borrowing may be an option should check their credit history. Also, any account holders should check savings and investments to ensure the best rate of return. Finally, look into financial aid. Remember, college lasts for several years, and even if you are too late for financial aid the first year of enrollment it may be available for subsequent years.

Saving money in advance is the most obvious way to prepare for the costs of college. Many young parents have good intentions but ultimately fail to save for a variety of reasons. Plus, saving money is no longer as simple as it used to be; the art of investing now includes a multitude of financial choices and terms that overwhelm many people. How much should your parents try to save? The answer is, of course, as much as possible. Table 5.1 illustrates what parents should save to have $10,000 available to pay college costs. As the table demonstrates, the amount a family needs to save varies depending on the interest rate and the number of years those dollars have been put aside. If your parents began saving regularly when you were born, they need only deposit a small monthly amount compared to someone who started saving when their child reached age 16.

COLLEGE SAVINGS METHODS

For parents with a short time frame the best advice is to concentrate primarily on safety. Investments designed for safety include certificates of deposit, which are government insured up to $100,000. They generally pay a higher rate of return than a passbook savings account, the most basic of saving vehicles, but there are also penalties for early withdrawal.

Money market deposit accounts, insured up to $100,000 by the FDIC, are another safe haven. They are a combination of a savings and checking account but require a minimum balance. These accounts routinely pay higher interest than regular savings and checking accounts and offer check-writing capabilities.

Savings bonds, often considered a simple savings vehicle, have become more complicated as the government continues to change the rules. In May 1995, Congress did away with the 4% flat rate the bonds earned

Table 5.1
Amount You Would Need to Save to Have $10,000 Available When You
Begin College

If your parents started saving when you were

Your age	Number of years until college	Monthly saving	Principal	Interest earned	Total savings
		(Assuming a 4% interest rate)			
Newborn	18	$ 32	$6,912	$3,187	$10,099
Age 4	14	$ 45	$7,560	$2,552	$10,112
Age 8	10	$ 68	$8,160	$1,853	$10,013
Age 12	6	$124	$8,928	$1,144	$10,072
Age 16	2	$401	$9,624	$ 378	$10,002
		(Assuming an 8% interest rate)			
Newborn	18	$ 21	$4,536	$5,546	$10,082
Age 4	14	$ 33	$5,544	$4,621	$10,165
Age 8	10	$ 55	$6,660	$3,402	$10,062
Age 12	6	$109	$7,848	$2,183	$10,031
Age 16	2	$386	$9,264	$ 746	$10,010

Source: U.S. Department of Education.

during their first five years and also did away with the guarantee that
the bonds would earn no less than 4% during those years. So the old
rule that you shouldn't buy U.S. savings bonds unless you intend to hold
them for five years or more no longer applies. Now the long-term rate,
or look-back rate, is no longer applied retroactively to the entire holding
period for bonds purchased on or after May 1, 1995. You can buy and
redeem series EE savings bonds at most banks. For current rates, which
change every May 1 and November 1, call 1–800–427–2663. (See Chapter
4 for more information on U.S. Savings Bonds.)

A mutual fund is a simple way to invest in a diverse group of stocks,
bonds, or other securities. Mutual fund shareholders basically are pooling their money with thousands of other shareholders in that fund to
reap the rewards of diversity without having to buy huge sums in a
portfolio of individual stocks. Safest and least expensive are the no-load
mutual funds, which do not charge for purchasing or selling their shares.
Load funds can charge commissions as high as 8.5%, and both kinds of
funds charge an annual management fee. Internet enthusiasts can find
lots of information online about mutual funds. (See Appendix B for Web
sites.) See Chapter 4 for more information on mutual funds.

Other saving and investment tools include whole life insurance policies, borrowing from a pension fund or 401(k), or taking out a home
equity loan. (See Appendix A for definitions of various savings vehicles.)

PREPAID TUITION PLANS

Many states also offer parents an opportunity to prepay college tuition; www.finaid.org gives details on each state's prepaid plan and how to contact them. The greatest concern families have about taking advantage of a state prepaid plan is the obvious one: How do students know where or if they will want to go to college? If you have any doubts discuss them with your parents. A prepaid plan may not be for you if you think you may want to attend a school out of state or a technical or vocational school.

Currently 33 states offer prepaid tuition plans. Seven states offer savings bond programs. Four states offer savings funds or savings plan trusts. Georgia offers the Georgia HOPE Scholarship Program, which uses proceeds from the state lottery. Twelve other states are currently planning, developing, or discussing the possibility of offering prepaid tuition plans. One state, Oregon, had its plan rejected by voters.

There are other questions to consider before investing in a prepaid tuition plan: Which schools participate in the plan? What happens if a student decides to attend a school in another state? Are the shares in the plan guaranteed by the state? What fees are associated with enrollment in the plan? What is the minimum or maximum investment? Who can purchase shares on behalf of the student? Families interested in prepaid plans should thoroughly evaluate them before making any commitment.

FINANCIAL AID

So how much can you and your parents expect to pay? Parents are expected to contribute up to 47% of their available income toward tuition, but only up to 5.6% of their savings, numbers that surprise many people. Students, however, must provide assets at a rate of 35% per year. This disparity makes sense because parents have other financial responsibilities. Families trying to decide whether to save in a child's name need to consider this information. For example, if $10,000 goes into a custodial account in your name under the standard financial aid formula, you, the student, would be required to pay 35% of that the first year, a $3,500 chunk. If that same $10,000 was held in your parents' name, their contribution would be no more than $560, which could have a direct effect on your financial aid eligibility.

Another factor to consider when deciding in whose name to save is that money put in a custodial account is a gift, and your parents might need to use the money for other purposes such as emergency medical or household bills. If those funds are in the student's name they cannot be used. Although it is tempting to keep money in a minor's account to take advantage of lower income tax rates, a tax savings of a couple of hundred dollars a year may not be enough to compensate for the loss of potential financial aid.

There are two financial aid forms currently in general use: PROFILE and FAFSA. Copies of these forms can be obtained from Web sites as well as from college financial aid offices and high school or college guidance counselors. (See Appendix B for more information on each individual site.) They include www.fafsa.ed.gov, www.finaid.org, and www.fastweb.com.

FAFSA, an acronym for Free Application for Federal Student Aid, is the application form required for federal government–funded need-based financial aid. Some colleges and universities also accept it as an application for their need-based aid, and some states also accept it for state government–funded need-based aid. Check with the financial aid office at the school you are interested in attending to see which form(s) they require. Since both are lengthy you may be able to save yourself work if one will suffice for your chosen school(s).

PROFILE (formerly called Financial Aid Form or FAF) is published by the College Scholarship Service (CSS), Princeton, New Jersey. Most colleges and universities that formerly accepted FAF now use PROFILE, but this form cannot be used to apply for federal aid.

Two classifications of financial aid are available to students; merit-based aid and need-based aid. Merit-based assistance given to students is not related to financial need. Good examples include merit scholarships for artistic or athletic talent or academic performance. Need-based aid is calculated based on the cost of the college the student will attend and on the ability of the student or their student's family to pay those costs.

In wading through financial aid information, help can come from high school guidance counselors, the local public library, and the financial aid office of the college you plan to attend. The World Wide Web is also filled with free information to help find money. But beware: there are plenty of scams out there from people saying they will help you get financial aid. A good place to check out common scams is www.finaid.org, which offers tips and warnings.

In deciding financial aid packages for students, parents' income and assets and the number of family members in college are important considerations. Calculating need for financial aid is a straightforward concept; the cost of college, minus the expected parent contribution, minus the expected student contribution, equals a dollar amount that signifies the students' need for financial aid.

Here is an example of how financial aid is calculated. Anne Green is a single mother with a daughter, Georgia, now a graduating senior in high school. Anne earned $25,000 last year and paid just over $5,000 in federal, state, and Social Security taxes. Anne has no savings and under

$10,000 in home equity. (Federal financial aid methodology no longer counts home equity among assets, but private schools sometimes add it to their financial aid calculations).

Georgia has $500 in a savings account. To arrive at Georgia's financial aid eligibility, Anne will subtract her taxes from her income. Federal methodology also allows an income protection allowance based on family size and number of children in college. And federal methodology also computes an employment-expense allowance from income for single-parent families and for two-parent families in which both parents work. Anne's income protection allowance is approximately $10,500; her expense allowance is approximately $2,500. When all that is subtracted from her yearly income, the figure is $7,000. In this scenario she is expected to contribute 20% of that remainder, or $1,400. Georgia is expected to contribute 35% of her savings, $175.

If Georgia wants to attend an expensive private school with a price tag of $30,000 a year, financial aid officers will subtract her expected family contribution of $1,575 and could offer her a $28,425 financial aid package. An average-priced public college with a $10,000 cost per year could put together a projected offer of $8,425. However, that aid could be in many forms including grants, scholarships, loans, and work-study.

The largest grant program is the Federal Pell Grant, and the amount students receive will depend on the cost of the school, eligibility based on need, and full-time versus part-time status. The Federal Supplemental Educational Opportunity Grant (FSEOG) is generally referred to by its initials or by the term Supplemental Grant. It's awarded by the colleges themselves to the neediest students, so it often goes hand in hand with a Federal Pell Grant.

There are a few other federal grants available in such programs as the Robert C. Byrd Honors Scholarship, the Paul Douglas Teacher Scholarship, Higher Education Grants for Indian Students, National Science Scholarships, and a few programs targeted to graduate students. These grants and scholarships are specifically targeted and may be merit-based rather than need-based. Institutional grants are awarded by the college or university, and criteria for eligibility vary from college to college. These may also be merit-based. FastWEB at www.fastweb.com and Scholarship Resource Network at www.rams.com are good searching tools for scholarship and grant resources. The College Board also offers a scholarship search site.

Students need to remember that grants are gifts and do not need to be repaid. However, before accepting an institutional grant from a particular school students should carefully review any documents they must sign. Some colleges put in language to convert grants to loans retrospectively if a student withdraws or is dismissed from the school.

Loan terms are more complex than grant, scholarship, or work-study terms because they are affected by interest rates, repayment terms, deferment options, prepayment penalties, and consolidation. Points to consider when deciding if a loan is affordable include whether the interest rate is fixed or variable; what fees are applied to the loan and whether they are deducted directly from the loan amount; the length of repayment; if you can repay early without penalty; if multiple loans can be consolidated; and what deferment options, if any, are available. Federal loans include the Perkins Loan, the subsidized and unsubsidized Stafford Loans, the PLUS Loan, and the William D. Ford Federal Direct Student Loan.

Eligibility for a Perkins Loan is based on need and is calculated using the federal need analysis formula. Colleges decide the amount of each loan from a pool of funds and choose recipients. The interest rate on this loan does not accrue while the student is in school, and borrowers have up to 10 years for repayment.

Of the two types of Stafford Loans, students with the greatest financial need determined by the FAFSA receive the subsidized loans. Need is not a factor in determining eligibility for the nonsubsidized loan. The government pays the interest on the subsidized loan while the student is in school, but interest accrues on the unsubsidized loan during the time the student is attending school. Like the Perkins Loan, repayment doesn't begin until six months after graduation.

The Federal PLUS Loan is an unsubsidized, non–need-based loan program for parents of undergraduate students. Parents with good credit can borrow up to the cost of education at the college, minus any financial aid received. The interest rate is set once a year in June, and repayment begins 60 days after the funds are disbursed. The borrowed PLUS money goes directly to the school, and repayment is required within 10 years.

Colleges that do not participate in the Stafford Loan program may provide the Federal Direct Student Loan program. The terms of the two loans are similar, but under the Federal Direct Student Loan the U.S. Department of Education, rather than a bank, is the lender. Another difference in the two loans is the repayment options for the direct loan, currently not available to Stafford Loan borrowers. Those choices include a standard repayment plan like that of the Stafford Loan that can be paid over 10 years; an extended repayment plan with lower monthly payments that extends up to 30 years; a graduated repayment plan with two or more levels of payments for up to 30 years; and an income-contingent option with repayment based on debt level. More and more colleges are signing up for this program. Interested students and parents should contact college financial aid offices.

Federal work-study (FWS) helps students with demonstrated financial need to earn money to pay education costs. The program is run through the individual school and arranges jobs for undergraduate students. The program attempts to place students in jobs related to their area of study. The student earns an amount not to exceed the FWS award. Because a portion of the student's salary is paid through federal funds, FWS recipients are in demand by employers. A few states also offer work-study programs. Check with the financial aid office at any state college for more information.

ADDITIONAL READING

Barron's Profiles of American Colleges. 21st ed. Hauppauge, NY: Barron's Educational Series, 1996.

Black, Richard. *The Complete Family Guide to College Financial Aid.* New York: Perigee Books, Berkley Publishing Group, 1995.

The College Handbook, 1999. 36th ed. New York: College Board Publications, 1998.

Deutschman, Alan. *Winning Money for College: The High School Student's Guide to Scholarship Contests.* 4th ed. Princeton, NJ: Peterson's Guides, 1997.

Gallagher, Stephanie. "Student Loans Are Cheaper Than Ever." *Kiplinger's Personal Finance Magazine* 53, no. 9 (September 1999): 52.

Halverson, Guy. "Tips on Saving for Grandchild's Education." *Christian Science Monitor,* April 12, 1999, 19.

Krefetz, Gerald. *Paying for College: A Guide for Parents.* New York: The College Board, 1995.

Leider, Anna, and Robert Leider. *Don't Miss Out! The Ambitious Student's Guide to Financial Aid.* Alexandria, VA: Octameron Associates, 1998.

Peterson's College Money Handbook 1999. 16th ed. Princeton, NJ: Peterson's Guides, 1998.

Peterson's Guide to Four-Year Colleges, 1996. 26th ed. Princeton, NJ: Peterson's Guides, 1995.

Quinn, Jane Bryant. "Of Scholars and Dollars." *Newsweek* 130, no. 14 (October 6, 1997): 82.

Shields, Charles. *The College Guide for Parents.* New York: The College Board, 1994.

6

A Budget: Your Friend for Life

It takes practically no brains to spend money. It does take careful thought and planning to budget your money. In the twenty-first century careful financial management will not just be sensible, it will be vital as more and more people must take charge and make decisions about their retirement investments and daily living expenses.

Even if you are new to the job market you should be saving for your retirement years. As life expectancy continues to improve, many people discover that their retirement life could span more than 20 years. Yet many young people have only a hazy idea of how much it costs them to live.

A 1999 survey by the Strong Funds, a mutual fund group, found that 18% of Americans save nothing and that another 21% save less than 10% of their annual income. Most planners recommend that individuals have three to six months' worth of expenses in savings or other liquid assets like cash, money market funds, or Treasury bills. And advisors caution that whether they are working or not, all adults should have a strong savings and investment program in place to build the security they will eventually need. In other words, financial security begins with a budget, and the sooner the better.

But why make a budget even before there's a job offer on the table? It's a good exercise that can help prepare young people to anticipate their means and gauge the expenses that can comfortably fit.

For those who have a career in mind, check the newspaper help wanted advertisements to get a range of what employers in the area pay. Or consult the list below, compiled from a July 1, 1999 press release issued by the National Association of Colleges and Employers, showing starting salaries for college graduates with majors in 10 fields.

It is generally true that the higher the educational level, the higher the salary. Students who continue with graduate education in medical, law, or business school will likely command higher starting salaries. They also typically carry higher student loan debts upon graduation.

Degree In	Job Average Starting Salary
Accounting	$34,475
Business administration	$33,790
Chemical engineering	$47,136
Civil engineering	$36,160
Computer science	$44,345
Electrical engineering	$45,121
English	$27,017
Information sciences	$39,248
Management information systems	$41,077
Marketing/marketing management	$31,542
Political science/government	$29,299
Software development jobs	$46,513

The best place to start with a budget is to create a spending plan. Make sure that it includes discussion of major purchases before they are made by anyone in the household. Regardless of income level, people benefit from beginning and staying with a spending plan, setting financial goals, determining income and expenses, and then, most important, keeping track of where money is being spent.

INCOME WORKSHEET

Complete this income worksheet to determine income and expenses.

Anticipated Income

1. Anticipated yearly salary: $_____
2. Spouse's anticipated yearly salary: $_____
3. Other income: $_____
4. Total lines 1–3 $_____
5. *Your monthly income* (Divide total yearly income by 12): $_____

Monthly Living Expenses

6. Housing (rent or mortgage payment): $_____

7. Transportation (car payment, gas, parking, insurance, $_____
train, bus, subway):

8. Student loan payments (you or your spouse): $_____

9. Employer benefits (your contribution toward medical $_____
insurance and company retirement plan):

10. Your monthly credit card payments (or your spouse's): $_____

11. Phone/Utilities (gas, electric, water): $_____

12. Food (grocery and restaurant): $_____

13. Entertainment:

14. Clothing:

15. Savings: $_____

16. Medical/Dental: $_____

17. Child care: $_____

18. Other: $_____

19. Amount you pay out each month (Add lines 6–18): $_____

What's Left?

20. Your monthly income from Line 5: $_____

21. Monthly expenses from Line 19: $_____

22. Amount of money available after expenses (Subtract $_____
Line 21 from Line 20):

WHEN TWO BECOME ONE

For wage earners in a two-income household the best choice is to design a plan to maximize the benefits of that second income. When developing a family budget, tailor it to the personal needs, values, and priorities of everyone involved. It is also important to be realistic when establishing expenses, both fixed and discretionary. And financial planners caution against letting credit obligations rise above 15% of take-home pay. A good rule of thumb for savings is to set aside at least 5% of take-home pay and keep records of where money is being spent by everyone involved.

There are many systems for those who live in a household of two or more wage earners, and there is no one best way to handle the money. Instead, all involved must work together to develop a system and then make a commitment to follow through. For couples, there are two basic checking and savings account options: jointly, where both people have access to the money, or separately, where only one person is listed as signer.

Although there are only two basic types of accounts, there are many ways couples put them together and split their earnings. One common practice for couples is to put an equal amount of their respective salaries into joint checking and savings accounts to cover household expenses. The remainder can be saved or spent as each sees fit. However, problems can develop when one partner earns much more than the other, leaving one person with more money for individual spending.

This leads some couples to pool all their income to use for both household and personal expenses. This has the advantage of valuing the work of each person equally regardless of salary levels. But problems again can develop if the partner with the lower income feels that he or she has less say in how the joint income is spent, or if one partner feels that the other is making frivolous purchases. Many financial advisors suggest that couples who pool their money retain an independent "allowance" of a set amount so that each may make discretionary purchases.

If couples find that pooling money creates too many problems they may elect to each contribute a percentage of their salaries to cover household expenses and joint savings. This leaves the remainder for each to spend as they please. Again, differences in income can cause resentment, but it allows both people to contribute to household expenses while retaining some independence in using their funds.

Financial planners also suggest that couples switch financial jobs occasionally. If one pays the bills each month, the second should take a turn to become familiar with the family finances. Some couples use a six months on and six months off system of rotation. Analysts suggest that the more an individual knows and understands about the family finances, the more likely he or she will be to cooperate and to follow a budget or financial plan.

STEPS TO BUDGETING

Pay Yourself First

One of the most important first steps in creating a budget is to set goals. Some examples might be starting a savings account, remodeling or redecorating your home, saving for continuing education, planning for a special vacation, or purchasing more insurance. Next, sit down with family members to identify what goals are most important, and prioritize them. If, for example, your goal is to save $600 in one year, then $50 must go into a savings account each month.

It is also important to have a clear picture of where you get your money. Income sources include salary, allowances, pensions, rental property, Social Security, child support, alimony, commissions or bonuses, and interest. A common mistake in budgeting is to include overtime pay in your calculations. Overtime pay, while nice, cannot be considered regular income.

You must also understand where you spend your money. Realistically identifying expenses is as important as identifying income. Obviously some expenses are easier to track than others. Review canceled checks, credit card statements, grocery store receipts, and bank statements. Divide expenses into two categories, fixed and flexible. Fixed expenses are payments that stay the same, like the rent or mortgage, insurance, automobile payments, loan payments, and long-term savings goals. Flexible expenses are costs that vary, and include food, clothing, household supplies, gifts, transportation, medical bills, entertainment and hobbies, and other miscellaneous purchases. Once you can identify where your money is going you can make informed spending decisions.

Advisors generally suggest writing down every penny you spend for a month. Try it. The results might surprise you. If you have a checking account, it's a little easier to do this exercise—assuming most of your checks aren't made out to "cash." If they are, or if you deal mostly in cash, buy a small notebook and keep it with you. Every time you buy something, write down what it is and what you spent on it. At the end of the month add it up.

When adding up the expenses, categorize them. For example, checks or cash given to the pizza delivery person and the ATM withdrawal that you needed to make to have lunch at the mall and the cash for the cafe lattes should all go under "dining out." The compact discs you bought, the movie tickets, popcorn, and soda, cover to see a band play, and the round of drinks you bought your friends that might go under "entertainment." The more you can categorize, the more precise your budget will be. Those ATM withdrawals and cash spent that simply can't be identified can go in the "miscellaneous" category, but don't forget to include them. Also remember to include payments that you make only occasionally. If you pay $600 for auto insurance twice a year, include it as a $100 a month expense.

The number one way to successfully save is to pay yourself first. Most people don't save on a regular basis because they wait to see what's left over at the end of the month. But financial planners agree that those who save think of that money as a fixed expense rather than a voluntary choice. In other words, their savings commitment is viewed like a mortgage payment or utility bill and is a part of each month's fixed expenses. For those who lack the discipline to do this every month, savings can be automatically deducted from a checking account or automatically deposited from a paycheck into a savings account. For example, 401(k) retirement plan contributions are regularly deducted from an employee's paycheck.

If past budgeting efforts have failed it may also be due to discretionary spending habits that now include easy access to cash via ATMs. There are also hidden budget breakers in everyone's day; $2 for coffee and a bagel every morning adds up to over $500 per year, money that could easily be saved. Also, be sure goals are realistic. Set modest goals first and gradually increase to a more ambitious savings amount if you find yourself feeling like a deprived dieter.

PAYING A LOAN

Even with a budget and careful spending, most people at some time in their lives will end up needing a loan. It may be to buy a home, pay for school, expand a business, or restructure their debt. The larger the loan, the more intimidating the process, although even credit card applications are a form of a small loan.

The easy availability of credit cards, consumer loans, and easy payment plans has made consumer debt one of the most serious financial threats facing Americans today. College students are among the most vulnerable targets for credit card recruiters who make it sound like they are offering free money. But that free money must be repaid with interest.

Loans are divided into two major groups: business and personal. Business loans may be needed for expansion, buying new equipment, financing a cash flow difference between income and expenses, or starting a new venture. Personal loans may be needed for mortgages, education, medical bills, debt consolidation, auto financing, or cash advances on credit cards.

There are also as many sources of money for loans as there are loans. Although we often think of banks originating a loan, there are two different types of banks, retail banks and commercial banks. Commercial banks usually handle loans for businesses and emphasize long-term business relationships. Retail banks generally loan smaller amounts for things like autos, boats, or other installment purchases.

Other sources of money include savings and loans institutions and finance companies, as well as mortgage brokers and credit unions. Savings and loans (S&Ls) were originally designed to provide money for mortgage loans. With the deregulation of the financial markets in the 1980s, some S&Ls then moved to offer loans beyond real estate. But many lacked experience handling these loans, and the 1980s saw many S&Ls fail.

Credit unions are nonprofit cooperative savings organizations. Members have a common bond, such as the same employer, same union, or same neighborhood, and the members own the institution. Credit unions offer services such as savings and checking accounts, and their loan rates may be lower and their qualifications less stringent than those of banks.

Finance companies are organizations of investors who seek to lend their own money or the money of their investors instead of using the money of depositors. They are not subject to the same laws as other lenders because they do not use depositors' money. They often make personal loans, but are considered to be aggressive lenders, and usually charge higher interest rates. Be aware that fees charged to process loans from finance companies can also raise interest rates substantially.

Mortgage brokers use fees from loans to make their money. Using a mortgage broker can save time and aggravation because he or she knows the ins and outs of preparing loan requests. Mortgage brokers save lenders from having to do a lot of paperwork because they will have the borrower complete all the necessary forms prior to submitting the mortgage application for approval to the lender. If the loan is approved, the lender then pays the broker a small percentage of the loan as a loan fee, also known as points. This fee can range from one to ten points, and although the lender pays the broker, the borrower ends up paying the points as part of the loan.

Do not pay a preapplication or up-front application fee to a broker. If the broker is legitimate and can find a lender, he or she will be paid for this service after the loan is approved.

UNDERSTANDING THE LOAN PROCESS

No matter why you are borrowing money, it is important to understand the three basic components of any loan: the interest rate, the security component, and the term. The interest rate is what the lender is going to charge for use of the money. Interest rates can be fixed or variable. A fixed percentage rate will not change over the life of the loan. A variable rate will increase or decrease over time. Variable rates are tied to other rates—usually the prime lending rate—and if that rate drops, your interest rate will also fall. However, if that rate rises, the cost of your loan will increase along with the rate.

All loans are either secured or unsecured. For a secured loan, you put up collateral to guarantee payment; for an unsecured loan, you do not need collateral. When you take out a secured loan, you guarantee that the lender will not lose money by giving them claim on something of value you own. Then, if you default on the loan, the lender can claim the asset used as collateral. Because of this guarantee, financial institutions charge lower rates for secured loans than for unsecured loans.

The term of the loan is the length of time given to repay it. Most personal loans have a payback time of between one and five years. Some loans do not have a term, such as lines of credit and credit cards, where you are only required to pay the interest on an ongoing basis and can keep owing on the principal indefinitely.

For any personal loan you will need to complete a detailed application and supply a number of documents, including a copy of your W-2 form showing your current income, as well as a current pay stub. You will often be asked to provide copies of your income tax returns for the last several years. Lenders want to see whether your cash flow is sufficient to cover the payments you are obligated to make. They also look to see if you have a history of timely payments of debts, and whether you have assets in case the loan fails.

MORTGAGES

For most people, a mortgage is their biggest and most important personal loan. Mortgages come in many different makes and styles. The most popular mortgage is the one that is amortized over 30 years, at which time it's paid in full. However, 15-year mortgages offer some attractive advantages, including saving thousands of dollars in interest costs. The monthly payments on 15-year mortgages are higher, but counselors suggest getting the shortest term you can afford to save you money.

Mortgage loans come with either fixed or variable rates. Variable rates by definition vary or change over the life of the loan depending on how they are structured. Fixed rates are harder to qualify for but may be easier to maintain because the payments do not change.

For a $100,000 30-year mortgage at 8%, the borrower would pay $733.77 principal and interest per month. Loans that are repaid gradually over their life are called amortizing loans. The borrower's money goes largely toward paying the interest in the early years of this loan, and most of the principal is not paid off until the later years.

The total interest paid on this loan would be $164,160. At the end of five years, the borrower would still owe $95,070 of the original $100,000 borrowed. That's because in those early years, the bulk of each monthly payment goes to interest. It is not until sometime in the fifth year that the amount allocated toward principal repayment tops $100 per month. By around the 20th year of the loan payoff, more of the monthly payment goes toward repaying principal than paying interest. Once that happens, of course, the payoff goes much more rapidly, but by then the borrower has already paid more than $143,000 in interest.

The 15-year mortgage has an obvious advantage if the borrower can afford higher monthly payments. By paying the total loan sooner, the borrower needs less money for less time and pays less interest over the life of the loan. The disadvantage to the shorter 15-year loan is that the monthly payments are much higher than for a comparable 30-year loan and borrowers need to have a higher income to qualify for it.

For example, a $100,000 15-year mortgage at 8% interest would have a monthly payment of $955.65. Over the life of the loan, the borrower would pay only $72,017 in interest. By the end of the fifth year, the balance on this loan would be just under $79,000, but by the end of the 10th year, it would be down to $47,000. In those last five years, the payoff accelerates because the payments go almost entirely toward principal repayments, not on paying interest.

Another way to save thousands over the lifetime of a loan is to make additional principal payments. Let's say you cannot afford the higher monthly payments of a 15-year mortgage. So you take a 30-year mortgage. At the same time, purchase an amortization chart or run one on some personal financial software such as Quicken. These charts show precisely how much money is going toward interest and principal for every payment. In this example, initial principal payments range around $70. So when you send in your monthly mortgage payment, add an extra $70 to it and note on the coupon or mortgage voucher that the additional money is to go toward the principal. You still have to pay the mortgage the next month, of course, but what you've done is effectively cut one payment off the life of the loan. Do that whenever you have additional money on hand and two things happen: the equity in your home builds faster, and the loan balance decreases. Some mortgagers require that these additional principal payments reflect the exact amount of the next month's due; others allow borrowers to contribute as much to additional principal payments as they wish.

The equity that you have in your home is the value of the home less the outstanding mortgage balance. The equity begins as your down payment and grows depending on the interest rate and length of the loan. If the home appreciates, or increases in value, equity likewise increases. If you need additional funds for college tuition payments, a home equity line of credit loan is a popular choice. Home equity loans are a line of credit with an adjustable rate you may draw on over time, secured by the equity in a home. Home equity lines of credit and second mortgages are similar in that the interest on both loans is tax deductible. However, a home equity loan is in essence a second lien against your property and must be paid off in full if and when you sell your home. A home equity loan works best for people with good credit who do not need all the money at once. That way they won't be paying interest on the money until it is actually withdrawn, and pay interest only on the outstanding balance.

A line of credit, if handled correctly, can effectively be used to purchase large items like cars. If you secure an attractive rate on the line of credit on your house, the best plan is to structure payments to pay it off in about three years. That way you enjoy the benefit of a tax deduction on the interest portion of your equity line of credit. Consult with a tax professional for specifics.

CAR LOANS

Next to a mortgage or student loan, a car loan is the most common debt for most people. It is important to get preapproval for a car loan before you go out to select the car. First, decide what appeals to you in a car, from safety features to gas mileage to repair costs. Research its price using various consumer sources such as the Kelley *Blue Book* or *Consumer Reports*. Then apply for a conventional loan at a local bank or credit union. Once you have preapproval for your loan, you will not be as easily swayed when bargaining because you have a firm figure in mind. This is more cost-effective than selecting a car on the showroom floor that you cannot afford.

Although auto loans run between 12 and 60 months, financial advisors suggest not going over 36 months or three years for many reasons. First, you will obviously pay more interest the longer the term of the loan. For example, a car that sells for $16,995, with a down payment of $1,700 and a 36-month loan, will have monthly payments of $486. This means that when you are finished paying the loan, the car will have cost a total of $19,196 when you include interest, some $2,000 above the cost of the car.

There is another reason not to prolong your loan. If something happens to the car, your insurance settlement is based on actual cash value instead of market value. The older the car, the smaller the cash value settlement you can expect from your insurance company. A good rule of thumb for first-time automobile buyers is that if you can't afford the payments on a 36-month loan, choose a less expensive car. And keep in mind that although dealers offer special financing programs, such offers may have hidden finance charges.

BUY OR LEASE?

You're standing in the auto showroom and your heart is beating faster as you envision yourself in this new car. Then the salesperson announces that the lease rates on the car are even less expensive than the monthly payments. Should you take the deal? Not before looking at the entire picture.

The Federal Trade Commission (FTC) and the Federal Reserve Board have created a guide on vehicle leasing, *Keys of Vehicle Leasing: A Consumer's Guide* (February 1998). This guide is for a closed-end lease, at the end of which you may return the vehicle, pay any end-of-lease costs, and walk away.

The agencies suggest you weigh the pros and cons of owning versus leasing.

Ownership

Leasing: You do not own the vehicle. You get to use it but must return it at the end of the lease unless you choose to buy it.

Buying: You own the vehicle and get to keep it at the end of the financing term.

Up-Front Costs

Leasing: Up-front costs may include the first month's payment, a refundable security deposit, a capitalized cost reduction (like a down payment), taxes, registration and other fees, and other charges.

Buying: Up-front costs include the cash price or a down payment, taxes, registration and other fees, and other charges.

Monthly Payments

Leasing: Monthly lease payments are usually lower than monthly loan payments because you are paying only for the vehicle's depreciation during the lease term, plus rent charges (like interest), taxes, and fees.

Buying: Monthly loan payments are usually higher than monthly lease payments because you are paying for the entire purchase price of the vehicle, plus interest and other finances charges, taxes, and fees.

Early Termination

Leasing: You are responsible for any early termination charges if you end the lease early.

Buying: You are responsible for any pay-off amount if you end the loan early.

Vehicle Return

Leasing: You may return the vehicle at lease end, pay any end-of-lease costs, and "walk away."

Buying: You may have to sell or trade the vehicle when you decide you want a different vehicle.

Future Value

Leasing: The lessor has the risk of the future market value of the vehicle.

Buying: You have the risk of the vehicle's market value when you trade or sell it.

Mileage

Leasing: Most leases limit the number of miles you may drive (often 12,000–15,000 per year). You can negotiate a higher mileage limit and pay a higher monthly payment. You will likely have to pay charges for exceeding those limits if you return the vehicle.

Buying: You may drive as many miles as you want, but higher mileage will lower the vehicle's trade-in or resale value.

Excess Wear

Leasing: Most leases limit wear to the vehicle during the lease term. You will likely have to pay extra charges for exceeding those limits if you return the vehicle.

Buying: There are no limits or charges for excessive wear to the vehicle, but excessive wear will lower the vehicle's trade-in or resale value.

End of Term

Leasing: At the end of the lease (typically 2–4 years), you may have a new payment either to finance the purchase of the existing vehicle or to lease another vehicle.

Buying: At the end of the loan term (typically 4–6 years), you have no further loan payments.

Consider Beginning, Middle, and End-of-Lease Costs

At the beginning of the lease, you may have to pay your first monthly payment; a refundable security deposit or your last monthly payment; other fees for licenses, registration, and title; a capitalized cost reduction (like a down payment); an acquisition fee (also called a processing or assignment fee); freight or destination charges; and state or local taxes.

During the lease, you will have to pay your monthly payment; any additional taxes not included in the payment such as sales, use, and personal property taxes; insurance premiums; ongoing maintenance costs; and any fees for late payment. You'll also have to pay for safety and emissions inspections and any traffic tickets. If you end your lease early, you may have to pay substantial early termination charges.

At the end of the lease, if you don't buy the vehicle, you may have to pay a disposition fee and charges for excess miles and excess wear.

The guide also suggests working to negotiate some lease terms, including:

   the agreed-upon value of the vehicle—a lower value can reduce your monthly payment

   up-front payments, including the capitalized cost reduction

   the length of the lease

   the monthly lease payment

   any end-of-lease fees and charges

   the mileage allowed and per-mile charges for excess miles

   the option to purchase either at lease end or earlier

   whether your lease includes "gap" coverage, which protects you if the vehicle is stolen or totaled in an accident.

STUDENT LOANS

Student loans for funding a college education are only part of the package, which can also come in the form of grants, scholarships, and work-study. Loans are more complex than grants and scholarships or work-study dollars because they must be paid back. Student loans contain many of the same components as conventional borrowing, including interest rates, terms of the loan, fees, and deferment options.

These loans are not secured, so there is no security component to student borrowing. Many students do not realize that once they sign the papers for a student loan it must be repaid even if they do not graduate, or if they have trouble finding a job or encounter other financial difficulties.

Under certain circumstances the federal government will cancel all or part of an education loan in a practice called loan forgiveness, but qualification can be time-consuming and costly in a personal sense. To qualify for loan forgiveness someone may perform volunteer work with AmeriCorps, the Peace Corps, or Volunteers in Service to America (VISTA). Another qualification can be through military service. Also, graduates who agree to teach or practice medicine in specific high-need communities can have a portion of a loan forgiven. However, loan forgiveness is based on meeting specific criteria and does not apply to all federal loans. Students interested in pursuing loan forgiveness can contact the specific volunteer organizations or obtain information from the financial aid office at the college they attend, or on the Web at www.finaid.org.

However, most students do not qualify for loan forgiveness and if faced with financial difficulties and missed payments may consider defaulting on their government student loans. Be aware that those who do default on government student loans face possible litigation, collection fees, and late penalties that are not included under a Chapter 7 bankruptcy. There is also no statue of limitations on government student loans, which means that no matter how old the original loan is you can be sued and taken to court if you default.

The best advice for anyone who misses payments or falls behind is to contact the loan holder to make arrangements for a deferment, forbearance, or loan consolidation. If you do not make payments on your loans for 180 days without contacting the lender, the loan will be in default. Consequences of default may include having federal and state income tax refunds withheld; being ineligible to receive any more federal financial aid until the loan is repaid or some portion is paid; being ineligible for deferments (discussed below); having your wages garnished; being liable for costs associated with collecting the loan, including court costs and attorney fees; and having the defaulted loan appear on your credit record.

Two options for postponing repayment are deferments, where the lender allows you to postpone repaying the principal for a specific period of time, and forbearances, where the lender allows you to postpone or reduce payments but the interest charges continue to accrue. Deferments are often granted for students who enroll in graduate school, for students who are unemployed or disabled and participating in a rehabilitation-training program, or for economic hardship. However, deferments are granted only after you submit an application and provide documentation to support your request. Forbearances are typically granted in 12-month intervals for up to three years and usually in cases of extreme financial hardship or unusual circumstances. When you can't qualify for a deferment, a forbearance is the next best choice.

Loan consolidation is another option if you have several student loans and want to roll them into one lower-interest loan. However, due to the complexity of servicing federal student loans, only a handful of lenders offer consolidation programs. In this situation you may also be able to extend the term of the loan in order to reduce the size of the monthly payments. But be careful: if a payment amount is too low to cover the interest portion, you could eventually end up with a bigger loan balance.

ARE YOU IN TROUBLE?

Once you have taken out a loan it is important to realize that it must be paid back on top of regular living expenses. Once again, try to save even if you are in debt. Chances are if you wait until you are debt-free it may never happen. However, remember that it makes sense to pay off the high interest debt first; you can end up earning 5% on your savings while paying 18% or 19% interest on credit card debts.

When bill collectors begin calling and you find that you routinely spend more than you earn, those are signs of financial trouble. Some other signals that you need to slow spending include paying for daily living expenses like groceries with credit cards because you don't have the money in your checking account, and paying only the minimum on monthly credit card bills. Ask yourself, if I lose my job, would I be able to pay next month's bills? If the answer is no, there are immediate steps to take to help stretch your dollars and spend more efficiently. When juggling finances to make ends meet there are two basic choices: either increase income or decrease expenses. While some people have the energy to land a part-time job or a second job in the evenings, many more would benefit from some simple reductions in spending. Food dollars are a category rich in savings; eat breakfast at home; brown bag lunch except for special occasions; use coupons when grocery shopping; reduce restaurant dining to once or twice a month; plan food shopping on a weekly basis and pay attention to store specials.

Other cost cutters include shopping for clothes at discount or outlet stores or during advertised sales; avoiding ATMs that charge fees per transaction; refinancing high-interest credit cards into lower-interest cards; downgrading or canceling cable TV; cutting down or discontinuing cellular phone usage; and giving up expensive habits like smoking.

For most people credit card spending is the biggest budget breaker. Financial planners suggest limiting credit cards to two or three at the most. They also suggest paying down current balances beyond the monthly minimum due even when money is tight. An extra $10 or $20 off the bill will help reduce the debt and save on finance charges. But the most important step to take when debt becomes a problem is to stop adding to it.

THE LONG VIEW: A RETIREMENT BUDGET

When should you start planning for your retirement? Whether you know it or not, you take the first step when you get your first full-time job. Once you are working you begin making contributions to Social Security via your paycheck, and you may be able to join your employer's pension plan. But during this early period, after graduation from high school or college, retirement is so far off in the very distant future that many fail to take it seriously. That delay can be a costly mistake for young workers due to increasingly complex retirement options. And financial planners warn that although income needs go down in retirement, the average person still requires at least 75% of his or her annual pre-retirement income to be comfortable. Newer estimates suggest that rising health care costs may raise that figure even higher.

Young people shouldn't expect all of that to come from Social Security. Social Security provides just over 41% of seniors' retirement income. The rest comes from income from assets (20%), pensions and annuities (nearly 20%), and earnings (nearly 17%). With traditional company pensions becoming less standard, and with the federal debate about the solvency of Social Security in the future, it pays to start thinking about retirement funding early.

The U.S. Department of Labor has created a guide called "Top 10 Ways to Prepare for Retirement." It contains the following suggestions:

1. *Know your retirement needs.* Retirement is expensive. Experts estimate that you'll need about 70% of your pre-retirement income—lower earners, 90% or more—to maintain your standard of living when you stop working. Understand your financial future.

2. *Find out about your Social Security benefits.* Social Security pays the average retiree about 40% of pre-retirement earnings. Call the Social Security Administration at 1–800–772–1213 for a free Personal Earnings and Benefit Estimate Statement (PEBES).

3. *Learn about your employer's pension or profit sharing plan.* If your employer offers a plan, check to see what your benefit is worth. Most employers will provide an individual benefit statement if you request one. Before you change jobs, find out what will happen to your pension. Learn what benefits you may have from previous employment. Find out if you will be entitled to benefits from your spouse's plan. For a free booklet on private pensions, call the U.S. Department of Labor at (800) 998–7542.

4. *Contribute to a tax-sheltered savings plan.* If your employer offers a tax-sheltered savings plan, such as a 401(k), sign up and contribute all you can. Your taxes will be lower, your company may kick in more, and automatic deductions make it easy. Over time, deferral of taxes and compounding of interest make a big difference in the amount of money you will accumulate.

5. *Ask your employer to start a plan.* If your employer doesn't offer a retirement plan, suggest that he/she start one. Simplified plans can be set up by certain employers. For information on simplified employee pensions, order Internal Revenue Service Publication 590 by calling (800) 829–3676.

6. *Put money into an Individual Retirement Account.* You can put $2,000 a year into an Individual Retirement Account (IRA) and delay paying taxes on investment earnings until retirement age. If you don't have a retirement plan (or are in a plan and earn less than a certain amount), you can also take a tax deduction for your IRA contributions. IRS Publication 590 contains information about IRAs. It's never too late to start. Start young. A look at the performance of $2,000 retirement plan investments over time at 4% shows the value of starting early.

Age	1995 Dollars grow to
30	$2,000
40	$24,012
50	$59,556
60	$112,170

7. *Don't touch your savings.* Don't dip into your retirement savings. You'll lose principal and interest, and you may lose tax benefits. If you change jobs, roll over your savings directly into an IRA or your new employer's retirement plan.

8. *Start now, set goals, and stick to them.* Start early. The sooner you start saving, the more time your money has to grow. Put time on your side. Make retirement saving a high priority. Devise a plan, stick to it, and set goals for yourself. Remember, it's never too late to start. Start saving now, whatever your age.

9. *Consider basic investment principles.* How you save can be as important as how much you save. Inflation and the type of investments you make play important roles in how much you'll have saved at retirement. Know how your pension or savings plan is invested. Financial security and knowledge go hand in hand.

10. *Ask questions.* These tips should point you in the right direction, but you'll need more information. Talk to your employer, your bank, your union, or a financial advisor. Ask questions and make sure the answers make sense to you. Get practical advice and act now.

The guide notes the following facts, supporting the idea that "financial security doesn't just happen, it takes planning, and commitment, and yes, money":

FACT—Less than half of Americans have put aside money specifically for retirement.

You can't retire with security unless you really prepare for it. That means facing up to reality, and beginning to take action for tomorrow as well as today.

FACT—In 1993, of those who had 401(k) coverage available, one-third didn't participate.

Putting away money for retirement is like giving yourself a raise. It's money that gives you freedom when you want it—and deserve it.

FACT—The average American spends 18 years in retirement.

Today, half of Americans guess when determining their retirement needs. Don't be one of them. Find out more. Save now and beat the retirement clock.

While many retirement decisions seem too far off in the future, there are early steps to take that will ultimately result in a more comprehensive plan. First and foremost, begin saving as soon as you begin working. It's never too soon to analyze information about your specific pension and savings plan and to consider seeking outside advice. Write down retirement goals and be prepared to make adjustments to reflect the changes you will face in the coming years, especially concerning health care plans. Also, try to maintain a savings plan that sets aside 10% of your income as you move into your 30s. Those years are typically a time of growing children and growing bills, but also a time of rising salaries. In your 40s—considered by many to be the peak earning years—as your salary increases, so should your retirement investments. Financial analysts suggest putting away the maximum allowable by law in a 401(k) or IRA. As retirement looms larger in your 50s, take the time to thoroughly review your overall plan and consider future insurance needs. This is also a good time, according to experts, to shift some money into more cautious fixed-income investments. Finally, in your 60s decide on a retirement date. With all that early planning and hard work you should be ready to relax and enjoy those golden years.

NET WORTH CHECK

One way to ensure that you're progressing with your financial goals is to do a periodic net worth assessment. Your net worth is the way to calculate the true value of your assets. First, list your assets: cash, checking and savings accounts, retirement accounts, real estate, cash value of your life insurance policy, investments, and anything else of value. In another column, list all your debts: the balance on any loans—student loans, car loans, personal loans, home loans, credit card balance, and anything else you owe. Total the two columns. Don't panic if your net worth is a negative number, particularly if you're paying back student loans and just took out a car loan, for example, or if you just bought a house with little money down. The loan is still large and the equity is small. Repeat this assessment every year or so, and you should see progress. Retirement accounts and investment accounts should be growing. If you've bought a house, you should start seeing more equity in it. In the meantime, some of those early loans will be paid off, and if other debts are entered into only as needed, the numbers will start to match up more. Ideally, you'd like to own more than owe, but it's important to track the trend. If the liability column outpaces the assets column, take action to turn it around.

The College Board created the following net worth worksheet.

NET WORTH WORKSHEET

The first step in developing a long-range financial plan is determining your net worth. Basically, your net worth is what's left after you've subtracted your liabilities from your assets. Check your net worth every year or so. If it is increasing each year, you're heading in the right direction!

Step 1: Add up your assets

Cash (money in the bank and in your pocket, money market funds, CDs, etc.) $_____

+ Estimated current value of stocks, bonds, and securities $_____

+ Current market value of your home plus any other real estate you own $_____

+ Current market value of your car(s) and other vehicles $_____

+ Estimated resale value of household goods and furnishings $_____

+ Market value of jewelry, antiques, art, etc. $_____

+ Cash value (not face value) of life insurance policies $_____

+ Your current share of company savings or profit-sharing plans $_____

+ Vested pension plan (i.e., actual amount due to you) $_____

+ Current balance in your IRA $_____

+ Current balance in your Keogh $_____

+ Fair market value of property held in trust $_____

+ Your interest in a business, partnership, or other investment $_____

+ Money that is owed to you $_____

+ Any other assets you own $_____

= Your Total Assets $_____

Step 2: Add up your liabilities

Unpaid balance on your home mortgage	$_____
+ Unpaid balance on any other real estate mortgages or loans	$_____
+ Total outstanding balances on other loans (e.g., car or personal loans)	$_____
+ Balance due on any loans against insurance policies	$_____
+ Total balance due on unpaid bills	$_____
+ Unpaid federal, state, and local taxes (income and property)	$_____
+ Any educational debt for which you are responsible	$_____
+ Any other liabilities	$_____
= Your Total Liabilities	$_____

Step 3: Estimate your net worth

Your Total Assets (result from Step 1)	$_____
+ Your Total Liabilities (result from Step 2)	$_____
= Your Net Worth	$_____

Source: CollegeCredit(R), a registered trademark of the College Entrance Examination Board

BUDGETING ABROAD

It's finally here—the long awaited trip overseas or across the border. It might be a bicycling adventure through Europe or an eco-adventure in South America. Whatever brings you beyond the U.S. borders, you'll need money and you'll need to watch your budget. First of all, the temptation is always there to live it up a little on vacation, but the conversion of U.S. money to foreign currency means you'll need to be even more careful that you're not blowing the budget without even knowing it.

Cash is not king on overseas trips. In fact, take very little U.S. currency with you. You'll want to carry enough to buy items at U.S. airports or buy your train ticket back home when you return, but that's about it.

What you need is traveler's checks. Traveler's checks are sold at most banks, and there are several major brands, such as American Express. Traveler's checks are sold in different denominations. Record the serial numbers and denominations of these checks so you can get replacements quickly if needed. It's best to try to calculate how much money you'll need on the trip and purchase enough traveler's checks to cover that. If you bring too much, you can simply deposit the traveler's checks in your own account when you return. But that's much easier than trying to access cash in a foreign country.

Another relatively simple way to pay for items abroad is by using a credit card. It might also be possible to obtain cash advances on credit cards. Take only the credit card(s) you'll really need and leave the others at home. Record the credit card number and carry the issuer's telephone number with you, just in case the card is stolen or lost. Take care to note the credit limit on your account and don't exceed it.

No matter how you pay for items, also take the time to calculate what you're paying for them. When paying by credit card, typically the charge will appear in that country's currency, not in U.S. dollars. Make sure you know what the exchange rate is so you can figure out how much you're spending.

That can be a little complicated, especially if you're traveling around different countries. For example, if $1 U.S. is exchanged for 1,800 Italian lira, items in Italian stores can look very expensive. A cup of coffee and a pastry could set you back several thousand lira. In contrast, go to Great Britain, where the U.S. dollar is worth about 0.6 British pounds and you might be lulled into thinking items are less expensive. Because the exchange rates are close—or at least closer than they are with other currencies, you might look at a t-shirt that costs 20 pounds and think it's about $20. But it's really more than $33. Take the time, indeed, take a calculator if you need it, to do the math so you know what you're paying.

Also figure out the formula for calculating the value of your purchases. If the foreign currency is exchanged at more than 1 for every $1 U.S., you divide by that currency. Recall that the exchange rate was 1,800 lira for every $1 U.S. Let's say the tab for the cup of coffee and pastry is 5,000 lira. Divide by 1,800 to determine the U.S. cost—about $2.77.

If the foreign currency exchanges for less than 1 unit for each U.S. dollar, the formula is obviously different. In the United Kingdom, we were getting 0.6 pounds for each U.S. dollar. Now we take our 1 and divide by 0.6. The answer is 1.66. So multiply the cost of an item by 1.66 to reach its cost in U.S. dollars.

These numbers were true exchange rates on one day in 1999, but exchange rates fluctuate often. The better value for American travelers is when the U.S. dollar gets you more foreign currency. Look what happens if you find a bank that will exchange your dollar, or the rates fluctuate so the dollar exchanges for 1,900 lira. That same cup of coffee and pastry now cost $2.63. And if the British pound is suddenly trading for 0.68, recalculate the conversion factor (1 divided by 0.68 = 1.47). Now that 20 pound t-shirt would cost you about $29.40 in U.S. dollars.

When in Rome or London, do as the Romans and Londoners do. Carry their currency. To do so, you'll have to exchange your traveler's checks. Many bureaus and banks are willing to exchange your traveler's check for the local currency—for a price. How much you pay depends on how willing you are to find the best deal. Those are usually found in larger banks within larger cities. The best deal will probably come from a bank that issues the same brand of traveler's checks you're carrying.

The worst deal? Airports, small exchange bureaus in tourist areas, hotels, restaurants, shops. To avoid paying these highest prices, obtain some money in the local currency before leaving the United States. That way, if you arrive after business hours, you'll have enough money to hop on a train or bus or to buy some food. Foreign currency can be purchased at some banks and even at some vending machines in larger international airports in the United States.

Most bureaus and banks post their exchange rates, so look around. But also find out what the fees are. Some places charge both a commission, a percentage of the amount they're exchanging, and a fee. If you can't avoid a fee, consider exchanging a little more money. Better to be hit with one fee in exchanging $100 than two fees in exchanging $50 twice in a week.

Exchange rates do fluctuate, so keep an eye out for a good value. Some countries have requirements about the amount of money you must exchange or limits on how much you can bring in. Border or customs agents may ask you to report how much money you have upon entering, and again upon leaving. Your travel agent might know of those types of restrictions.

ADDITIONAL READING

Bolles, Richard Nelson. *What Color Is Your Parachute?* Berkeley, CA: Ten Speed Press, 1996.

Glossbrenner, Alfred, and Emily Glossbrenner. *Smart Guide to Managing Personal Finance.* New York: John Wiley & Sons, 1998.

Hetzer, Barbara. *How Can I Ever Afford Children? Money Skills for New and Experienced Parents.* New York: John Wiley & Sons, 1998.

Lidz, Richard, and Linda Perrin, editorial directors. *Career Information Center.* 6th ed. New York: Macmillan Library Reference USA. 1996. (An 11-volume series describing jobs, starting and average salaries, prospects for growth, and training required.)

Mellan, Olivia. *Money Harmony: Resolving Money Conflicts in Your Life and Relationships.* New York: Walker, 1994.

The Occupational Outlook Handbook, 1996–97 Edition. Washington, DC: U.S. Department of Labor, Bureau of Labor Statistics, 1996.

Pybrum, Steven. *Money and Marriage: Making It Work Together. A Guide to Smart Money and Harmonious Communications.* Santa Barbara, CA: Abundance Publishing Co., 1996.

Schurenberg, Eric. *401(K): Take Charge of Your Future.* New York: Warner Books, 1996.

Schwab, Charles R. *Charles Schwab's Guide to Financial Independence*. New York: Crown, 1998.

Skousen, Mark, and JoAnn Skousen. *High Finance on a Low Budget*. 2nd ed. Chicago: Dearborn Financial Publications, 1997.

Steinmetz, Thomas C. *The Mortgage Kit*. 4th ed. Chicago: Dearborn Financial Publications, 1998.

Tyson, Eric. *Personal Finance for Dummies*. San Mateo, CA: IDG Books, Worldwide, 1996.

Consumerism and Saving:
Opposing Forces

It's no wonder some young Americans are spending themselves into serious debt. Advertisers love young adults because they have disposable income and they are generally impressionable. If everyone else in the school is wearing the latest greatest style, they should too. So what if sneakers cost the same as two weeks worth of groceries? Advertisers and peer pressure have put certain items on the must-have list.

And advertisers are targeting younger audiences. Advertising in schools is still relatively rare today, but may become more standard in coming years. For school districts struggling with their budgets, turning to advertisers for help can seem very appealing. Examine what Channel One Communications offers its participating schools. Schools commit to air for three years a 12-minute news show for students in grades 6 through 12 every day—including two minutes of youth-oriented advertisements. In exchange, they receive a satellite dish, a cable hookup, a television monitor for each classroom, and an agreement to service the equipment for three years. By 1995, Channel One Communications programs were being viewed in 350,000 classrooms.

ADVERTISING IN THE CLASSROOM

More advertising gets into schools indirectly—through ads in magazines or teaching materials. It's a trend that concerns organizations like Consumers Union, whose Education Services department published *Selling America's Kids: Commercial Pressures on Kids of the 90's*. In its analysis of advertising and its effect on students, the group made three recommendations:

1. Make schools ad-free zones, where young people can pursue learning free of commercial influences and pressures. The group recommended restricting the use of business-sponsored materials. Any material that is used should be accurate, objective, complete, nondiscriminatory, and noncommercial (no brands or trademarks or explicit sales messages).
2. Promotions that target kids must meet higher standards than those aimed at adults. They should not exploit the inexperience and vulnerabilities of kids, and they should clearly identify themselves as advertising.
3. Educate children about the nature of commercial messages directed at them and build their ability to resist sales pressures. Schools and parents need to balance some of the promotional influences on kids' development as consumers and citizens.

Even without school-based advertising, American teenagers are typically exposed to 360,000 advertisements by the time they graduate from high school, according to Alan Thein Durning, author of *How Much Is Enough? The Consumer Society and the Future of the Earth.* The result of this push toward consumerism—to buy what we think we need or deserve right now—is that we excel at spending money. According to Lawrence Shames in *The Hunger for More,* 93% of American teenage girls reported store-hopping as their favorite activity.

Credit cards make it so easy to buy on the spur of the moment and without the cash on hand. And then when the bills come, there are too many other bills that take priority. So some people pay only the minimum due, and because of additional purchases and growing interest charges, their debt gets bigger and bigger. With no savings to turn to, when that financial hole gets too deep, many Americans see filing for bankruptcy as their only way out. In 1986, about 333,000 Americans declared bankruptcy. Ten years later, the number had tripled and more than 1 million Americans declared bankruptcy. By 1998, it was up to nearly 1.5 million.

THE HIGH COST OF KEEPING UP

The odd thing is that even though Americans are spending more and, in the late 1990s, the country was in a period of amazing economic growth as a result, it doesn't necessarily mean that they feel richer. Keeping up with the Joneses, that idea of having what others have, is a losing battle. As some people upgrade to better products, houses, styles, and cars, others feel they have to just to keep up. But how important is that to one's financial and psychological health? If your three-year-old car runs great, do you really need a sport utility vehicle just because they're the current trend? Look at the consequences. You have just one year left to pay on your current car loan. If you sell it now, while it has fairly low mileage and still looks great, you'll be able to pay off the loan and still have a little left for a down payment on the new SUV. But you'll be back to square one, paying another car loan. And you've given up a perfectly good car. Still, consumers rationalize that kind of purchase every day. "I'd have to get a new car in the next two years anyway, so I might as well do it now." "I have a new job; I should be seen in a new car." "I've been buying used cars my whole life. I deserve a new car I like." "It's my money, I'll spend it how I like." "The interest rates are so low and I got such a good trade-in, I couldn't afford not to."

In fact, per capita consumption—the amount of money spent per person—has risen 45% in the United States in the last 20 years. But since 1970, according to the Index of Social Health, quality of life has decreased 5%. In fact, those who report the highest quality of life, the highest level of satisfaction with their lives, are those who can live within their budget. Financial concerns are a tremendous stress for almost anyone, no matter what their income level. And it's a struggle for most people. Only 5% of Americans earning less than $15,000 a year say they've achieved the American dream. But only 6% of those earning more than $50,000 say they've achieved the American dream, according to *Harper's* magazine (October 1998). When the dream is chasing the next bigger or better item—computer, home entertainment system, vacation, house, car, Ivy league education—it can become more like a nightmare.

So more is not necessarily better. Sometimes more is simply more expensive. For example, look at where we live. In 1948, the median size of a new house built in this country was 1,100 square feet. By 1993, it was 2,060 square feet. It's not that our families are bigger, or that we need the space for ourselves. We just want it. We want it because we've always dreamed of a house with a big kitchen. We want it because all the children want separate bedrooms. We want it because we need the space for all our stuff.

What is that stuff? Chances are, most people could go through their closets or storage areas and find things they've long since forgotten they own. Things they haven't used in years. Broken parts of things. Things they or someone else spent good money on. Chances are, it's too much stuff. Take a look at the "storage solutions" area of a hardware or department store. It has become an industry to provide people with ways to store stuff—stackable boxes, clear boxes, rolling trays, dozens of ways to squeeze in a few more feet of storage space.

Is that necessary? Why not cull through the stuff that's there, keep what you need, and get rid of the rest? Donate it to charity, or have a yard sale. The result is less clutter, better access to the things you want, and no more need to spend money on storage. The exercise might also add to your skepticism about consumer advertising. Most people will uncover an item they simply had to have—something they saw advertised and couldn't wait for. They begged, or simply coughed up the money themselves, bought the item, used it a few times, found out it wasn't what they had hoped for, and stuck it away. Look at it now. Remember the $45 price tag on it. Remind yourself to be more cautious next time you feel the urge to buy something now.

That's not to say that buying consumer products is a bad thing. People need clothes and food and cars. But buying food and clothes and cars because advertisers have convinced you that it's what you want—even if you can't afford it—is a recipe for financial trouble. And spending, at the sacrifice of saving, is also a problem.

According to the U.S. Bureau of Labor Statistics, in 1998 the average "consumer unit"—which averaged 2.5 people, of which 1.3 were income earners, with an average age of 47.6 and an average income of $41,622— spent $35,536, an increase of 2% over the year before. Here is what the money was spent on:

Food: $4,810
  At home: $2,780
  Away from home: $2,030
Housing: $11,713
Apparel and services: $1,674
Transportation: $6,616
Health care: $1,903
Entertainment: $1,746
Personal insurance and pensions: $3,381
Other expenditures: $3,693

That leaves that "consumer unit" with very little to save. And that's exactly what has been happening.

HOW MUCH DO AMERICANS SAVE?

The American savings rate was at a 65-year low in 1998. Table 7.1 shows personal savings as a percentage of disposable personal income. Some historical footnotes to this chart: the Great Depression lasted from 1929–1933 and World War II, during which Americans hunkered down and got serious about saving, lasted from 1939 to 1945. Because of lower savings rates and increased spending, many people that find they have to work harder. They feel tired and frustrated at the end of the day. Fully 69% say they'd like to slow down and live a more relaxed life, according to *Time* magazine (April 8, 1991).

That points to an interesting issue in the American economy: if the

Table 7.1
U.S. Savings Rate

Year	Percent saved	Year	Percent saved	Year	Percent saved
1929	4.3	1952	8.1	1975	9.3
1930	3.8	1953	7.9	1976	7.9
1931	3.5	1954	7.1	1977	6.9
1932	−1.4	1955	6.6	1978	7.5
1933	−2.1	1956	8.0	1979	7.7
1934	0.6	1957	8.1	1980	8.5
1935	3.7	1958	8.2	1981	9.4
1936	5.6	1959	7.2	1982	9.0
1937	5.3	1960	6.6	1983	6.7
1938	1.1	1961	7.7	1984	8.6
1939	3.7	1962	7.6	1985	6.9
1940	5.0	1963	7.0	1986	5.9
1941	11.7	1964	7.9	1987	5.0
1942	23.8	1965	7.8	1988	5.4
1943	25.2	1966	7.5	1989	5.0
1944	25.7	1967	8.7	1990	5.1
1945	19.9	1968	7.7	1991	5.6
1946	9.3	1969	7.2	1992	5.7
1947	3.9	1970	8.5	1993	4.4
1948	6.6	1971	8.8	1994	3.5
1949	4.6	1972	7.6	1995	3.4
1950	6.7	1973	9.5	1996	2.9
1951	8.1	1974	9.5	1997	2.1
				1998	0.5

Source: U.S. Department of Commerce, Bureau of Economic Analysis.

economy showed unprecedented growth in the past few decades, why don't more people feel financially well off? The conundrum doesn't surprise a San Francisco–based organization, Redefining Progress, because it is among those who argue that the way the country has measured prosperity is flawed.

MEASURING ECONOMIC PROSPERITY: THE GDP VERSUS THE GPI

In 1994 Redefining Progress developed the Genuine Progress Indicator (GPI) to measure the economy differently. In their 1998 summary, the authors, journalist Jonathan Rowe and public policy analyst Mark Anielski, called it a measure of economic well-being rather than simply a monetary tally.

The current measure, the gross domestic product (GDP), shows how much money Americans spend each year. "If the amount is greater than in the previous year then economists call it 'expansion' or 'growth.' The more money people spend the more the economy grows. But how this spending translates into human well-being, and whether the additional outlays suggest that life is getting better or worse, are totally different questions. About these, the GDP says virtually nothing at all. It says even less about the implications of current patterns of growth for the generations that will come after us" (Rowe and Anielski, "Genuine Progress Indicator," Section I).

One of the problems is that the GDP was never designed to become a gauge of economic performance. It was developed at the beginning of World War II to measure production by the country's industrial plants. Even Simon Kuznets, the Nobel Prize–winning economist who was the chief architect of what is now the GDP, encouraged a better and more inclusive measure to assess a national economy.

Why? Because higher spending doesn't necessarily reflect a better quality of life. For example, a person diagnosed with cancer and requiring expensive chemotherapy increases the GDP by spending more money on health care that year. A couple that divorces and sets up two households increases the GDP.

The GDP also includes business investment and government payrolls, but about two-thirds of the measurement is attributable to household and individual expenditures. And increased household spending doesn't necessarily equal a better quality of life, as Rowe and Anielski see it.

The GDP regards every expenditure as an addition to well-being, regardless what that expenditure is for or the effects. By this reasoning the nation's economic hero is the terminal cancer patient going through an expensive divorce, whose car is totaled in a twenty-car pile-up. The economic villain is the healthy person in a solid marriage who cooks at home, walks to work, and doesn't smoke or gamble. The hero borrows and spends; the villain pays cash and saves for the kids' education. What economists call "growth," in other words, is not always the same as what most Americans would consider good. (6)

The GDP also "ignores the crucial economic functions that lie outside the realm of monetary exchange." Only when there are problems— storms that wipe out entire communities, floods that destroy property, troubled kids who need counseling—does the GDP count them, because then the cost of replacing or providing these services is counted. "When the city cuts down shade trees to widen a street, and homeowners have to buy air conditioners for cooling, the GDP goes up again. It looks like economic growth, but in reality no increase has occured. Instead, something that used to be free now costs money; social and environmental decay have been transmogrified into 'growth' through the myopic lens of the GDP" (6). Because of its focus on the present, and not the future, the GDP presents an unrealistic picture. "The GDP counts the depletion of natural resources as current income rather than as the liquidation of an asset.... Similarly, saving doesn't add much to the GDP ... [b]ut maxing out on credit cards makes it soar" the authors wrote in Section III of the report "Fallacies of the GDP."

The fourth problem they see is that the GDP ignores the distribution of income. One thousand dollars means little to the ultra wealthy and makes a world of difference to the poor. "Add these fallacies together, and it helps explain why the opinion establishment thinks the future is rosy, and why many Americans are worried nevertheless."

The GPI, on the other hand, tries to acknowledge that money can be spent on negative circumstances—medical costs for a dangerously premature baby are much higher than for a healthy full-term baby—and also try to account for elements in the economy that aren't measured by money—parents who stay home to care for a child, for example. And the GPI tries to account for the impact of today's spending on the future.

And according to the GPI, the American economy isn't nearly as rosy as the GDP portrays it, as Figure 7.1 demonstrates. "Where the GDP portrays continual economic advance from the 1950s to the present, the GPI rose in tandem with the GDP until the mid–1970s but then turned downward. The economy has been 'growing' during that time. People have been spending more money. But a closer look suggests that the costs of this expansion—especially the social and environmental costs— have begun to outweigh the benefits, such as they may be" (Section II).

In its 1998 update to earlier research, Redefining Progress says that the GPI shows a continued downward trend. Costs in some categories, such as those associated with air pollution and crime, have declined. But overall:

• The gap between the rich and everyone else is expanding.
• The nation is borrowing more and more from abroad, a symptom of an anemic savings rate and mountains of household debt.
• The costs of reliance on nonrenewable energy resources continue to mount, as do the costs of the environmental damage that results. Household capital continues to wear out rapidly, the result of shoddy construction or rapid obsolescence. (Section II, "The Genuine Progress Indicator, 1998 Update")

While the developers of the GPI say it is not a perfect measurement, they argue that it corrects some flaws in the GDP. "It starts with personal expenditures as a baseline, the way the GDP does. But it then adjusts for numerous factors to start to translate those gross expenditures into a reckoning of net economic gain. In essence, the GPI moves towards the

Figure 7.1
GDP versus GPI, 1950–1997

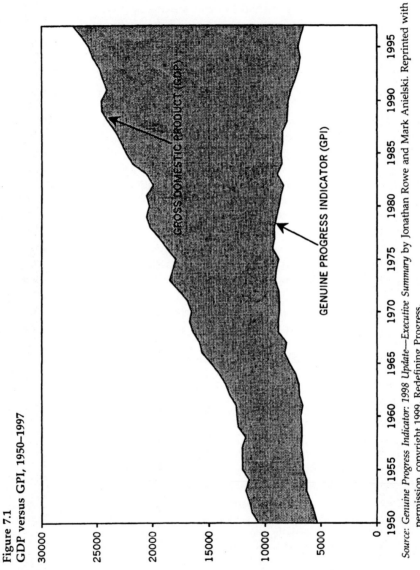

Source: Genuine Progress Indicator: 1998 Update—Executive Summary by Jonathan Rowe and Mark Anielski. Reprinted with permission, copyright 1999, Redefining Progress.

kind of common sense accounting that a household or a business would do" (Section IV "A New Measure of Progress: The GPI").

The report explains how that's done.

1. The GPI adds a cost side to the growth ledger. It subtracts so-called "defensive expenditures" such as the costs of crime and environmental decay. It accounts for such things as long-term environmental damage and the loss of leisure time. The GPI also subtracts certain kinds of outlays that few Americans would regard as evidences of well-being, such as those related to family break-down and commuting.

2. The GPI begins to account for the aspects of the economy that lie outside the realm of monetary exchange. It assigns value to the life-sustaining functions of households, communities, and the natural environment so that the destruction of these, and their replacement with commoditized substitutes, no longer appears as growth and gain. It also counts the value of services from public infrastructure such as highways and bridges that the GDP ignores.

3. The GPI acknowledges that the economy exists for future generations as well as for the present ones. When we deplete the earth's resources, degrade the natural environment, and weaken the social structure by displacing it with things and services people have to buy, we are robbing our grandkids' trust fund. The GPI treats such destruction as cost rather than as gain.

4. The GPI adjusts for income disparities. A growing income gap involves real costs that the nation's economic accounting should not ignore. Large disparities in income tend towards social breakdown and even bodily disease.

The organization is concerned about the booming economy reflected in the GDP because it suspects that the erosion in the economy is being masked by the financial boom and "the associated shopping spree. . . . Yet high-level commentators maintain that the main economic threat is that Americans might somehow cease borrowing and spending money" (Section IV).

And if Americans stop spending and start saving, the GDP will drop. "Politicians keep trying to 'stimulate' the economy to solve the nation's problems; but increasingly what they are really stimulating are the problems themselves" (Section II). According to the GDP, the average per person spending in 1997 was $27,163. According to the GPI, the figure was much lower. And according to the GPI, per capita spending grew very little over the past 50 years and, in fact, has been dropping since the 1980s. "The economy appears to have expanded almost three times over on a per capita basis. This would suggest that Americans are three times better off" (Section V "Summary of GPI Results").

Why did the GPI start to fall while the GDP continued to rise?

A number of factors lie behind this trend. Environmental damage, dependence on fossil fuels, loss of leisure, and the income gap all played a part. So too did crime and family breakdown. In the 1990s the divergence between the GDP and the GPI has become more pronounced. While the GDP has increased per capita at about 1.4 percent a year, the GPI has fallen at about twice that rate. The stock market has boomed. Americans have been spending (and borrowing) more money than at any time in history. But beneath the buoyant surface of this transactional increase, there have been countercurrents that don't register on the GDP and other official indicators. (Section V)

Along with income disparity, another major factor has been the loss of leisure time.

Historically, [leisure] time has always been associated with wealth. Yet the financial boom of the 1980s and 1990s has had the opposite effect; it has put Americans on a treadmill on which they have to run faster and faster to keep the boom in motion. Americans have less leisure today than at any time since the Second World War.
As a result, people have less time for their kids and families, less time for civic and community needs. In the short term this tends to boost the GDP, as people contract out to the expanding "service sector" what they no longer have time to do themselves. But in the long term, it represents the depletion of the social capital upon which an economy ultimately depends.

Environmental damage and the depletion of nonrenewable resources such as oil and coal also contribute to the decline of the GPI.
Even though the GDP has its critics, the system seems fairly well entrenched. That's not surprising, according to Rowe and Anielski. "A new measure would imply a whole new way of understanding the economy, with all the inconvenience that involves. Economic interest also plays a role. Industries that inflict costs upon the public bask in the warm glow of the GDP because it casts all economic activity in a flattering light. They are not eager for an honest accounting that begins to distinguish costs from gains" (Section IV).
It's not that Redefining Progress wants to get rid of the GDP entirely. "The government does need a gross tally of monetary transactions for purposes of monetary policy, fiscal planning, and the like. . . . The problem is not that the GDP exists, but that it has become a conceptual dead-end." They acknowledge the difficulty in trying to create a different measurement.

Some argue that the effort is inherently misguided. To try to express the care of a parent or the quiet of a virgin forest in terms of a dollar price only degrades them. We agree. Yet there's danger in the other direction too. To continue to exclude such things from the economic accounting helps the engines of policy to ride roughshod over them. When the GDP portrays the destruction of the social structure and the environment as growth and gain, it justifies the policies that bring about that destruction. . . . The question is not whether to make value judgments but rather which ones to make. We contend that it is more honest and responsible to meet this difficulty head on than to sweep it under an accounting rug called the GDP. (Section VI "Conclusion")

Similar issues were raised in *Shifting Fortunes: The Perils of the Growing American Wealth Gap*, a 1999 publication by United for a Fair Economy. According to the overview announcing the publication:

From 1983 to 1998, the stock market grew a cumulative 1,336 percent. The wealthiest households reaped most of the gains. . . . The top 1 percent of households have more wealth than the entire bottom 95 percent. Financial wealth is even more concentrated. The top 1 percent of households have nearly half of all financial wealth (net worth minus net equity in owner-occupied housing). . . . The percentage of households with zero or negative net worth (greater debts than assets) increased from 15.5 percent in 1983 to 18.5 percent in 1995—nearly one out of five households. That's nearly double the rate in 1962, when the comparable figure was 9.8 percent—one out of ten households.

VOLUNTARY SIMPLICITY

Is the savings rate low because people spend too much, or because economic measurements aren't measuring the right thing, or because the distribution of wealth is completely skewed? Or is it some combination of all three?

Without necessarily trying to figure out the economic reasons why they suffer from financial stress, some people have taken action and said enough is enough. They reached the conclusion that they were trying too hard to earn money and enjoying life less and less, so they're taking a big step back from the rat race. The movement is called voluntary simplicity. It encompasses a variety of philosophies, characterized by spending less, saving more, scaling back on possessions, using only what you need, and generally treading more lightly on this earth. It emphasizes frugality—not poverty.

It can be as simple as riding a bicycle to work or to the train station. While that seems like an environmentally based action, it has enormous financial implications. How many families have two cars, one which sits at a train station or office parking lot for 10 hours a day? Deciding to ride a bike to work opens up the option of getting rid of the second car—a move that has additional positive environmental and financial consequences.

Indeed, voluntary simplicity is driven in part as a reaction to Americans' overconsumption of earth's resources. While Americans account for only 5% of the world's population, they use 30% of the world's resources and 25% of the fossil fuel burned annually (*Seattle Weekly*, November 10, 1993). The amount of energy used by 1 American is equivalent to that used by 3 Japanese, or 6 Mexicans, or 14 Chinese, or 38 Indians, or 168 Bengalis, or 531 Ethiopians (*Philadelphia Inquirer*, January 17, 1990).

Voluntary simplicity, listed as one of the top 10 trends of 1994 by Trends Research Institute, also draws on the romantic value of people spending time with their own thoughts, doing the things they like to do. That's why Henry David Thoreau's *Walden* remains a classic in American literature. But frugality doesn't necessarily mean heading out to a cabin in the woods and getting away from it all. It begins with scaling back, such as getting rid of credit cards or winnowing the credit card collection down to one.

Some people practice their thrift quietly. Others are a little more outspoken about it. For example, Adbusters, a British Columbia–based anticonsumerism group, organizes an annual Buy Nothing Day on the day after Thanksgiving, traditionally the first day of the holiday shopping bonanza. It began in the Pacific Northwest in the early 1990s, and by 1998 it is estimated, more than 1 million people made a personal pact with themselves and joined the consumer fast for 24 hours.

Those interested can go to the group's Web site (www.adbusters.org) and download copies of Buy Nothing Day posters or the group's "uncommercials" or copy the idea of gift exemption certificates to give to friends to encourage them to spend time with you, not spend money on you. Some Adbusters-inspired groups have staged credit card–cutting booths in front of shopping malls and handed out stickers to nonshoppers to proudly proclaim they bought nothing. The Web site also posts its *Adbusters* magazine online.

Being a smart consumer doesn't require people to boycott all advertised products. But a healthy dose of skepticism is a good attribute for consumers. Remember that it is the job of marketers to make people think they will be better looking, sexier, and have the greatest friends if they have a certain car, shoe, cereal, or housecleaning product.

There are other ways to save, too. The Consumer Literacy Consortium, a group coordinated by the Consumer Federation of America, has identified the top 10 consumer purchase mistakes:

1. Leasing rather than buying a car because you believe that leasing costs less.
2. Not carefully searching for a competent, honest auto mechanic.
3. Assuming your insurance agent will "shop the market" to find you the best auto or homeowner's policy.
4. Not holding a cash-value life insurance policy for at least 15 years.
5. Not maintaining the minimum balance required to avoid checking fees.
6. Holding many credit cards.
7. Taking out a 30-year mortgage loan, rather than a 15-year loan, just because the monthly payments are lower.

8. Paying in full for a home improvement before the work has been completed to your satisfaction.
9. Purchasing new appliances that are not energy efficient.
10. Not comparing unit prices found on supermarket shelves.

The Consumer Literacy Consortium publishes "66 Ways to Save Money," a brochure available free and online (see Appendix E).

Another tip for saving is to avoid compulsive purchases—leave the item in the store. If you still feel you have to have it the next day, return and buy it then. That's a better option than having buyer's remorse the next day and lacking the initiative to return the item for store credit or cash.

TELEMARKETERS COUNT ON COMPULSIVE BUYING

Indeed, compulsive purchases are what telemarketers count on. And while telemarketing is a legal—if annoying—way to market products or services, the opportunity for getting ripped off is greater. A consumer partnership, National Futures Association has produced "Swindlers Are Calling," a brochure on how to avoid fraud in telemarketing. "Phone fraud is a multi-billion dollar business that involves selling everything from bad or non-existent investments to the peddling of misrepresented products and services. Everyone who has a phone is a prospect; whether you become a victim is largely up to you," the brochure warns.

Don't think you can outsmart a swindler. They have slick answers ready and will try to dissuade you from asking for more information. That's a red flag because reputable businesses are willing to share written information. The brochure states, "Perpetrators of phone fraud are extremely good at sounding as though they represent legitimate businesses. They offer investments, sell subscriptions, provide products for homes and offices, promote travel and vacation plans, describe employment opportunities, solicit donations, and the list goes on. Never assume you'll 'know a phone scam when you hear one.' Even if you've read lists of the kinds of schemes most commonly practiced, innovative swindlers constantly devise new ones."

Buying products or services over the phone requires some extra caution. The National Futures Association's brochure also lists the following tip-offs that a caller may be dishonest.

High-pressure sales tactics. The call may not begin that way, but if the swindler senses you're not going to be an easy sale, he or she may shift to a hard sell. . . . This is in contrast to legitimate businesses, most of which respect an individual's right to be "not interested." . . . High-pressure sales tactics take a variety of forms but the common denominator is usually a stubborn reluctance to accept "no" as an answer.

Insistence on an immediate decision. If it's an investment, the caller may say something like, "the market is starting to move even as we talk." For a product or service, the urgency pitch may be that "there are only a few left" or "the offer is about to expire." The bottom line is that swindlers often insist that you should (or must) make your decision right now. And they always give a reason.

The offer sounds too good to be true. [P]hone swindlers are becoming more sophisticated. They may make statements that sound just reasonable enough (if only barely) to keep you from hanging up. Or they may make three or four statements you know to be true so that when they spring the big lie for what they're selling, you'll be more likely to believe that, too. That's where the verbal camouflage comes in.

A request for your credit card number for any purpose other than to make a purchase. A swindler may ask you for your credit card number—or, in the most brash cases, several credit card numbers—for "identification," or "verification" that you have won something, or merely as an "expression of good faith" on your part. Whatever the ploy, once a swindler has your card number it is likely that unauthorized charges will appear on your account.

An offer to send someone to your home or office to pick up the money, or some other method such as overnight mail to get your funds more quickly. This is likely to be part of their "urgency" pitch. It could be an effort to avoid mail fraud charges by bypassing postal authorities or simply a way of getting your money before you change your mind.

A statement that something is "free," followed by a requirement that you pay for something. While honest firms may promote free phone offers to attract customers, the difference with swindlers is that you generally have to pay in some way to get whatever it is that's "free." The cost may be labeled as a handling or shipping charge, or as payment for an item in addition to the "prize." Whatever you receive "free"—if anything—most likely will be worth much less than what you've paid.

An investment that's "without risk." Except for obligations of the U.S. Government, all investments have some degree of risk. And if there were any such thing as a risk-free investment with big profits assured, the caller certainly wouldn't have to dial through the phone book to find investors!

Unwillingness to provide written information or references (such as a bank or names of satisfied customers in your area) that you can contact. Swindlers generally have a long list of reasons: "There isn't time for that," or "it's a brand new offer and printed material isn't available yet," or "customer references would violate someone's privacy." Even with references, be cautious, some swindlers pay off a few customers to serve as references.

A suggestion that you should make a purchase or investment on the basis of "trust." Trust is a laudable trait, but it shouldn't be dispensed indiscriminately—certainly not to unknown persons calling on the phone and asking that you send them money. Even so, "trust me" is a pitch that swindlers sometimes employ when all else fails. ("Swindlers Are Calling" 1990. National Futures Association in association with the Commodity Futures Trading Commission, Federal Trade Commission, and Alliance Against Fraud in Telemarketing, c/o National Consumers League, 1990.)

The brochure offers these sensible tips to keep you from becoming a victim of investment fraud:

Don't allow yourself to be pushed into a hurried decision. No matter what you're told to the contrary, the reality is that at least 99 percent of everything that's a good deal today will still be a good deal a week from now! And the other one percent isn't generally worth the risk you'd be taking to find out.

There may be times when you'll want to make a prompt decision, but those occasions shouldn't involve an irrevocable financial commitment to purchase a product or make an investment that you're not familiar with from a caller that you don't know. And purchase decisions should never be made under pressure.

Always request written information, by mail, about the product, service, investment or charity and about the organization that's offering it. For legitimate firms, this shouldn't be a problem. Swindlers, however, may not want to give you time for adequate consideration, may not have written material available, or may not want to risk a run-in with legal or regulatory authorities by putting fraudulent statements in writing.

Also insist on having enough time to study any information provided before being contacted again or agreeing to meet with anyone in person. Some high-pressure telephone sales calls are solely for the purpose of persuading you to meet with an even higher-pressure sales person in your home!

Don't make any investment or purchase you don't fully understand. A beauty of the American economy is the diversity of investment vehicles and other products available. But it's a diversity that includes the bad as well as the good. Unless you fully understand what you'd be buying or investing [in], you can be badly burned. Swindlers intentionally seek out individuals who don't know what they are doing! They often attempt to flatter prospects into thinking they are making an informed decision.

Ask what state or federal agencies the firm is regulated by and/or is required to be registered with. And if you get an answer, ask for a phone number or address that you can use to contact the agency and verify the answer yourself. If the firm says it's not subject to any regulation, you may want to increase your level of caution accordingly.

Check out the company or organization. If you assume a firm wouldn't provide you with information, references, or regulatory contacts unless the information was accurate and reliable, that's precisely what swindlers want you to assume. They know that most people never bother to follow through. Look at it this way: Most victims of fraud contact a regulatory agency after they've lost their money; it's far better to make the contact and obtain whatever information is available while you still have your money.

If an investment or major purchase is involved, request that information also be sent to your accountant, financial advisor, banker, or attorney for evaluation and an opinion. Swindlers don't want you to seek a second opinion. Their reluctance or evasiveness could be your tip-off.

Ask what recourse you would have if you make a purchase and aren't satisfied. If there's a guarantee or refund provision, it's best to have it in writing and be satisfied that the business will stand behind its guarantee before you make a final financial commitment.

Beware of testimonials that you may have no way of checking out. They may involve nothing more than someone being paid a fee to speak well of a product or service.

Don't provide personal financial information over the phone unless you are absolutely certain the caller has a bona fide need to know. That goes especially for your credit card numbers and bank account information. The only time you should give anyone your credit card number is if you've decided to make a purchase and want to charge it. If someone says they'll send a bill later but they need your credit card number in the meantime, be cautious and be certain you're dealing with a reputable company.

If necessary, hang up. If you're simply not interested, if you become subject to high-pressure sales tactics, if you can't obtain the information you want or get evasive answers, or if you hear your own better judgment whispering that you may be making a serious mistake, just say good-bye. ("Swindlers Are Calling," 1990)

ADDITIONAL READING

Andrews, Cecile. *Circle of Simplicity: Return to the Good Life.* New York: HarperCollins, 1997.

Benham, Barbara. "Why Have We Lost Confidence?" *Investor's Business Daily,* June 12, 1992.

Blix, Jacqueline, and David Heitmiller. *Getting a Life: Real Lives Transformed by Your Money or Your Life.* New York: Viking Penguin, 1997.

Bolonik, Kera, and Jennifer Griffin. *Frugal Indulgents: How to Cultivate Decadence When Your Age and Salary Are Under 30.* New York: Henry Holt, 1997.

Brandt, Barbara. *Whole Life Economics.* Philadelphia: New Society, 1995.

Captive Kids: Commercial Pressures on Kids at School. Consumers Union Education Service, 1995.

Castro, Janice. "The Simple Life." *Time,* April 8, 1991.

Celente, Gerald. *Trends 2000.* New York: Warner, 1997.

Collins, Chuck, Betsy Leondar-Wright, and Holly Sklar. *Shifting Fortunes: The Perils of the Growing American Wealth Gap.* Boston: United for a Fair Economy, 1999.

Cross, Gary. *Time and Money: The Making of Consumer Culture.* New York: Routledge, 1993.

Daly, Herman. *Steady State Economics.* Washington, DC: Island Press, 1991.

Dominguez, Joe, and Vicki Robin. *Your Money or Your Life.* New York: Penguin Books, 1992.

During, Alan Thein. *How Much Is Enough? The Consumer Society and the Future of the Earth.* New York: W. W. Norton, 1992.

Elgin, Duane. *Voluntary Simplicity.* New York: Morrow, 1981.

Goldberg, Carey. "The Shopping Addicts: When the Urge to Spend Overtakes the Rational Processes of Mind and Budget." *New York Times*, October 8, 1995.

Goodwin, Neva, Frank Ackerman, and David Kiron, eds. *The Consumer Society*. Washington, DC: Island Press, 1996.

Hunnicutt, Benjamin. *Work Without End*. Philadelphia: Temple University Press, 1988.

Jacobsen, Michael, and Laurie Mazur. *Marketing Madness*. Boulder, CO: Westview Press, 1995.

Korten, David. *When Corporations Rule the World*. West Hartford, CT: Kumarian Press, 1995.

Levering, Frank, and Wanda Urbanska. *Simple Living*. New York: Penguin, 1992.

Linder, Staffan. *The Harried Leisure Class*. New York: Columbia University Press, 1970.

Luhrs, Janet. *The Simple Living Guide*. New York: Broadway Books, 1997.

McNeal, James. *Kids as Customers*. New York: Lexington Books, 1992.

Meadows, Dennis, and Jorgen Randers. *Beyond the Limits*. Post Mills, VT: Chelsea Green Publishing, 1992.

Meadows, Donella, and Ferenc Mate. *A Reasonable Life*. New York: W. W. Norton, 1993.

Menzel, Peter. *Material World*. San Francisco: Sierra Club Books, 1994.

Millbank, Dana. "Hooked on Plastic: Middle-Class Family Takes a Harsh Cure for Credit-Card Abuse." *Wall Street Journal*. January 8, 1991.

Molnar, Alex. *Giving Kids the Business*. Boulder, CO: Westview Press, 1996.

Naylor, Thomas, William Willimon, and Magdalena Naylor. *The Search for Meaning*. Nashville, TN: Abingdon Press, 1994.

O'Neill, Jessie H. *The Golden Ghetto*. Center City, MN: Hazelden, 1997.

Otten, Alan L. "Young Adults Now Are More Pessimistic." *Wall Street Journal*. September 27, 1993.

Phillips, Kevin. *The Politics of Rich and Poor*. New York: Random House, 1990.

Rifkin, Jeremy. *Biosphere Politics*. New York: Crown, 1991.

———, ed. *The Green Lifestyle Handbook*. New York: Henry Holt, 1990.

Rowe, Jonathan, and Mark Anielski. *Genuine Progress Indicator: 1998 Update— Executive Summary*. San Francisco: Redefining Progress, 1998.

Schor, Juliet B. *The Overspent American*. New York: Basic Books, 1998.

———. *The Overworked American*. New York: Basic Books, 1993.

Selling America's Kids: Commercial Pressures on Kids of the 90's. Washington, DC: Consumers Union Education Services, 1990.

Shames, Lawrence. *The Hunger for More*. New York: Times Books, 1989.

Shi, David. *The Simple Life*. New York: Oxford University Press, 1985.

Smith, Carol. "More Seek Meaning in a Simpler Life." *Seattle Post-Intelligencer*, February 25, 1994.

Stein, Herbert, and Murray Foss. *The American Economy*. Washington, DC: American Enterprise Institute Press, 1995.

Strasser, Susan. *Satisfaction Guaranteed*. New York: Pantheon Books, 1989.

Swenson, Richard. *Margin*. Colorado Springs, CO: Navpress, 1992.

Travid, John. *Global Wellness Inventory*. Mill Valley, CA: Wellness Associates, 1990.

Wachtel, Paul. *The Poverty of Affluence.* Philadelphia: New Society Publishers, 1989.

Wallechinsky, David, *The People's Almanac Presents the Twentieth Century: History With The Boring Parts Left Out.* New York: Overlook Press, 1999.

Strategies that Make Sense

This presents advice from experts—financial planners, family counselors, and clergy who have seen firsthand the dismay and destruction that poor financial management can cause. These include bad decisions that squander savings, the sudden realization that there won't be enough money for retirement, or even marriages that fall apart because of the wedge driven in by financial worries.

Of course, these same counselors have seen the advantages of early planning and good communication. And they generally remain optimistic—it is never too late to set out on the right financial path. They shared their recommendations in interviews for this volume.

DEVELOP THE SAVINGS HABIT EARLY

Saving money is a lot like exercising. We know we need to do it, but some people struggle, while others enjoy it. The hard part, with both exercise and saving, is making it a habit. Once that's done, it simply becomes part of what you do.

That's why certified financial planner William B. Howard, Jr., president of William B Howard Co., Financial Advisers Inc., of Memphis, Tennessee, feels it's so important to form the habit early. "If young people make a habit of saving 10 to 15% of everything they get, that would be a great start." That means for every dollar received, 10 or 15 cents gets put away. "It's not that they'll get a lot of money saved that way, but over a period of time it will grow. And when that young person gets more pay, they'll automatically think in terms of saving 10 to 15%."

Howard has seen that motivation in action. One of his nephews is saving to buy a car by putting away the bulk of the money he's earning doing yard work and other odd jobs. He has also asked friends and family for cash gifts rather than other presents for birthdays and holidays. "This has been going on for three years," said Howard, impressed with the teen's ability to set a goal and work toward it. His nephew knows that the strategy pays off. He used it several years before when he wanted to buy a bass guitar. After he had accumulated half the cost of the guitar, his father paid the other half. "That was his reward."

When young people start making that kind of commitment to saving, and seeing the results—whether it's a longed-for high-ticket item or helping to pay for college—it puts them in the mode for saving lifelong. Howard encourages students to find part-time work. For example, he hires college students to work about 20 hours a week in his office. "They receive spending money and they get experience. When they handle spreadsheets and filing for our clients, they get to see real numbers," he said.

And Howard's experience with real numbers is that people can get into trouble with debt, no matter how much money they make. "I have a client making $500,000 a year and struggling with debt."

That's not to say that debt is necessarily a bad thing. "It's how you manage it." After all, most people will incur some long-term debts, such as car loans, student loans, or mortgages. "There's nothing wrong with student loans or having a mortgage, but it's when you abuse credit that you get in over your head," warned Howard. A high school or college graduate earning $20,000 to $25,000 a year and accumulating $5,000 to $10,000 a year in debt is "digging a hole that's going to be very difficult, if not impossible, to get out of. If you can live on less than you make, that's a built-in cushion for saving money," he said.

In addition, those savings help offset unexpected expenses for which many people rely on credit. For example, a big car repair may cost $750. Someone with $400 in savings only needs to put $350 of that repair on a credit card. The person who has no savings needs to pay the entire sum on credit. The saver will be more likely to pay off the credit balance faster, and incur much less interest as a result. People "who can use their savings as an emergency fund will be so far ahead of the game," said Howard.

That's important because young people have become targets for credit card companies. It's a good thing to build up a good credit rating. That could result in better terms for loans and lower interest rate offers in the future. But the danger for people not careful with managing their money is the temptation to put major purchases on credit cards and only pay the minimum amount due each month.

"It's easy to fall into the trap because of the way it's presented. Credit card companies by design kind of lure people into making minimum payments and then it will take years to pay off the debt," Howard said. His advice: write checks instead. If you need to use a credit card or want to use it because it's more convenient, pay the entire bill each month.

That requires self-control—for example, not putting the tab on a credit card when you go out to dinner. "Don't use it for discretionary spending," he advised. Writing a check at the clothing store and seeing the money immediately subtracted from an account often helps that self-control.

In turn, reduced spending means increased savings. "Money is a tool we can use to buy financial freedom. Look at it that way, rather than just as something with which we buy things." That's the advice he gives his clients, many of whom are wealthy and successful. Those that are most successful are often those who started the savings habit early. (*Note*: Concepts in this section are detailed in Chapters 3 [compounding savings and credit cards] and 6 [budgeting and saving toward a specific goal].)

SAVER OR SPENDER: YOUR CHOICE

According to certified financial planner Roger T. Smith, a partner with Planned Solutions Inc., of Sacramento, California, there are two types of people in the world: savers and spenders. "The saver will do well at retirement; the spender won't. I don't care how much money they make."

Smith feels that whether someone is a saver or spender is often ingrained during childhood. That's one reason he has established this rule with his two children: Save 25% of everything you make. "That's the rule. Just do it." That policy isn't always popular, especially when his children want to spend all their holiday or birthday money or paycheck on a particular item. But it's less harsh than the rule he grew up with: save 50% of everything. And it has its rewards. "My 17-year-old son can see his cash accumulating," he said.

Even so, there's the challenge of looking ahead. When his son approaches him, saying he wants to buy a high-ticket item and dip into his savings, Smith asks him, "How do you plan to pay for a car? How do you plan to pay for college?"

"You have to get into the mental attitude of looking to the future and not just today." When it becomes a habit, it stays that way. For example, he and his wife continue to put 29 to 39% of their gross income per year toward savings or investments. That's gross—the entire amount—not net, the amount left over after taxes and other withholding.

The major reason for saving is to be prepared for what Smith calls "Oh my God" reasons: the engine on the car blows out or other unexpected major expenses. He advises his clients to keep at least 10% of their annual income as a cash reserve and sees no reason why young adults and children can't keep 25% as a reserve.

Part of the reason so many young people end up in financial hot water is that they simply don't understand basic money management strategies and the costs of living. For example, he recalled one client couple where the husband was a state employee and the wife was a buyer for the school district. The husband was diagnosed with spinal cancer and confined to a wheelchair. He began to collect disability payments; that money and his wife's income should easily have covered their expenses. But it didn't. The couple was struggling.

Smith went to the house to counsel them. He found the couple's three children, all college graduates, living at home. "They wanted to live there because it was free. But what I saw was lights on in three bedrooms, the dining room, the kitchen, and the living room, and four stereos running. I could see the problem right away."

Smith told the children that their parents couldn't pay the bills. He suggested that the children start to pay rent and their share of the electric bills. What happened in the coming months was the classic result: the electric bills went down dramatically.

"Get the meter running," he said, meaning that once these young people understood what they were spending, they became motivated to save. If you don't know your usage, there's no incentive to control.

"It's the same with young people. If there's no 'meter' on your allowance or your paycheck, people will simply spend it all. We include our kids in discussions on our expenses. I show them what it costs to heat and air condition the house."

That way, they get a sense of everyday costs. Most young people leave college with a smattering of knowledge about "what it costs to get a meal at a restaurant or to rent a car, but it ends there." That's why it's important that young people leave high school and college with an understanding of what things cost. Look through a newspaper and see how much it costs to rent an apartment in the area. Does that price include utilities? Which ones? Add in cable, phone lines, gas or bus money, and groceries. Now you'll have an idea of what you'll need each month just to cover costs.

While Smith is fairly confident his children will grow up to be savers, he's seen the problems of perpetuating the spender mentality. "I have a client who inherited $750,000. Yet he and his wife never have cash around. I've met both of their children, and one is a 28-year-old attorney, single with no children, making $80,000 and still can't make ends meet."

"Either you're a saver or a spender. And I've rarely been able to teach a spender to be a saver," he said. The one exception he recalls is a couple with modest incomes. He was a correctional office and she worked for the state. He wanted to retire at age 55 and came in to see Smith 12 years before that. Smith told them it couldn't happen at the rate they were going. He outlined a strict savings plan—the only possible way they could make it. "They were passionate about retiring and made it. For 12 years they scrimped and saved every penny and he did retire at 55 and she was 44. They've been living in Maui since then."

But in most cases, that's not how it works. The course is set early, and the decision is yours: be a saver or a spender. (*Note*: Concepts in this section are detailed in Chapters 6 [creating a budget] and 7 [consumerism and spending].)

DEBUNK MONEY MYTHS; STUDY THE TOPIC

Money and sex are two topics many adults are reluctant to discuss with their children. Answers they do give are often incomplete or patronizing, such as "You're too young to know or worry about that." That kind of secrecy can create fear about money. Certified financial planner Ross Levin, president of Accredited Investors, of Minneapolis, Minnesota, suggested that it would be better if parents were a little more open about what their financial objectives are and the kind of choices they'll have to make to reach them. "Even young kids know there are choices to make and a choice in one direction may close the door to another option," he said.

The point that comes across from these discussions is that parents are intentional with their spending. In other words, if parents share the thinking that goes into making their financial choices, children will absorb some of that knowledge.

Because there are so many choices, making good decisions can be difficult. But it's worse not to make decisions at all. For example, let's say a family wants to make some kind of charitable contribution. Overwhelmed by the number of organizations and charities out there, they do nothing.

Levin suggested looking at the three kinds of resources people have: material, physical, and spiritual. Material resources include money or other items we can donate. Physical resources are those things we can do for others: help build houses or playgrounds, rake lawns or shovel walks for elderly neighbors, make cookies for bake sales. And spiritual resources are the options that enliven others' lives as well as our own. "Marshaling those can be productive. Maybe rather than write a check, spend a weekend with the Habitat for Humanity group building a house. Or maybe you do both."

"The best atmosphere for making these decisions is in family meetings. At the beginning of the year, the family can hold a meeting and develop a mission statement for philanthropy. Determine what you want to achieve and what actions you'll take to do that."

So what does giving to charities have to do with one's own financial management? A lot, said Levin, who sees the process of setting goals and figuring out how to achieve them a paramount in managing money. "If young people can develop a process early on by which they can make good decisions, it will suit them well. That's especially true for those who are getting ready to join the work force. Up until now, they've been earning maybe $2,000 a year, and that will probably jump to about $2,000 a month. At this point, their income needs haven't jumped to the level of financial resources, so it's the perfect time to establish a pattern of savings, investing and charity contributions."

For younger people, the same kind of decisionmaking skills can be put to use. Levin himself is working on that with his young twin daughters. "I put myself through college and even though my wife and I can afford to pay for their college education, we believe there are benefits and lessons from paying for your own education. It drove me in my career." As his daughters get older, he'll likely implement a matching program for the money they save.

That's been an effective strategy for others. For example, for most young people in school or college, summers are the prime earning time. Some parents have a program whereby they match 100% of what the child saves during the summer. "The adult rewards good decision making. And the young person starts the school year with twice as much money saved," he said.

To reward decision making, however, parents have to be grounded in their own money management skills. "Young people can look for financial role models" either inside or outside the family. In other words, if a parent balks at answering questions about household bills, income, and savings, the young person can turn to a banker or an investment broker. "Find an adult who doesn't have hangups about money. The message needs to be that it's OK to talk about money. We need to break the taboo that it's something we can't discuss. If a young person starts showing an interest in money and interviewing others, the parents will become interested in what they're learning. Their hands will almost be forced to participate."

Levin added that it's appropriate for young people with access to computers to use them for money management. Quicken is an easy program that lets users categorize where and how money is spent. "Eighteen to twenty one-year-olds can get a program like Turbo Tax. By the time they're that age, they can know how to complete tax returns and understand how it comes in and goes out and what the tax implications are. These lessons are cumulative and they're almost all experiential," he said. In other words, learn by doing when the stakes aren't as high.

"There are few permanent mistakes you can make around money. The biggest mistake is not exploring it to a level with which you're comfortable." (*Note*: Concepts in this section are discussed in Chapters 3 [saving and taxes] and 6 [budgeting] and 7 [quality of life issues].)

LET MONEY WORK FOR YOU

Investing money sounds like a scary proposition. How do you figure out what good investments are? How much money do you need to invest? What happens if the stock market collapses?

Investing is actually much easier than most people think, suggested Jim Putman, a certified financial planner and president of Wealth Management, LLC, in Appleton, Wisconsin. That's because so many companies offer 401(k) plans, in which a specified amount of income is put directly into a tax-deferred retirement plan. "When my son got a job at 18, there was a 401(k) option with it," said Putman. "Now young people are starting to invest as soon as they get a job." And that's good news for the future.

Many 401(k) plans have a number of choices that the employee has to make. There may be a few or there may be multiple different funds from which to choose. And employees get to pick the percentage of income they contribute to the plan. Putman recommends putting away the highest percentage, especially when the employee is young and cost of living expenses aren't as high. Many employers also match employee contributions, so contributing the highest percentage allowed takes most advantage of the plan.

Young people have time on their side. "Invest in the aggressive stock option, whatever it happens to be," he said. The choices, in descending order of risk—and potential reward—are aggressive, conservative, balanced funds, or money markets. Many company-sponsored retirement plans provide a pool from which employees make their investment selection.

While aggressive funds do hold more risk, Putman said that young people shouldn't worry about periodic drops. Over a long span of years, most investors will come out way ahead. "If they are educated properly, and the market corrects, they should be thinking, 'Oh, good, I'll be buying more this month than last month.' It's a mind set that stems from good education."

Young employed investors aren't completely on their own. The government requires that employers educate employees on fund choices and options. "That gets participants curious and once they start putting money in and hear the grumblings or bragging at the lunch table, they'll become even more interested in their investment performance."

If an employer doesn't offer a 401(k), the employee can open an Individual Retirement Account (IRA) or a Simplified-Employee Pension Plan (SEP-IRA). There are a number of qualified plans that allow employed people to save pretax earnings. That benefits the investor in two ways. First, it reduces the amount of taxable income for the current year. Second, the money grows tax-deferred until it is withdrawn from the account at retirement age. Presumably, one's income after retirement will be lower than it was during peak earning years.

IRAs or SEP-IRAs are only available to employed people. "You can be six years old and if your parents pay you to take out the garbage, and they report it to the Internal Revenue Service, you can open an IRA." And 100% of earned income, up to a maximum of $2,000 a year, can be contributed to an IRA. For example, a 12-year-old is paid $2,000 a year by his or her parents for lawn maintenance, twice-monthly car washes, bill filing, and other odd jobs. The parents report the income on federal forms and the entire sum is invested in an IRA and is therefore completely tax free to the youngster. After six years, $12,000 will have been invested in the IRA. At 8% interest, the account will be worth $14,671 by the time the child is 18. Fifty years later, the value of the account will be $688,134 if the fund continues to earn 8% interest. That's without another penny being added. "Time has a major impact on compounding money. Even two, three, or four years can make a huge difference."

That's precisely the reason a young person should be interested in saving money for retirement. "If at 18, you put $2,000 into an IRA each year for 10 years, by the time you reach 65, you'll have $1.3 million. That's the same as putting away $18,650 per year starting at age 45."

Many young investors seem keen on investing in socially conscious funds—Some invest in "green" or environmentally friendly companies; others invest only in companies that meet certain social criteria.

Pretax savings available through individual or company-sponsored retirement plans are a way that young investors can have their cake and eat it too. Not only can they reduce current taxes, they enjoy the advantage of dramatic compounding over the years. And with the wide choice of available funds, chances are there are investment strategies that can suit everyone's social or political conscience.

WHY INVEST EARLY?

Putman shows the advantage of investing early. Table 8.1, Benefits of Early Saving, shows what happens when a young person invests just $2,000 a year for the first 10 years of his or her working life: he or she ends up with a nest egg of about the same value as someone who starts investing $18,650 a year at age 45. Both accounts earn 10% interest, compounded annually. While the two have equal amounts in their accounts at age 65, the person who started young invested only $20,000; the person who waited invested $391,650. (*Note*: Concepts in this section are

Table 8.1
Benefits of Early Saving

Age	Starting Early		Postponing Savings	
	Invested Jan. 1	*Balance: Dec. 31*	*Invested Jan. 1*	*Balance: Dec. 31*
18	$2,000	$2,200	$0	$0
19	$2,000	$4,620	$0	$0
20	$2,000	$7,282	$0	$0
21	$2,000	$10,210	$0	$0
22	$2,000	$13,431	$0	$0
23	$2,000	$15,974	$0	$0
24	$2,000	$20,872	$0	$0
25	$2,000	$25,159	$0	$0
26	$2,000	$29,875	$0	$0
27	$2,000	$35,062	$0	$0
28	$0	$38,569	$0	$0
29	$0	$42,425	$0	$0
30	$0	$46,668	$0	$0
31	$0	$51,335	$0	$0
32	$0	$56,468	$0	$0
33	$0	$62,115	$0	$0
34	$0	$68,327	$0	$0
35	$0	$75,159	$0	$0
36	$0	$82,675	$0	$0
37	$0	$90,943	$0	$0
38	$0	$100,037	$0	$0
39	$0	$110,041	$0	$0
40	$0	$121,045	$0	$0
41	$0	$133,149	$0	$0
42	$0	$146,464	$0	$0
43	$0	$161,110	$0	$0
44	$0	$177,222	$0	$0
45	$0	$194,944	$18,650	$20,515
46	$0	$214,438	$18,650	$43,082
47	$0	$235,882	$18,650	$67,905
48	$0	$259,470	$18,650	$95,210
49	$0	$285,417	$18,650	$125,246
50	$0	$313,959	$18,650	$158,286
51	$0	$345,355	$18,650	$194,629
52	$0	$379,890	$18,650	$234,507
53	$0	$417,879	$18,650	$278,583
54	$0	$459,667	$18,650	$326,956
55	$0	$505,634	$18,650	$381,167
56	$0	$558,197	$18,650	$438,699
57	$0	$611,817	$18,650	$503,083
58	$0	$672,998	$18,650	$573,907
59	$0	$740,298	$18,650	$651,812
60	$0	$814,328	$18,650	$737,509

61	$0	$895,761	$18,650	$831,775
62	$0	$986,337	$18,650	$935,467
63	$0	$1,083,871	$18,650	$1,049,529
64	$0	$1,192,258	$18,650	$1,174,997
65	$0	$1,311,484	$18,650	$1,313,011
Totals Invested:	**$20,000**		**$391,650**	

detailed in Chapters 4 [mutual funds and investing] and [budgeting for retirement].)

MONEY CAN'T BUY YOU LOVE

Money is not the key to happiness, and it is not the root of all evil. But money, for better or for worse, is one of the top three problems facing couples and families today. According to Family Educational Consultant and syndicated columnist Tracey Barnes Priestley, founder and executive director of Contemporary Family Education, "Money represents so many things to people within the context of their relationships. It's love, power, control, independence, security and ambition."

Because money is so many things to people it is being used to fill in more and more gaps in our personal lives. "This is an especially difficult problem for those people who feel very disconnected from family and friends," Barnes Priestley said. People often use money and material possessions to compensate for their lack of close relationships. When a loss of intimacy is combined with the slow disintegration of community and family, the problem of spending for fulfillment can get out of control quickly. "People today follow isolated career paths and lack human connections in their lives. In an effort to feel good about themselves they end up buying things to try and fill that space."

The problem worsens with the increase in media messages and advertising, making it easy to see why personal bankruptcy rates are climbing and more people are overwhelmed by debt. But Barnes Priestley feels it's unfair to blame the advertising industry for fostering bad spending practices. "All the ad industry did was to understand how people were feeling, tap into it and sell their products by convincing consumers they would be happier, more attractive or more successful if they made a purchase."

Today's advertising also includes the message of entitlement. "You deserve a break today" according to one commercial slogan. Another shows an attractive actress telling listeners, "I'm worth it." This sense of entitlement promoted to adults, teens, and young children manifests itself as the need for immediate gratification. "I often hear people tell me 'I deserve this' or 'I earned that' as a justification for their debt or poor spending choices. Another justification for reckless spending is when people choose to define themselves by their surroundings, meaning the better my things are, the better I am," Barnes Priestley said.

The growing need for immediate gratification is a byproduct of several decades of working families. "Some parents feel guilty for being away and tell themselves, 'I'm not home but I am doing this to provide for my family so I can give them great things.' " Consequently, parents with more disposable income then make large purchases upon request. "Because the adults are away more, if their child asks for something they want to be able to provide it without any waiting." This reinforces two wrong messages: that you can buy happiness and that you should have what you want without having to wait or think about the practicality of the purchase.

For Barnes Priestley, mother of three children, the first step when working with individuals or families is to ask people to look realistically at how they use money to meet psychological needs. "Ask yourself what money is doing for you." She suggests keeping a journal. "I call it mapping your spending habits. Write down what you buy, how you feel afterwards and how you feel a few days later about that purchase."

Next, learn to meet your needs in other, healthy, ways. "This is difficult for people, especially those who say 'I deserve this' or 'I should have this.' Counseling is often helpful." It's also helpful to realize that with couples in a relationship each partner brings different family values to the table. One person may come from a family where money was never discussed or was very carefully spent; the other person may have been raised by parents who spent money lavishly. There is an inevitable clash of styles, and when things get tough, people revert to what they learned as children.

Those lessons of childhood are where important changes can be made for future generations. "Parents today have a responsibility to teach their children about money and most importantly to let their kids fail with money. Those small failures can be the best and most enduring lessons," she said. Consistency of message is also important when teaching children about money. Parents should encourage children to save and then model the same saving and planning behavior.

The biggest challenge for teenagers today is to develop the strength to go against the popular culture of spending and buying. She suggested that parents talk about their spending mistakes. "It would be empowering for their children if they would; the kids could see how they handle money and how they handle mistakes."

Lastly, and most important, families must create a budget. "Sit down with your children, especially the teenagers, and figure out how much money they need each week and how much allowance you will provide. Then decide together where the money will come from to meet their weekly expenses." When parents take the time to teach and model good financial planning, their children can reap the benefits of increased self-confidence and improved self-esteem. "When there is thought behind it, money can teach good lessons," she said—lessons that will last a lifetime. (*Note*: Concepts in this section are detailed in Chapters 6 [creating a budget] and 7 [consumerism and spending].)

HIS, HERS, AND THEIRS

Young people in love want to shout it from the mountaintops. When they decide to get married, it is generally because they are convinced they are lucky enough to have found someone they can spend their lives with. Infatuation has given way to true love, and now it's time to make preparations for a lifetime together.

Those preparations go far beyond the wedding day—and talking about money is an important factor, said J. J. Bodine, pastor and teacher at Stratham Community Church, Stratham, New Hampshire. Many young people don't want to talk about something as mundane as money at a time like this, but Bodine leads them through these discussions during premarital counseling. That's because conflict over money is like the canary in the coal mine—it can foreshadow serious conflict over larger issues.

While he's neither a financial counselor nor able to divine which couples will survive difficulties in their marriage, Bodine is convinced that it is worth his effort to get young people to talk about finances and their future. Too often, he finds himself mediating and counseling with couples whose love for each other has been overshadowed by conflict over money.

"Young people need to recognize the symbolic and real value of money in our culture and the ease with which secrecy about finances can submerge a marriage," he said. "And if one is a spendthrift and the other frugal, they're going to have to learn conflict resolution."

In his community, the high tech sector is booming. As a result, many young people are landing lucrative jobs right after college. That means there's a lot of cash on hand—and no solid experience in how to handle it. He sees young people overextending themselves by buying expensive homes and other luxuries. Rather than deferring gratification, they're indulging. That's not necessarily bad, but marriage is about compromises, thinking beyond one's own small world. Saddling oneself with debt early in life is usually an indication that these people are not looking toward the future, when they have children and one parent might want to stay home with them. They're locking themselves into jobs that demand high salaries to keep up with the lifestyle they've established.

Granted, it's hard for young couples to look beyond the event of getting married. Bodine estimates that only about one-third of the couples he talks with take the financial planning activities he suggests seriously. But those that do have a better understanding of themselves and each other. Here are some of the ways he approaches the conversations.

Bodine has a young couple create a budget. For many, this is the first time they've done it, and almost certainly the first time they've done it with someone else's income and expenses in mind. Do one or both have student loans to pay off? Who takes responsibility for those? Is one person still in school? Does either own property? How is money invested? How much money is invested?

He also encourages them to think about whether they will have joint or separate bank accounts. Some couples simply assume that they will merge their accounts, but that's not the answer for everyone. And if money is held in joint accounts, who will serve as the primary bookkeeper? Is one person a more fastidious record keeper? Is one person notoriously sloppy with finances? How will the couple handle that?

He also has them list their goals, short-term and long-term. Do they want children? If so, will one parent stay home? How will that affect their finances and the choices they're making now? What kind of house will they live in? Will one or both go back to or continue with school? If so, how will they support themselves during that time?

And what are they doing to ensure financial stability? "I always talk about life insurance and wills. Most young people look at me as if I have three heads when I bring that up, but it's important," he said.

These kinds of exercises show how comfortable a young couple is with money and talking through differences of opinion. He's found some that are very good and who practice sound financial planning right from the start. He's found others who are extremely hesitant to talk about finances—even to the point where they've been unwilling to share exactly how much they earn with their future spouse.

When he does encounter areas of potential or obvious conflict, "as empathetically as possible, I'll tell them what I'm hearing or seeing. If it's just that they're talking past each other, I can be a third ear for a little while, but if it's a serious communication difficulty, I'll send them to a real expert—especially if it's an issue that uses money as the tip of the iceberg."

An example: One person will laughingly mention that the other spends an atrocious amount of money on a hobby or interest and will say, "After we're married, I'm going to refuse to let her do that anymore." It sounds like a money issue, but it's a red flag that there are bigger problems—maybe bigger financial issues, control over finances or even of the other person's hobbies and habits.

What he's also found in his counseling of married couples and parishioners is that "where it really begins to hit the fan is when the first child comes along. That represents such incredible life changes for everyone. It's like adding a new tap to a closed plumbing system. The pressure change is palpable." And many people use money to alleviate stress. Before, when there were two income-producing people, stress-induced splurges could be better absorbed. But a couple's financial stresses change dramatically after a child arrives.

Bodine also spends a little time talking about credit and debt. He's finding that more young people already own credit cards and often have revolving debt or student loans outstanding. He'll review the basics: finding the best interest rate, explaining that debt is compounded and if they're only paying the minimum balance, they're falling behind. He'll advise couples with more serious credit issues to see a credit counselor. The bigger the debt or the money management conflicts he's noticed, the more strongly he'll encourage that step.

It's not that Bodine wants to throw a wet blanket over a young couple's most optimistic moment. But through his premarital counseling, his hope is that he can help identify areas of potential conflict. If counseling uncovers serious differences in philosophy, it's better to do so early. If it helps the couple approach their future together more realistically, all the better. And if financial issues arise later in marriage, Bodine hopes that simply letting young people know that money management is a struggle for everyone at some point will encourage them to get help before it submarines a marriage. "It's one thing to say love conquers all, but these are issues every couple needs to work at." (*Note*: Concepts in this section are detailed in Chapters 6 [creating a budget] and 7 [consumerism and spending].)

GOAL-SETTING: A GOLDEN RULE

It seems so obvious, so intuitive. Yet it's a fundamental principle of money management: In order to save more, you have to spend less. Sure, you can increase your earnings, but that's a little harder to do.

That's not to say that spending less is easy. "From an early age, we're trained to be consumers and we're very good at it," said Rob Billingsley, an attorney who works as a financial advisor in Fredericksburg, Virginia. In fact, Americans have one of the lowest savings rates in the world. Some studies show that Americans save only about 4% of their annual salaries, but recent studies have reported that with credit card debts mounting, the savings rate has dipped below zero.

Billingsley points to the savings and spending habits of immigrants. "You hear about people from other countries coming here and getting wealthy. It's not because they're making more money, but they're coming in without the baggage—the mentality to buy things. They come in with the mentality that it's worth it to save. That's why first generation immigrants are able to become financially independent relatively quickly."

Financial independence relies much more on your spending patterns than on your income. To illustrate that point, Billingsley uses the real life example of two Gladyses—women with the same name but extremely different saving and spending habits.

One Gladys died in 1996 at the age of 86. In her will, she left $18 million to her favorite charity, a children's hospital. What struck Billingsley most was that she never earned more than $15,000 a year.

The other Gladys hit it big—winning the Virginia state lottery. Her share of her winnings comes out to one $388,000 check per year. But in a newspaper interview, she confessed that prior to the arrival of the annual check, she often spends several months living hand to mouth. "She can't effectively live on $388,000 a year."

While it might be difficult to sympathize with someone who squanders that much money, the point is that on a smaller scale, many Americans are doing the same thing. The first Gladys had a goal and a plan to achieve it. The second Gladys is tremendously disorganized financially, and chances are that is reflected in other parts of her life.

"The same sorts of things that enable you to become successful in a career and other parts of your life are transferable to the financial arena and vice versa," said Billingsley. The sooner that young people develop a mind-set to defer gratification today to achieve something better tomorrow or down the road, the better. "Most people have a tendency to go through life like going down the river in a raft. We tend to bounce from rock to rock," he said. That's reacting. But goal setting is proactive.

And it pays off. Billingsley cited a study of 1952 graduates of Ivy League schools. Respondents were asked if they had established and written down their goals. Only 3% had. Twenty years later, researchers followed up with the same graduating class. "The three percent that had established goals were worth more than the 97 percent of the rest of the class combined. What people are beginning to discover is that the gray matter between our ears is like a sophisticated computer. Our brain requires programming—and goal setting is a key part of that programming."

In the seminars Billingsley holds on financial planning, he encourages people to "dust off their dreams"—to find what it is they would like to accomplish and start figuring out how to get there. Time is the biggest asset young people have because they can benefit from years of compounding interest.

To illustrate the way money grows exponentially, look at the magic penny theory. Start with one penny and double it every day for a month. At the end of the month, you have more than $5.3 million. Doubt it? Look at Table 8.2. For the first two weeks the money accumulates slowly; however, look what happens as time goes on. Of course, money doesn't double every day, but the example vividly illustrates what can happen to savings over a long period. And as Billingsley points out, a savings account or investment of $100 doubles at the same rate as a savings account or investment of $10,000. The sooner the money starts compounding, the better. It's no wonder Albert Einstein called compounding interest the eighth wonder of the world. It is an amazing phenomenon.

Table 8.2
The Magic Penny

Day	Amount
1	$ 0.01
2	$ 0.02
3	$ 0.04
4	$ 0.08
5	$ 0.16
6	$ 0.32
7	$ 0.64
8	$ 1.28
9	$ 2.56
10	$ 5.12
11	$ 10.24
12	$ 20.48
13	$ 40.96
14	$ 81.92
15	$ 163.84
16	$ 327.68
17	$ 655.36
18	$ 1,310.72
19	$ 2,621.44
20	$ 5,242.88
21	$ 10,485.76
22	$ 20,971.52
23	$ 41,943.04
24	$ 83,886.08
25	$ 167,722.16
26	$ 335,544.32
27	$ 671,088.64
28	$1,342,177.28
29	$2,684,354.56
30	$5,368,709.12

Saving is a discipline—and those who recognize it early reap larger rewards. "I see lots of people who haven't learned the lesson," Billingsley said. It makes him think of two rugged movie characters played by Marlon Brando and Sylvester Stallone. At the end of *On the Waterfront* ex-boxer Terry Malloy laments, "I coulda been a contender." Contrast that to Rocky, who "understood how important it was to get up early, drink that awful concoction, run all over the city and pound the meat in the slaughterhouse. He understood winning takes discipline."

If young people learned the lesson early, Billingsley wouldn't see so many people in a financial fix. But the learning comes through making choices. He encourages his children to take part of their allowance and put it aside for charity and put another portion into savings. As his parents did for him, he matches the amount they put into college savings. "My parents gave me an allowance with no strings attached, but they matched dollar for dollar everything my siblings and I put into a college fund. That demonstrated to us that they considered saving an important thing. And I discovered quickly that if I went along with that, I'd get far more out of my money than I did if I spent it on baseball cards."

"It's a lesson you have to learn by spending money. Young people who haven't had to make those choices are ill equipped to handle them and they get into debt with credit cards."

The clearer your goals, the better the discipline to achieve them. (*Note*: The concepts in this section are detailed in Chapter 3 [savings], 6 [creating a budget] and 7 [consumerism and spending].)

9

In Over Your Head

The worst thing about debt is that it tends to snowball. Some people are able to get out of that predicament fairly quickly. They forgot to pay a bill on time and made amends as soon as they recognized the error. That's simply an error. Even though the mistake may have cost them some extra money in penalties or late fees, it was correctable.

But when paying bills late or paying one bill and leaving others unpaid becomes habitual, it's a sign of a much more serious problem: runaway debt. And like a runaway train, when that runaway debt gets on down the track, it gains momentum.

A mountain of debt can seem overwhelming. But it's not hopeless. That's what makes those stories about young adults who took their own lives as they sank further into debt all the more depressing. Too much debt is obviously a problem. It's a sign that one needs help handling one's finances. Do the responsible thing: take steps to reduce debt. If that means telling your parents you've made mistakes, do so. If it means finding professional help, do so.

Don't think that you can hang on until it gets so bad you can just declare bankruptcy. Even though 1.5 million Americans did so in 1998, declaring bankruptcy should be an absolute last resort. Why? First of all, bankruptcy can stay on your credit record for 10 years, meaning that it almost certainly will become more difficult to qualify for a mortgage or other loan, and that the terms of credit cards will be much less appealing. Bankruptcy should not be seen as an escape hatch.

For those who have some income, and have fallen into the habit of spending more than they're earning, financial recovery may be a matter of imposing strict financial discipline. Such a change of heart might be difficult, but staring down the chasm can create crystal clear focus and initiative. If you can't do it alone, there are professional credit counselors who can help you create a debt management plan to pay off your creditors.

First try some steps for yourself. Review all your outstanding bills and make sure they're accurate. If you think any are wrong, contact the creditor immediately.

ORGANIZE YOUR DEBTS

Find out exactly what you owe to whom. Contact the creditors and let them know you're having difficulty. This can be a hard step to take; most people would rather hide from their creditors than acknowledge their inability to pay. But creditors will have more respect for those who come clean. If there are circumstances, such as a recent job loss or high medical bills you're paying off, let them know them that as well. "Managing Your Debts," a booklet by a consortium of financial and consumer companies, gives the following advice: "Try to work out an acceptable payment schedule with your creditors. Most are willing to work with you and will appreciate your honesty and forthrightness. The Fair Debt Collection Practices Law prohibits a debt collector from showing what you owe to anyone but your attorney, harassing or threatening you, using false statements, giving false information about you to anyone, and misrepresenting the legal status of your debts."

CREATE A BUDGET

Determine how much money you must pay every month for rent, utilities, and travel to and from work. Add to that the amount you've worked out with creditors to pay off the balance on debts. Then work to economize on the rest of your expenses. How much have you been spending on dining out? Cut it down to zero for a while so you can channel that money into debt repayment. What have your entertainment expenses been? Cut them. Vacations? Postpone them. These might seem like drastic measures at the moment, but the feeling of relief and accomplishment will soon outweigh the sacrifice. Put off all unnecessary expenses for a while. Take a look at your possessions. While selling off grandma's jewelry probably isn't a good idea, selling a second car, a second bike, or other accumulated and unused items might be.

USE YOUR SAVINGS

While it's generally recommended that you keep a savings safety net, high debt might be an exception to the rule. Look at the numbers. Your savings account in the local bank is drawing 4.5% interest. On your debts, you're paying 14.5% interest. As soon as you're able, you can start funneling money back into the savings account, but for now, you're better off paying down the debt. If a CD is due to mature soon, it might be better to wait than pay the penalty for early withdrawal.

CUT UP YOUR CREDIT CARDS

Enough said. If credit cards are what got you in trouble in the first place, stop using them. At a minimum, stop using them for everything except emergencies. Above all, don't apply for new credit cards. This is not the time to get creative with borrowing from one card to pay another. It's time to get serious about repayment.

WHERE TO FIND HELP

Determine if you qualify for any government or private assistance. Government assistance includes unemployment compensation, Aid to Families with Dependent Children (AFDC), food stamps, low-income energy assistance, Medicaid, and Social Security including disability.

If you can't do it alone, there are professional credit counselors who can help. The National Foundation for Consumer Credit (NFCC) provides education and counseling to families and individuals, often free or for a low fee. The organization can put you in touch with a Consumer Credit Counseling Service (CCCS) agency in your area. These CCCS programs are certified by the NFCC.

The counselor will work with you on developing a budget. The counselor can also negotiate a financial management plan with creditors who are pressing for repayment. "Managing Your Debt" describes it this way: Under this plan, creditors often agree to reduce payments, lower or drop interest and finance charges, and waive late fees and over-the-limit fees. After starting the plan, you will deposit money with CCCS each month to cover these new negotiated payment amounts. Then CCCS will distribute this money to your creditors to repay your debts.

LAST RESORT: BANKRUPTCY

As a last resort, bankruptcy is a legal procedure to provide a fresh start. There are two types of bankruptcy filings.

Chapter 7 (so called because the rules governing these types of filings are found in Chapter 7 of the bankruptcy code) is a "straight" or "liquidation" bankruptcy, requiring that the debtor liquidate or sell all assets that are not exempt in that state. These exemption amounts vary from state to state, but could include work-related tools and basic household furnishings.

Chapter 13 is known as a reorganization plan. It allows debtors to keep property, such as a house or car, that they might otherwise lose. These types of filings often allow debtors to pay off an existing loan, over three to five years. This type of plan can work for people who have consistent income and need time to pay off debts, as well as relief from creditors while they're trying to pay their debts down. Both types of bankruptcy filings may get rid of those debts to which creditors don't have specific rights to properties. They can stop foreclosures, repossessions, garnishment of wages, utility shutoffs, and debt collection activities.

However, bankruptcy does not eliminate the debtor from all financial obligations. Typically, it does not affect taxes, child support, alimony, fines, and some student loan obligations. Because bankruptcy is a federal legal proceeding, the cases must be filed in federal court. There's a filing fee of $160 and additional attorney fees. Contact your local bar association for a referral to an attorney who specializes in bankruptcy filings. Some communities have legal services programs or law school programs that can assist with bankruptcy filings for low or no fees.

Most credit counseling agencies want to help people, but even in this area there is opportunity for less honest people to profit from the vulnerability of someone in financial stress. Beware a counselor who asks for a large sum of money up front. "Managing Your Debt" recommends checking an organization's reputation with the state attorney general, consumer protection agency, or Better Business Bureau.

"Fiscal Fitness," a 1999 brochure published by the U.S. Consumer Information Center, advises consumers to interview several counseling agencies and check with state and consumer agencies in the state to see if complaints have been filed before choosing a counseling agency. It further notes that "any reputable credit counseling agency should send you free information about itself and the services it provides without requiring you to provide any details about your situation. If not, consider that a red flag and go elsewhere for help."

These questions can help you make a decision about which counseling agency to use:

Services and Fees

• What services do you offer?

• Do you have educational materials? If so, will you send them to me? Are they free? Can I access them on the Internet?

• In addition to helping me solve my immediate problem, will you help me develop a plan for avoiding problems in the future?

- What are your fees? Do I have to pay anything before you can help me? Are there monthly fees? What's the basis for the fees?
- What is the source of your funding?
- Will I have a formal written agreement or contract with you?
- How soon can you take my case?
- Who regulates, oversees, and/or licenses your agency? Is your agency audited?
- Will I work with one counselor or several?
- What are the qualifications of your counselors? Are they accredited or certified? If not, how are they trained?
- What assurance do I have that information about me (including my address and phone number) will be kept confidential?

Repayment Plan

- How much do I have to owe to use your services?
- How do you determine the amount of my payment? What happens if this is more than I can afford?
- How does your debt repayment plan work? How will I know my creditors have received payments? Is client money put in a separate account from operating funds?
- How often can I get status reports on my accounts? Can I get access to my accounts online or by phone?
- Can you get my creditors to lower or eliminate interest and finance charges or waive late fees?
- Is a debt repayment plan my only option?
- What if I can't maintain the agreed-upon plan?
- What debts will be excluded from the debt repayment plan?
- Will you help me plan for payment of these debts?
- Who will help me if I have problems with my accounts or creditors?
- How secure is the information I provide to you?

STOLEN CREDIT CARDS AND IDENTITY THEFT

Imagine the following. You receive a bill from your credit card company reflecting hundreds or even thousands of dollars worth of purchases you didn't make. What happened? Chances are that someone used your credit card. With catalog and online shopping possibilities, someone can easily use a stolen or unauthorized credit card number to make purchases. That's the reason credit card issuers encourage the following steps for securing your credit card:

Sign your card as soon as it arrives. Keep the agreement and other papers that came with the card in a safe place. You'll need these to reach customer service and to learn what to do if the card is lost or stolen.

Don't give your credit card number to anyone who asks over the phone. Generally safe exceptions are ordering from catalogs for which you've made the call.

Don't lend a credit card to anyone.

Keep copies of sales slips and compare them to the charges when the bill arrives. Don't throw receipts with credit card numbers printed on them in the trash where they might be stolen. Save them until you've compared them to your bill.

If a credit card is stolen, notify the company immediately. That protects both you and the credit card company. The credit card company will cancel the card right away so that someone trying to use it will not be able to do so. And if you reach the credit card issuer before the stolen card is used, you will not be held responsible for any transactions the criminal makes. However, if a stolen card is used before you notify the company, you may be held responsible for up to $50 for any or every card the thief uses.

Always look at the monthly bill when it arrives. If there are charges on it that you think are wrong, act immediately. The same is true if you receive credit card bills from an account you can't remember opening, or if a billing cycle goes by and a bill you were expecting doesn't come at all. Then it's possible that you're a victim of identity fraud. That means someone has used your name, Social Security number, credit card, or other personal information and used your identity to purchase items. It's a crime and needs to be reported right away.

First, contact the fraud departments of the three major credit bureaus and tell them to flag your file with a fraud alert. Include an instruction to creditors to call you before they open any new accounts in your name. Do this immediately, because the person or people who stole the card often try to open new accounts based on your good credit record.

Contact the issuers of any credit card that has been used or any account that has been opened without your authorization. Speak to someone in the security or fraud department and follow up with a letter.

File a police report and keep a copy of the report as proof.

Messing with someone else's mail is a crime. If you believe that a thief has intercepted credit card offers, bank or credit card statements, newly issued credit cards, or tax information, contact the local postal inspector. If an identity thief has changed the billing address on an existing account, close it. Sometimes thieves do this to delay detection. After all, if you don't get a bill for a cycle, you won't see that unauthorized charges have been made. That buys the thief an extra month or more.

When creating passwords or personal identification numbers (PINs) for use with ATMs or online purchasing, avoid using obvious ones or readily available information, such as your mother's maiden name or the last four digits of your Social Security number. Some online companies encourage a password that mixes letters and numbers.

Tear up or shred any credit card applications or offers, expired cards, and papers that contain financial or personal information that could be used by an identity thief. A little information goes a long way. That's why it's important to keep numbers like your Social Security number to yourself. States that use Social Security numbers for driver's license numbers will create another number for you upon request.

Identity theft is insidious because the thief can affect more than you can imagine. He or she can set up a telephone account and charge long distance calls. In that case, call the phone company. The thief can use your Social Security number to get a driver's license. If you suspect that, contact the state's department of motor vehicles. Someone could even use your Social Security number when applying for a job.

In all cases, as soon as identity fraud is identified, report it. You and these creditors share the common goal of finding and stopping the thief.

ADDITIONAL READING

Consumer Literacy Consortium. "66 Ways to Save Money." Washington, DC: Consumer Federation of America, 1996.
"Managing Your Debts: How to Regain Financial Health." American Association of Retired Persons, Consumer Action, Consumer Federation of America, National Consumer Law Center staffers, National Foundation for Consumer Credit, U.S. Consumer Information Center, U.S. Office of Consumer Affairs, Visa U.S.A. Washington, DC, 1994
Snyder, Don. *The Cliff Walk: A Memoir of a Job Lost and a Life Found.* Boston: Little, Brown 1997.

ADDITIONAL RESOURCES FOR IDENTITY THEFT

Federal Trade Commission
Consumer Response Center
600 Pennsylvania Ave. NW
Washington, DC 20580
(202) 382–4357
TDD: (202) 326–2502

There is also an online complaint form:

Privacy Rights Clearinghouse
www.privacyrights.org
(619) 298–3396

Provides information on how to network with other identity theft victims:

Social Security Administration
Check the blue pages of your local phone book for address.

If you continue to have problems with identity theft, the SSA could issue you a new Social Security number. The agency can also review your earnings and profile to ensure that someone hasn't been using your Social Security number fraudulently.

U.S. Secret Service

While the Secret Service typically investigates cases of large dollar loss, your information about financial fraud might provide them with evidence.

10

Conclusion

The lesson of money management is really quite simple: Save as much as you can as often as you can. Having a cushion of savings and some money invested means your money is working harder for you. That means that your goals are more easily within reach. Financial security transcends having a savings account, however. Knowing that you're on the right path so that money will be there when you need it provides emotional and psychological security as well.

So before making that next big purchase—or even the little ones that add up—ask yourself the following questions: Do I need this? If I do need it, do I need it now? Delaying purchases can often save lots of money. Technological improvements in computers, for example, often mean that you can get more computer for the same amount of money. Delaying the purchase until you have the full amount, or close to it, in cash also saves money. Since you're not buying with credit, you're saving interest charges. And you've achieved the satisfaction of planning for a purchase and saving toward that goal.

Delaying or passing up larger purchases also helps get you in the habit of passing up smaller purchases. Saving money doesn't mean self-denial. It's trading one pleasure for another. If the goal is to buy a new entertainment system, it might mean passing on lunches at the nearby café every day. Think about it. If those lunches cost nearly $10 a day, you could have almost $200 saved up in one month. It's a relatively painless way to get to the goal.

How do you decide where you can cut? Keep track of your spending. Pull out a notebook and write down all your expenses. Especially keep track of those smaller ones—the $2 for coffee, the $1.50 for a midday snack at the vending machine. At the end of the month, look at where the money's gone. What were your good decisions? What were the bad ones? Try to cut out those expenses.

Be careful with credit cards. They're wonderfully easy to use, but their major attraction is also their major downside. They can be too easy to use. It doesn't feel like spending money when you say, "Charge it." But each time you charge, you are spending money—and it's an expensive loan if you let charges build up without paying them off.

Remember that overusing credit cards—especially when you start transferring balances from one to another—is in direct contradiction to the goal of saving. And if you get into trouble with credit card debt, let someone know right away. The sooner you start working to solve the problem, the sooner you can be on the right path.

Whatever your financial goals are, there's a way to get there. If the goal is a long time away—retirement, for example—you can afford to take greater risks with the investments allocated toward that goal. If the goal is to save $250 in the next month so you can buy a new VCR, tuck it in an account where you won't touch it. It's awfully hard to keep money in your checking account earmarked for something more than a few days away.

Read about money management. The goal of this volume has been to give you the interest and confidence to read financial magazines and business sections of newspapers. They're filled with great information about trends in investing, personal savings, and the stock market. The concepts shouldn't be foreign anymore, so take advantage of the knowledge of others. Apply what seems right for you. The experts and financial columnists often provide excellent advice—at only the cost of a magazine or newspaper or a visit to the library. But they can only lead you. You're the one who has to supply the initiative to save and invest. The sooner you start, the sooner you see rewards. You can make it a habit for life.

Appendix A: Glossary

Ability to pay: A criterion of tax fairness holds that people with different amounts of wealth or different amounts of income should pay different rates of taxes. Wealth may include assets or property, such as houses, cars, stocks, bonds, savings accounts, or valuables. Income includes wages, rents, interest, profits, or other payments.

Acquisition fee: A charge included in most lease transactions that is either paid up front or is included in the gross capitalized cost. It may be called a bank fee or an assignment fee. This fee usually covers a variety of administrative costs, such as the costs of obtaining a credit report, verifying insurance coverage, checking the accuracy and completeness of the lease documentation, and entering the lease in data processing and accounting systems.

Additional insured: A party who is covered by another party's insurance policy. In a lease, the lessor typically requires you to name the lessor as an additional insured under your vehicle insurance policy.

Adjusted gross income: Your income reduced by contributions to retirement accounts, alimony payments, and certain other exclusions.

Ad valorem tax: *See* personal property tax.

AMEX: The American Stock Exchange.

Amortization: The reduction of the principal of a loan by regular payments. Amortization tables allow you to see how much of each month's payment is interest and how much is principal.

Amount due at lease signing or delivery: The total of any capitalized cost reduction, monthly payments paid at signing, security deposit, title and registration fees, and other amounts due before you take delivery of a leased vehicle.

Annual fee: A flat, yearly charge for owning a credit card.

Annual percentage rate (APR): A measure of the cost of credit on a yearly basis expressed as a percentage rate, including interest, transaction fees, and service fees.

Annual percentage yield (APY): The amount of interest you will earn on a deposit on a yearly basis expressed as a percentage.

Annuity: A contract sold by life insurance companies that guarantees the purchaser fixed or variable future payments, usually upon retirement.

Asset: Anything a person owns, including property, that has value.

Assignee: A third party that buys a lease agreement from a lessor. You become obligated to the assignee, and the assignee generally assumes the responsibilities of the lessor, although some obligations may remain with the lessor.

Assignment: The sale of a lease agreement and transfer of the ownership rights for the leased vehicle from the lessor to an assignee. Many leases are assigned at the time the lease is signed.

Assignor: A lessor that sells the lease agreement and transfers the ownership rights for the leased vehicle to an assignee.

Automobile insurance: Protection against financial losses resulting from collision, theft, vandalism, fire, acts of nature, or injury to the driver, passengers, or others.

Average daily balance: The most common method of calculating interest. The lender adds up the amount owed for each day of the billing cycle and divides that number by the number of days in the billing cycle.

Bank: An establishment where money is stored for saving or for commercial purposes or is invested, supplied for loans, or exchanged.

Bankruptcy: A legal procedure to get rid of debts to which creditors don't have specific rights to properties. Bankruptcy filings can stop foreclosures, repossessions, garnishment of wages, utility shut-offs, and debt collection activities. However, a bankruptcy filing stays on a person's credit report for up to 10 years and will negatively affect that person's credit rating.

Base monthly payment: The portion of a monthly lease payment that covers depreciation, any amortized amounts, and rent charges. It is calculated by adding the amount of depreciation, any other amortized amounts, and rent charges and dividing the total by the number of months in the lease. Monthly sales/use taxes and other monthly fees are added to this base monthly payment to determine the total monthly payment.

Bear: An investor who sells his stocks and gambles on buying them back at a lower price.

Bear market: A market where stock prices are falling, favoring a bear.

Beneficiary: A person who receives an insurance payment.

Benefits, or employee benefits: A package designed by employers to help employees. Benefits packages might include holiday and vacation pay, tuition reimbursement, a retirement plan, and health insurance.

Block trade: A transaction involving over 10,000 shares.

Blue chip: The highest priced and best shares to buy. The term comes from poker, where a blue chip is the most valuable.

Blue chip stock: Higher-priced, dividend-paying shares of large corporations like IBM and General Motors. The nickname comes from the highest value poker chip, the blue chip.

Bond: An IOU issued by a corporation or government with regular interest payments and repayment at a later time.

Broker: A licensed professional who offers investment advice and helps individuals buy and sell stocks, bonds, mutual funds, etc., for a commission. Broker can also refer to the person or agency that arranges for the sale or lease of vehicles through another party.

Budget: An organized plan of spending and saving.

Bull: An investor who buys stocks and gambles on selling them at a higher price.

Capital gain: A profit made on the sale of stocks, bonds, real estate, or other assets.

Certificate of deposit: A savings account in which an individual agrees to leave money on deposit for a specific period of time in return for a specified amount of interest; minimum deposits are required.

Chapter 7: A "straight" or "liquidation" bankruptcy, requiring that the debtor liquidate or sell all assets that are not exempt in that state. It's called a Chapter 7 because the rules governing these types of filings are found in Chapter 7 of the bankruptcy code. The exemption amounts vary from state to state, but could include work-related tools and basic household furnishings.

Chapter 13: A reorganization plan that allows debtors to keep some of the bankruptcy code property, such as a house or car, that they might otherwise lose. These types of filings, governed by Chapter 13 often allow debtors to pay off an existing loan, or cure one on which they defaulted, over three to five years. This type of plan can work for people who have consistent income and need time to pay off debts and who need relief from creditors while they're trying to pay their debts down. Like Chapter 7 bankruptcy filings, Chapter 13 filings may be used to get rid of those debts for which creditors don't have specific rights to properties. They can stop foreclosures, repossessions, garnishment of wages, utility shut-offs, and debt collection activities.

Claim: A statement requesting payment of an insured's loss.

Close: The final price of a stock at the end of the trading day.

Closed-end lease ("walk-away" lease): A lease in which you are not responsible for the difference if the actual value of the vehicle at the scheduled end of the lease is less than the residual value, assuming that you have stayed within the mileage and wear limits stated in your lease agreement. However, you are responsible for other lease requirements.

Closely held corporation: A corporation that only allows a few people to invest in it, such as friends and relatives of the corporation's principals.

Collateral: Property that a borrower promises to pay the lender if the borrower cannot repay a loan.

Collectibles: Objects such as art, jewelry, baseball cards, and antiques that are held by people in hope that their value will increase.

Commission: The fee a broker or stockbroker collects for helping people buy and sell a stock.

Commodities: Raw materials, such as oil, wheat, pork, and gold, bought by a speculator in a specific quantity for a specific price with the expectation that the price will rise so that the commodity contract can be sold to someone else for a profit.

Compound interest or compounding interest: Earnings on savings that include previously earned interest. The frequency that earned interest is added to the principal so that you begin to earn interest on that amount as well as on the principal. The more often interest is compounded, the greater the annual percentage yield.

Consumer lease: A lease of personal property to an individual to be used primarily for personal, family, or household purposes for a period of more than four months and with a total contractual obligation of no more than $25,000. A lease meeting all of these criteria is covered by the Consumer Leasing Act and Federal Reserve Regulation M. If any one of these criteria is not met— for example, if the leased property is used primarily for business purposes or if the total contractual obligation exceeds $25,000—the Consumer Leasing Act and Regulation M do not apply.

Consumer Leasing Act: A 1976 amendment to the Truth in Lending Act that requires disclosure of the cost and terms of consumer leases and also places substantive restrictions on consumer leases. *See also* consumer lease.

Consumer Price Index (CPI): A measure of the changes in price of all the goods and services that urban households purchase for consumption. The CPI is used as an economic indicator and a policy guide.

Cosigner: A person who agreed to pay a loan if the borrower fails to do so.

Credit: A loan that enables people to buy something now and to pay for it in the future. Another meaning: the Internal Revenue Service provides credits as a direct reduction of the tax owed. Credits may be allowed for purposes such as child care, higher education costs, and qualifying children.

Credit counselor: A person or agency that can help people in financial trouble develop a plan to repay debts.

Credit limit: The maximum amount you may charge on a credit card; many lenders may let you spend more, but may charge you a fee for doing so.

Credit union: A savings and lending institution owned by its members, the people who use the credit union. Deposits in credit unions are typically insured up to $100,000.

Credited interest: Interest to which you have access, usually after it is posted to your account.

Cyclical stock: A stock whose price tends to rise and fall with changes in the economy.

Dealer preparation fee: A fee charged by some auto dealers to cover the expenses of preparing a vehicle for lease. The dealer may be reimbursed by the manufacturer for this expense.

Debt: Any money you owe.

Debt consolidation: When an obligation or loan is merged with another obligation or debt for the purpose of creating a single debt.

Debt repayment plan: A formal plan to pay back creditors. Often arranged with the help of a professional credit counseling service.

Deductible: A clause in an insurance policy which states that a portion of a loss is to be paid by the insured.

Deduction: A subtraction allowed from your adjusted gross income. All taxpayers are allowed a standard deduction, but those with other high qualifying payments, such as home mortgage interest or very high medical bills, could reduce taxes further by itemizing these deductions.

Default: The failure to fulfill or meet a financial obligation or pay money when it is due.

Deferment: When payments are postponed or delayed until a future date.

Demand: The popularity of a resource, good, or service that consumers are willing and able to buy at various possible prices during a specific time period. Low supply and high demand can work together to drive up the price of a product or service.

Dependent: An individual for whom the taxpayer provides over half of the support for the calendar year. This could be a child, spouse, relative, or nonrelative living as a member of the taxpayer's household.

Depreciation: The loss in value. Automobile lease agreements charge for this projected depreciation of the car during the lease term.

Dip: A drop in the price of a stock that is temporary, making it the ideal time to buy the stock.

Direct deposit: The employee's paycheck is automatically deposited by the employer in a savings institution.

Direct tax: A tax that cannot be shifted to others. The federal income tax is an example of a direct tax.

Disability insurance: Protection against expenses incurred in the event you become disabled.

Disclosures: Information on money and terms. In a lease, required disclosures must be made about terms and conditions of the lease. A sales agent should disclose whether he or she receives a commission on the sale of a product.

Discount broker: A simple broker that only takes orders on buying and selling.

Disposable income: Income available for saving or spending after taxes.

Disposition fee or disposal fee: In an auto lease, a fee often charged by a lessor to defray the cost of preparing and selling the vehicle at the end of the lease if the vehicle is not purchased and is returned to the lessor.

Dividend: A payment made by a company to a stockholder, usually based on the company's profits.

Documentation fee: A fee charged to cover the cost of preparing documents, such as a lease.

Dow Jones Industrial Average: A market indicator that averages 30 industrial stocks. Dow Jones also has a transportation index of 20 stocks and a utility average of 15 stocks. The 65-stock Composite Average is seen as one indicator of market performance.

Downgrade: To lower the rating score of an investment or a company.

Downsize: To lay off employees or not hire replacements.

Early termination: Ending of the lease before the scheduled termination date for any reason. The reason may be voluntary or involuntary (for example, the vehicle is returned early, stolen, or totaled, or you default on the lease). In most cases of early termination, you must pay an early termination charge.

Early termination charge: The amount you owe if your lease ends before its scheduled termination date, calculated as described in your lease agreement. The earlier your lease is terminated, the greater this charge is likely to be. The charge is generally the difference between the early termination payoff and the amount credited to you for the vehicle.

Early termination payoff: The total amount you owe if your lease is terminated before the scheduled end of the term. The payoff is calculated as described in your lease agreement before subtracting the value credited to you for the vehicle. The early termination payoff may include the unpaid lease balance and other charges.

Earned income: Wages or salaries paid (earned) for labor services, including tips.

Earned income credit: A refundable credit for low-income workers. This credit may be paid to the worker even if no income tax was withheld from the worker's pay. To receive the earned income credit, a taxpayer must file a tax return.

Education IRA: Called an IRA, but not actually a retirement account, this account can be set up for a child under age 18 and accumulates earnings tax-free. If the principal and interest are used to pay education expenses for that child, the money can be withdrawn tax-free. Contributions are limited to $500 per year per child.

Educational loan: A type of financial aid available to students and to the parents of students. An educational loan must be repaid, but payments often do not begin until the student finishes school.

Electronic filing: Filing an income tax return via computer rather than mail. Refunds may be directly deposited into a savings or checking account.

Electronic funds transfer (EFT): When money passes from one person's account to another without actually changing hands.

Employee: Someone who works for another person.

Employer: Someone who has others working for him or her.

Equal Credit Opportunity Act: A federal law that prohibits discrimination in credit transactions on the basis of race, color, religion, national origin, sex, marital status, age, source of income, or the exercise of any right under the Consumer Credit Protection Act.

Equity: The money realized when property is sold and all claims upon it are paid. This equals sales price minus present mortgage and closing costs.

Excess mileage charge: A charge by the lessor for miles driven in excess of the maximum specified in the lease agreement. The excess mileage charge is usually between $0.10 and $0.25 per mile. Suppose, for example, that your lease specifies a maximum of $36,000 miles and a charge of $0.15 per mile over the maximum. If you drive 37,000 miles, the excess mileage charge will be $0.15 × 1,000, or $150. Open-end leases typically do not include an excess mileage charge.

Excessive wear and use charge (excess wear and tear charge): Amount charged by a lessor to cover wear and tear on a leased vehicle beyond what is considered "normal." The charge may cover both interior and exterior damage, such as upholstery stains, body dents and scrapes, and tire wear beyond the limits stated in the lease agreement. Open-end leases typically do not include an excessive wear and use charge.

Exchange rate: The conversion rate from U.S. dollars into foreign currency and vice versa.

Exemption: You may take an exemption from your adjusted gross income for yourself, your spouse, and any dependents. An exemption excludes money from taxation.

Expected family contribution (EFC): An amount determined by a formula specified by law that indicates how much of a family's financial resources should be used to pay for higher education. The EFC is used in determining eligibility for federal need-based aid, and calculations are based on factors including taxable and nontaxable income, assets, and benefits.

Extended warranty: A contract that can be purchased to cover the costs of parts and service on a vehicle beyond the manufacturer's original warranty period.

Fair Credit Reporting Act: A 1997 act, enforced by the Federal Trade Commission, designed to promote accuracy and ensure privacy of information used in consumer reports used or seen by crediters, employers and others.

Fair market value: The amount that a willing buyer would pay to a willing seller to purchase certain property at a particular point in time.

Fair market value purchase option: Your right to purchase the vehicle you have leased according to terms specified in your lease agreement for a price determined by referring to a readily available guide to used car values or to another independent source.

Federal Deposit Insurance Corporation (FDIC): Insures protected accounts up to $100,000.

Federal Reserve Bank: The central bank of the United States. It was created in 1913 by Congress to stabilize the nation's economy. It is divided into 12 regional banks that are located throughout the country. The bank holds a percentage of the funds of commercial banks and lends money to them when needed.

Federal Trade Commission: The federal agency responsible for enforcing the Truth in Lending Act, of which the Consumer Leasing Act is part, among leasing companies, finance companies, and lessors not regulated by other federal agencies. The Federal Trade Commission also performs other functions related to its role of ensuring that the nation's markets function competitively, enforcing other statutes affecting consumer financial services, and enforcing the Federal Trade Commission Act, which prohibits unfair or deceptive acts or practices.

Fees: These are charges that cover college costs not including tuition, such as athletic activities, clubs, and special events.

Fees and taxes (or official fees and taxes): The total amount you will pay for taxes, licenses, registration, title, and official (governmental) fees over the term of your lease. Because fees and taxes may change during the term of your lease, they may be stated as estimates.

Filing a return: Mailing or electronically submitting a tax return form to the IRS.

Filing status: Based on a taxpayer's marital status and other factors, the filing status determines the tax bracket and rate at which income is taxed.

Finance charge: The dollar amount paid to use credit; it includes interest, transaction fees, and service fees.

Finance company: A loan company.

Financial aid: The money available from various sources to help students pay for college.

Financial need: A student's financial need is equal to the cost of education (estimated costs for college attendance and basic living expenses) minus the expected family contribution or EFC.

Fiscal policy: The use of federal government spending and taxation programs to affect the level of economic activity by promoting price stability, full employment, and economic growth.

Fixed expenses: Expenses which cannot be easily changed and which remain essentially the same from month to month, such as housing and transportation.

Fixed price purchase option: Your right to purchase the vehicle you have leased for a fixed price as specified in your lease agreement.

Flat tax: Proportional tax. A tax that takes the same percentage of income from all income groups.

Forbearance: The act of a creditor who refrains from enforcing a debt when it falls due.

Foreclosure: The legal action taken to extinguish a homeowner's right and interest in a property, so that the property can be sold in a foreclosure sale to satisfy a debt.

Form W-4 (employee's withholding allowance certificate): A form that helps an employer determine how much to withhold from an employee's paycheck for federal income tax purposes.

Full maintenance lease: A lease in which the lessor assumes responsibility for all manufacturer-recommended maintenance and service on the vehicle. The lease may also cover additional mechanical repairs and servicing during the term of the lease. The cost of this service usually is included in the gross capitalized cost or is added to the base monthly payment.

Gap amount: In the event a leased vehicle is stolen or totaled, the difference between the early termination payoff and the amount for which the vehicle is insured before the insurance deductible and any other policy deductions are subtracted. The definition of gap amount may vary in different states or in different lease agreements.

Gap coverage (guaranteed auto protection, or GAP): A plan that provides you with financial protection in case your leased vehicle is stolen or totaled in an accident. There are two types of gap coverage. One is a waiver by the lessor of the gap amount if the vehicle is stolen or totaled. The other is a contract by a third party to cover the gap amount. Under either type, you may remain responsible for the insurance deductible and for other amounts deducted from the insured amount of the vehicle by your insurance company.

Genuine Progress Indicator: A method used as an alternative to the gross national product (GNP) to measure the strength of the U.S. economy. GPI has been created by Redefining Progress, San Francisco.

Grace period (on credit cards): The time, usually about 25 days, in which you can pay your credit card bill without incurring a finance charge.

Grace period (on deposits): A limited period after an automatically renewing time deposit, such as a certificate of deposit, matures, during which you may withdraw funds without being charged a penalty.

Grant: A grant is a sum of money given to a student for the purpose of paying at least part of the cost of college and does not have to be repaid.

Gross: Value before tax.

Gross capitalized cost (gross cap cost): The agreed-upon value of the vehicle, which generally may be negotiated, plus any items you agree to pay for over the lease term (amortized amounts), such as taxes, fees, service contracts, insurance, and any prior credit or lease balance.

Gross domestic product (GDP): The measure of how the economy is doing based on the total consumption of goods and services. *See also* Genuine Progress Indicator.

Gross income: Money, goods, and property you receive that must, generally, be reported on a tax return and may be included in taxable income.

Growth stocks: Stocks that pay low dividends, but are expected to grow.

Health insurance: Protection against expenses incurred due to illness, injury, or disability.

Health maintenance organization (HMO): An organization that provides a wide range of comprehensive health care services for a specified group at a fixed periodic payment.

High: The highest price of a stock during the trading day.

Home run: A term referring to an investor's large gain in a short period.

Homeowner's insurance: Property insurance that protects against the loss of a dwelling and its contents due to fire, theft, or acts of nature.

Incentives: Amounts rebated or credited, or special programs offered, to consumers or lessors to encourage the lease of certain vehicles.

Income stocks: Stocks that have consistently paid high dividends.

Income taxes: Taxes on income, both earned (salaries, wages, tip, commissions) and unearned (interest, dividends). Income taxes can be levied both on individuals and businesses.

Independent leasing company: A leasing company that offers leases directly to consumers and businesses and is generally not affiliated with a particular automobile manufacturer.

Indirect tax: A tax that can be shifted to others. The one who pays the tax to the government may be able to shift it; business property taxes are an example of an indirect tax.

Individual Retirement Account (IRA): A personal retirement account for employed individuals allowing a contribution of up to $2,000 a year (or $4,000 for a couple). Contributions may be tax-deductible, and earnings are not taxed until the funds are withdrawn after age 59 1/2 or later. Variations are the SIMPLE IRA, Roth IRA, and Simplified Employee Pension Plan (SEP-IRA).

Inflation: A sustained increase in the average price level of the entire economy.

Initial public offering (IPO): The formal name for going public.

Insurance: A contract in which one party agrees to pay for another party's financial loss resulting from a specified event (for example, a collision, theft, or storm damage). Lease agreements generally require that you maintain vehicle collision and comprehensive insurance as well as liability insurance for bodily injury and property damage.

Insurance verification: The process of obtaining verbal or written confirmation of required coverage from your insurance agent or company.

Insured savings: Accounts in which the deposit is insured (up to $100,000) by the Federal Deposit Insurance Corporation (FDIC).

Interest: The price paid for the use of someone else's savings. It could be interest a credit card user pays an institution or money an institution pays you for its use of your funds.

Interest income: Income received from certain bank accounts or from lending money to someone else.

Interest rate: The rate of interest, expressed as a percentage, that an account will earn if funds are kept on deposit for a full year. It does not reflect the effect of compounding interest.

Investment: Using money to invest in something that will earn interest or dividends over time.

IRS: Internal Revenue Service, the government agency that oversees taxation.

Keogh plan: A tax-deferred pension account for self-employed workers or employees of unincorporated business.

Late charge: A fee charged for a past-due payment. This charge is usually either a percentage of the lease payment or a fixed dollar amount.

Late payment: A payment received after the specified due date. In most cases, a late payment triggers a late charge after any grace period.

Lease: A contact between a lessor and a lessee for the use of a vehicle or other property, subject to stated terms and limitations, for a specified period and at a specified payment.

Lease charge: *See* rent charge.

Lease extension: Continuation of a lease agreement beyond the original term, often one month at a time. There may be a charge for extending the lease. If the extension continues beyond six months, new lease disclosures must be provided.

Lease factor: *See* money factor.

Lease rate: A percentage used by some lessors to describe the rent charge portion of your monthly payment. No federal standard exists for calculating the lease rate. Any rates or factors used in lease calculations do not have to be disclosed under federal law. If a lease rate is given as a percentage in an advertisement or on any lease form, the ad or form must also state, "This percentage may not measure the overall cost of financing this lease."

Lease term: The period of time for which a lease agreement is written.

Lemon laws: State laws that provide remedies to consumers for vehicles that repeatedly fail to meet certain standards of quality and performance. Lemon laws vary by state and may not cover leased vehicles.

Lender: A person, company, corporation, or entity that lends money for the purchase of real estate.

Lessee: The party to whom a vehicle is leased. In a consumer lease, the lessee is you, the consumer. The lessee is required to make payments and to meet other obligations specified in the lease agreement.

Lessor: Person or entity who owns the vehicle or property being leased.

Life insurance: Protection against financial losses resulting from death.

Liquidity: The ease with which a saving option is convertible to cash. A highly liquid asset is a savings account.

Loan: A prearranged amount of money lent to someone. Many loans are tied to a specific purchase—for example, a car loan or a home loan called a mortgage. Loans are paid back in installments, typically monthly, that include principal payments (to cover the amount borrowed) and interest.

Loan origination fee: A one-time fee charged by the mortgage company to arrange the financing for the loan.

Luxury car tax: A federal excise tax assessed on vehicles with a gross vehicle weight of less than 6,000 pounds and a value exceeding a threshold amount, which is adjusted periodically for inflation.

Maintenance: Care for the vehicle required by the lease agreement. Maintenance may include manufacturer-recommended servicing and any repairs needed to keep the vehicle in good operating condition.

Maintenance lease: A lease agreement in which some or all of the vehicle maintenance and servicing is the responsibility of the lessor.

Marginal benefit: The additional benefits received from something.

Marginal cost: The additional cost of something.

Market order: An order to buy or sell at the best price available.

Market trend: The upward or downward movement of a market for six months or more.

Maturity: The full value of a bond or certificate of deposit at its termination date.

Medicare: A program of hospital insurance (Part A) and supplemental medical insurance (Part B) protection provided under the Social Security Act.

Merit-based financial aid: Financial aid given to students who meet requirements not related to financial need. Most merit-based aid is awarded on the basis of academic, artistic, or athletic performance and is given in the form of scholarships or grants.

Mileage allowance or mileage limitation: The fixed mileage limit for the lease term. If you exceed this limit, you may have to pay an excess mileage charge.

Minimum payment: The smallest amount you are required to pay the lender each month.

Monetary policy: Policy made by the Federal Reserve System that seeks to affect the amount of money available in the economy. The activities and policies of the Federal Reserve influence the interest rates set by banks for loans to borrowers and for returns on savings.

Money factor: A number, often given as a decimal, used by some lessors to determine the rent charge portion of your monthly payment. This number is not a lease rate and cannot be converted to a lease rate by moving the decimal point.

Money market account: A savings account that requires a minimum balance and pays a varying rate of interest. Withdrawals may be limited, and minimum deposits are required.

Monthly payment: On a leasing agreement, this term may refer to one of two required federal disclosures. *See* Base monthly payment; total of payments.

Monthly sales/use tax: State and local tax that you must pay monthly when you lease a vehicle. These payments, if any, are added to your base monthly payment and paid as part of your total monthly payment.

Mortgage: A home loan, often configured to be repaid in monthly installments for 15 or 30 years.

Mortgage broker: A company or individual that brings together lenders and borrowers and processes mortgage applications.

MSRP: Manufacturer's suggested retail price, sometimes called the sticker price.

Mutual fund: A savings option that uses cash from a pool of savers to buy a wide range of securities. The fund is managed by professionals and permits small amounts of money to be invested.

Need-based financial aid: Financial aid given to students who are determined to be in need of financial assistance based on their income and assets as well as family income, assets, and other factors.

Net worth: Value of a person's wealth, calculated by subtracting total debts from total assets.

No-load: These are mutual funds that charge no fees to buy in or cash out.

NYSE: The New York Stock Exchange.

Open-end lease: A lease agreement in which the amount you owe at the end of the lease term is based on the difference between the residual value of the leased property and its realized value. Your lease agreement may provide for a refund of any excess if the realized value is greater than the residual value. In an open-end consumer lease, assuming you have met the mileage and wear standards, the residual value is considered unreasonable if it exceeds the realized value by more than three times the base monthly payment (sometimes called the "three-payment rule"). If you believe the amount owed at the end of the lease term is unreasonable and refuse to pay, the lessor may attempt to prove that the residual value was reasonable when it was set at the beginning of the lease. However, if you cannot reach a settlement with the lessor, you cannot be forced to pay the excess amount unless the lessor brings a successful court action and pays your reasonable attorney's fees.

Opportunity cost: The next best alternative that is given up when a choice is made.

Option to purchase: *See* purchase option.

Overconsumption: Using or buying more than is necessary.

Overdraft charge: A fee charged by banks when there are insufficient funds in the checking account for one or more checks.

Payoff: Bringing a loan amount to zero, paying off the principal. *See also* early termination payoff.

Penny stock: A nickname for extremely speculative stocks. They usually have a low price per share and are considered highly risky.

Pension: A plan established by an employer or a labor union to provide retirement income for workers. Funds accumulate income and capital gains tax-free, used to pay benefits.

Perkins loan: A federal financial aid program that consists of low-interest loans for undergraduates and graduate students with exceptional financial need. Loans are awarded by the individual schools.

Personal income tax: A tax based on the amount of taxable income that people receive annually. Taxable income is less than total income because of exemptions and deductions.

Personal property tax (or ad valorem tax): A tax on personal property. State laws govern whether personal property taxes apply to a leased vehicle; your lease agreement governs whether you or the lessor will pay these taxes.

Policy: A written insurance contract.

Portfolio: A collection of stocks and investments that is owned by an investor.

Premium: The amount paid for insurance protection.

Principal: The amount of money you borrow if you are getting a loan.

Prior credit balance (negative equity or negative trade-in balance): The portion of the gross capitalized cost representing the amount due under a previous credit contract after crediting the value of the vehicle trade in on the lease.

Prior lease balance: The portion of the gross capitalized cost representing the balance due from a previous lease agreement after crediting the value of the previously leased vehicle.

Privately held corporation: A corporation that allows only a select group of people to purchase stock.

Progressive tax: A tax that takes a larger percentage of income from high-income groups than from low-income groups.

Property insurance: Protection against financial losses resulting from damage to property or possessions.

Property tax: A tax levied by a county or local authority on the value of real estate or high value personal property, such as automobiles and boats and business inventories.

Proportional tax: Flat tax. A tax that takes the same percentage of income from all income groups.

Proxy ballot: A voting ballot that allows you to have a say in what happens with the company you have stock in.

Publicly held corporation: A corporation that allows any member of the public to purchase their stock.

Purchase option: Your right to buy the vehicle you have leased, before or at the end of the lease term, according to terms specified in the lease agreement. Your lease agreement may or may not include a purchase option.

Purchase option fee: An amount, in addition to the purchase price, you may have to pay to exercise any purchase option in your lease agreement.

Quality of life: A measurement of how satisfied someone is with his or her condition.

Realized value: (1) The price received by the lessor for the leased vehicle at disposition, (2) the highest offer for the leased vehicle at disposition, or (3) the fair market value of the leased vehicle at termination. The realized value may be either the wholesale or the retail value as specified in the lease agreement.

Reasonableness standard: The requirement of the Consumer Leasing Act that charges for delinquency, default, or early termination be reasonable in light of the lessor's or assignee's (1) anticipated or actual harm caused by such delinquency, default, or early termination, (2) difficulties in proving loss, and (3) inconvenience in obtaining a remedy.

Rebate: An amount offered by some manufacturers, dealers, or lessors that may be paid to you separately or credited to your lease agreement.

Recession: Negative growth of the economy for a period of six months or longer resulting in decreases in production, income, and employment.

Reconditioning: The process of preparing a vehicle for resale or re-lease if you return it.

Reconditioning reserve: An amount that you may pay at the beginning of the lease that may be used by the lessor to offset any amounts you may owe at the end of the lease term for excessive wear and use and excess mileage. Any remaining amount may be refunded to you.

Registration fee: A fee charged by a state motor vehicle department to register a vehicle and authorize its use on the public roadways.

Regressive tax: A tax that takes a larger percentage of income from low-income groups than from high-income groups.

Rent: Payment made by a tenant at designated intervals in return for the right to occupy or use another's property.

Rent or rent charge: The portion of your base monthly payment that is not depreciation or any amortized amounts. This charge is similar to interest on a loan.

Renter's insurance: Property insurance for protection against the loss of contents in a rented dwelling due to fire, theft, and acts of nature.

Repossession: Original owner reclaiming ownership for failure to pay installments due.

Residual value: The end-of-term value of the vehicle established at the beginning of the lease and used in calculating your base monthly payment. The residual value is deducted from the adjusted capitalized cost to determine the depreciation and any amortized amounts. It is an estimate that may be determined in part by using residual value guidebooks. The residual value may be higher or lower than the realized value at the scheduled end of the lease.

Retirement age: Refers to the age at which an individual becomes eligible to receive Social Security benefits, 62. Full retirement age is 65, at which time an individual can begin to collect full Social Security benefits.

Return: The amount of money a saver receives from a saving option, usually expressed as a percentage yield.

Roth IRA: The Tax Relief Act of 1998 created this individual retirement account, which allows nondeductible, after-tax contributions of up to $2,000 per year. There is no minimum contribution each year and no age limit for additional contributions.

Rule of 72: A principle that can help you determine how many years it will take your money to double at a given interest rate. By dividing the interest rate into 72, you can roughly determine the number of years it will take for your investment to double.

Sales tax: Tax on retail products, based on a set percentage of retail cost.

Savings account: A bank account that pays interest on the money deposited.

Savings bond: U.S. Treasury bonds that pay a variable interest. These bonds are sold at half of their face value.

Scarcity: The condition that results from the imbalance between unlimited wants and limited resources.

Schedule: A form on which taxpayers list or itemize specific sources of income or specific expenses for which they claim deductions or credits.

SEC: Securities and Exchange Commission, the federal agency that regulates the investment industry.

Secured debt: Debt that is tied to an asset—a house or a car, for example. If you stop making payments, the lender can repossess or foreclose.

Securities: Another term for stocks and bonds.

Security deposit: An amount you may be required to pay, usually at the beginning of the lease or rental term, that may be used in the event of default or at the end of the lease to offset any amounts you owe under the agreement. Any remaining amount may be refunded to you. Security deposits are common in auto leases and apartment or house rentals, but the amount of the deposit might be negotiable.

Service contract: A contract that you may purchase to cover such expenses as the repair or replacement of components for high-cost products, such as automobiles or electronic equipment. In purchasing products, service contracts are optional. In leases, they may be required.

Shareholder: A person who buys stocks in a corporation, and therefore becomes a part owner of the corporation.

Simplified Employee Pension Plan (SEP): A pension plan in which both the employee and the employer contribute to an individual retirement account (IRA). Also referred to as SEP-IRA.

Single-payment lease: A lease that requires a single payment made in advance rather than periodic payments made over the term of the lease. This lump-sum payment may be less than the total amount you would pay were you to make periodic payments over the term of the lease.

Social Security: A federal program established in 1935 to provide retirement, survivor's, disability, and medical benefits through a payroll tax paid by both employers and employees.

Standard & Poor's (S&P): A large financial service company that publishes the S&P 500, a popular indicator of overall stock market performance. The S&P 500 represents a wide variety of industries and company sizes.

Standard deduction: An amount fixed by law and based on filing status, age, blindness, and dependency that taxpayers may deduct from their adjusted gross income before tax is determined.

Standard of living: The level of material well-being of an individual or group.

Stock: A certificate representing a share of ownership in a company.

Stock certificate: The actual piece of paper that is evidence of stock ownership, usually watermarked and patterned to make it hard to forge.

Stock market: A market in which the public trades stock it already owns.

Stockbroker: A broker that, in addition to taking orders, also offers advice on investing.

Sublease: Oral or written contractual transfer of your right to use the leased vehicle to another person. Such a transfer is usually prohibited without the lessor's approval.

Supply: The quantity of a resource, good, or service that lenders are willing to produce and sell at various possible prices during a specific time period. High demand and low supply can work together to drive the cost of a product or service.

Tax credit: A dollar-for-dollar amount subtracted directly from the taxes you owe.

Tax deductions: A part of a person's or a business's total expenditures that can be deducted in determining taxable income.

Tax Freedom Day: Announced annually by the Tax Foundation. Tax Freedom Day represents the day that the average worker meets his or her tax liability for the year. In 1999, Tax Freedom Day was May 11.

Tax liability: Total tax bill.

Tax shift: The process that occurs when a tax that has been levied on one person or group is in fact paid by others.

Tax withholding: Money that an employer takes from an employee's paycheck to pay part or all of the employee's taxes.

Tax-deferred: An investment that accumulates earnings that are not subject to taxes until they are withdrawn. The taxes are deferred until the investor taps into the accounts, usually at retirement, when the individual's tax bracket is generally lower than during his or her peak earning years.

Term insurance: Life insurance that provides coverage for a specific period. It provides protection only, with no cash buildup or loan provisions.

Termination date: The date at which a bond or certificate of deposit reaches its full value.

Tiered rates: An interest rate structure by which the rate paid on an account is tied to a specified balance level.

Time deposit: An account, such as a certificate of deposit, with a maturity of at least seven days, from which you are not generally allowed to withdraw funds unless you pay a penalty.

Tips: Income received for services directly from customers. Tip income should be reported on income tax filings.

Title: Legal document that identifies the owner of the vehicle. The lessor, not you, holds title to the leased vehicle.

Total of payments: In a lease, the sum of the periodic payments, the end-of-term disposition fee, any "other charges," and all "amounts due at lease signing or delivery," minus refundable amounts such as a security deposit and any monthly payments included in the "amount due at lease signing or delivery."

Trade-in: The net value of your vehicle credited toward the purchase or lease of another vehicle. If you own the vehicle being traded in, you sell it to the dealer or lessor. If you are leasing the vehicle being traded in, you are turning in the vehicle (either at the scheduled end of the lease or upon early termination) to the dealer or lessor. The amount credited may be positive or negative depending on the value of the vehicle and any remaining balance on your credit, loan, or lease agreement.

Unearned income: Income received that is not a result of labor or services, such as interest from a savings account.

Unsecured debts: Debts that are not tied to any asset. Examples include most credit card debt, bills for medical care, signature loans, and debts for other types of services.

Variable expenses: Expenses which can be controlled and which change from month to month, such as entertainment, food, and clothing.

Vesting: The legal right of an employee to share in the company's qualified pension plan. Vesting can occur gradually over a period of years or all at once. When fully vested, all contributions the company has made to the employee's retirement fund are the employee's.

Voluntary compliance: A system of compliance that relies on individual citizens to report their income freely and voluntarily, calculate their tax liability correctly, and file a tax return on time.

Wages: Money earned from a job.

Walk-away lease. *See* closed-end lease.

Warranty: A guarantee that the vehicle will function and perform as specified. A warranty usually covers specified mechanical problems during a specified period of time or number of miles.

Whole-life insurance: Also known as permanent life. The policy stays in force as long as the premiums are paid and the insured is alive. Premiums are the same throughout the life of the policy.

Will: The declaration of a person's wishes covering the disposition of the person's property after death. A will is executed in accordance with certain legal requirements.

Withholding: Money the employer takes out of a paycheck on your behalf and sends to the Internal Revenue Service (IRS).

Withholding allowance: Claimed by an employee on Form W-4. An employer uses the number of allowances claimed, together with income earned and marital status, to determine how much income tax to withhold from wages.

Yield: The percentage rate paid on a stock in the form of dividends, or the rate of interest paid on a bond or note.

Appendix B: Resource Guide

EDUCATION RESOURCES AND WEB SITES

Name: American Economic Association
  Address: 2014 Broadway, Suite 305, Nashville, TN 37203
  Phone: (615) 322-2595
  Web address: www.vanderbilt.edu/AEA/org.htm
  Web site: The AEA was organized in 1885 and incorporated in 1923. Its members are economists, with over 50% associated with academic institutions, 35% with business and industry, and the remainder largely with federal, state, and local government agencies. The association works to encourage economic research and publications on economic subjects but supports no formal position on economic issues. Developed for adults.

Name: American Savings Education Council
  Address: Suite 600, 2121 K Street, NW, Washington, DC 20037
  Phone: (202) 775-6364 / (800) 998-7542 (the U.S. Department of Labor's Publication Hotline, which distributes several ASEC brochures)
  Web address: www.asec.org
  Web site: Features a savings tool page which links to an interactive calculator designed to show how to set saving goals and reach them. Also includes a survey of 1,000 16 to 22-year-olds on issues concerning money management. Information is appropriate for older students and adults.

Name: College Board
  Address: Two College Way, P.O. Box 1100, Forrester Center, WV 25438
  Phone: (212) 713-8165 / (800) 323-7155
  Web address: www.collegeboard.com

Web site: An association of schools, colleges, universities, and other educational organizations providing programs and services for students and families. Information covers a wide array of topics including academic preparation,
understanding college applications, financial aid information, plus publications
and research data. This site caters to students and parents as well as school
and college educators.

Name: Economics America
Address: 1140 Avenue of the Americas, New York, NY 10036
Phone: (212) 730–7007 / (888) 338–5106
Web address: www.economicsamerica.org
Web site: This program provides curricula to train teachers and to use Internet
resources. Also provides a directory of state councils and centers on economic
education. Assists in the development of national, state, and local standards-
based curriculum; publishes classroom-tested materials for teachers and students. Resource materials developed for educators. *See also* National Council
on Economic Education (NCEE).

Name: Economic Education Web (EcEd Web)
Address: University of Nebraska at Omaha Center for Economic Education,
Omaha, NE 68182
Phone: (402) 554–3654
Web address: ecedweb.unomaha.edu/
Web site: Includes information, lessons on money and personal finance, and a
"K–12 Teach" page. Topics range from personal investing to understanding
money and interest rates. Also includes an index to useful links, connecting to
a variety of sites. Information is geared toward adults, especially educators.

Name: FastWEB
Address: 2550 Commonwealth Avenue, North Chicago, IL 60064
Phone: (847) 785–8000
Web address: www.fastweb.com
Web site: Provides free information including a database of over 400,000 schol-
arships that can match students to available scholarships based on their profile
questionnaires. This site is developed for a student audience.

Name: FinAid! The smart student guide to financial aid
Address: Not available
Phone: Not available
Web address: www.finaid.org
Web site: This free financial aid resource includes information ranging from a
glossary of terms to a calculator students may use to determine the cost of
college as well as the amount of debt new grads can reasonably repay. Also
provides information on student loan forgiveness requirements. Users can
search for scholarships and also look at tips on avoiding scholarship scams.
The site is operated by the National Association of Student Financial Aid Ad-

ministrators and written by Mark Kantrowitz. Information is appropriate for middle school students on up.

Name: Financial Literacy 2001
Address: 1901 North Fort Myer Drive, Suite 1012–1014, Arlington, VA 22209
Phone: (703) 276–1116
Web address: www.FL2001.org
Web site: A joint project of the nonprofit Investor Protection Trust (IPT), the National Association of Securities Dealers (NASD) Office of Individual Investor Services, and the North American Securities Administration Association (NASAA). Financial Literacy 2001 offers a printed or online teaching guide and works to encourage financial literacy educators. Also has a chat and forum for sharing tips and ideas among high school teachers. Developed for educators. *See also* National Institute for Consumer Education.

Name: Jump$tart Coalition for Personal Financial Literacy
Address: 919 18th Street, Suite 300, NW, Washington, DC 20006
Phone: (888) 45–EDUCATE
Web address: www.jumpstartcoalition.org
Web site: This nonprofit coalition evaluates the financial literacy of young adults; works with other organizations to develop guidelines; promotes teaching of personal finance; and maintains a clearinghouse of information, resources, and lesson plans which meet its recommended guidelines and can be accessed by grade level, keyword, title, and media type. For young adults as well as adults.

Name: National Association of Colleges and Employers
Address: 62 Highland Avenue, Bethlehem, PA 18017–9085
Phone: (610) 868–1421 / (800) 544–5272
Web address: www.jobweb.org
Web site: The home page of the National Association of Colleges and Employers reports trends in hiring and starting salaries with information for students and graduates involved in job searches, interviews, and career planning as well as for career counselors and human resource professionals who hire college graduates. Includes online version of its *Journal of Career Planning and Employment*. Information assists students as well as adults.

Name: National Council on Economic Education (NCEE)
Address: 1140 Avenue of the Americas, New York, NY 10036
Phone: (212) 730–7007 / (888) 338–5106
Web address: www.nationalcouncil.org
Web site: Founded in 1949, the NCEE is a major source of teacher training and materials with a goal of improving understanding of economic principles for students in kindergarten through grade 12. Includes a directory of a nationwide network of state councils called Economics America. Also includes information on Economics International, a global economics training initiative.

Publishes classroom-tested materials for teachers and students. Resource materials developed for educators. *See also* Economics America.

Name: National Endowment for Financial Education (NEFE)
   Address: 5299 DTC Boulevard, Suite 1300, Englewood, CO 80111–3334
   Phone: (303) 741–6333
   Web address: www.nefe.org
   Web site: The NEFE works to educate all Americans about personal finance. This nonprofit organization provides educational information to financial service professionals and the general public. Offers more than 20 courses and over a dozen programs. Materials are geared for an adult audience.

Name: National Institute for Consumer Education
   Address: Eastern Michigan University, 559 Gary M. Owen Building, 300 W. Michigan Avenue, Ypsilanti, MI 48197
   Phone: (734) 487–7153
   Web address: www.emich.edu
   Web site: NICE is a professional development center and clearinghouse in consumer, economic, and personal finance education and is an outreach program at Eastern Michigan University. NICE works with elementary and secondary school teachers plus community, business, and labor educators. NICE is also part of the network of centers of the Michigan Council on Economic Education, part of the Economics America program. Information is geared toward an adult audience.

Name: Resources for Economists on the Internet (RFE)
   Address: Department of Economics and International Business, University of Southern Mississippi, Hattiesburg, MS 39406
   Phone: (601) 266–4484
   Web address: www.rfe.org
   Web site: This guide lists resources on the Internet of interest to academic and practicing economists. Includes a list of organizations and associations, a calendar of conferences, information on related software, and teaching resources. Also included is a section titled "Neat Stuff," which includes jokes about economists and economics, and an online video lecture series by famous economists from the Center for Economic Studies in Munich. Developed for adults but appropriate for students from middle school on up. *See also* American Economic Association.

Name: Scholarship Resource Network
   Address: 555 Quince Orchard Road, Suite 200, Gaithersburg, MD 20878
   Phone: (301) 670–1260
   Web address: www.rams.com/srn/
   Web site: Offers software program and database of college financial aid and scholarship information. The database also includes information on student loan repayment as well as tips on avoiding scholarship scams. This information is geared toward students.

Name: USA Group, Inc.
  Address: P.O. Box 7039, Indianapolis, IN 46207–7039
  Phone: (317) 849–6510 / (800) 428–9250
  Web address: www.usagroup.com
  Web site: This Indiana-based nonprofit company provides education loan services. It insures lenders against default on federal education loans and also offers tuition payment plans and provides consulting services for families interested in managing tuition expenses. For students and adults.

Name: U.S. Department of Education, FAFSA on the web
  Address: 400 Maryland Avenue, SW, Washington, DC 20202–0498
  Phone: (800) 801–0576
  Web address: www.fafsa.ed.gov
  Web site: This site provides an online form that can be used to file a free application for federal student aid (FAFSA). Links to various financial aid sites as well as other Department of Education sites. Provides tips and shortcuts, lists records needed for applications, and offers general student aid information. For students and adults.

Name: Wall Street Journal Classroom Edition Program
  Address: Dept. 6AAR, P.O. Box 7019, Chicopee, MA 01021
  Phone: (800) 544–0522, ext. 6AAR
  Web address: http://info.wsj.com/classroom
  Web site: The program, created in 1991 by Dow Jones & Company, seeks to improve the business, economic and financial literacy of American middle school and high school students. Those enrolled in the program receive a monthly student newspaper, a monthly Teacher Guide with lesson plans, a subscription to the daily *Wall Street Journal*, optional videotapes produced by CNBC, and educational posters with activity guides.

Name: Wills and Estate Planning, Nolo Press
  Address: 950 Parker Street, Berkeley, CA 94710
  Phone: (510) 549–1976
  Web address: www.nolo.com
  Web site: Includes information on wills, probate and executors, living trusts, estate and gift taxes, living wills, and power of attorney. Contains a free legal encyclopedia, a legal dictionary, and a variety of legal publications for adult consumers. Described as "a living room law machine."

GOVERNMENT AGENCY RESOURCES AND WEB SITES

Name: America's Job Bank, U.S. Department of Labor
  Address: 200 Constitution Avenue, NW, Washington, DC 20210
  Phone: (202) 693–4650
  Web address: www.ajb.dni.us/
  Web site: Developed by the U.S. Department of Labor and state employment service agencies, this site lists more than 800,000 domestic and international

job opportunities. The job bank also offers a resumé listing of candidates with a wide range of skills and experience in a variety of employment fields. Job and resumé listings are indexed by industry, location, requirements, duration, and salary range. Information is appropriate for students and adults.

Name: The Consumer Information Center
Address: Pueblo, CO 81009
Phone: (888) 878-3256
Web address: www.pueblo.gsa.gov
Web site: The CIC is part of the General Services Administration (GSA) and has a catalog that lists some 200 consumer publications currently in print. Anyone can order a free consumer catalog, which includes the publication *Prepay Your Child for College*, by calling (888) 878-3256.

Name: Consumer Price Index/Bureau of Labor Statistics (BLS)
Address: BLS, Division of Information Services, 2 Massachusetts Avenue, NE, Room 2860, Washington, DC 20212
Phone: (202) 606-7000 (information and analysis)
Web address: http://stats.bls.gov/cpihome.htm
Web site: The Consumer Price Index (CPI) is a measure of the average change in prices paid by urban consumers for goods and services. This site provides a way for consumers to compare the price of goods from months or years past. The CPI is used as an economic indicator and as a means of adjusting dollar values. The site also includes a detailed look at the CPI, how it is used, and other information, as well as revisions and announcements. The Bureau of Labor Statistics, the government's principal fact-finding agency in the field of labor economics and statistics, oversees the CPI and this site.

Name: Federal Deposit Insurance Corporation
Address: 550 Seventeenth Street, NW, Washington, DC 20429-9990
Phone: (202) 393-8400
Web address: www.fdic.gov
Web site: The FDIC has a quarterly consumer newsletter filled with tips on how to handle banking issues, resolve complaints, and protect yourself against fraud or scams, as well as reports on what new legislation means to you. The Web address www.fdic.gov/consumers/consumer/news/index.html brings you directly to the index of all issues available online.

Name: Federal Trade Commission
Address: CRC-240, Washington, DC 20580
Phone: (202) 382-4357
Web address: www.ftc.gov
Web site: Contains a variety of publications on subjects such as credit, buying, working at home, investments, and telemarketing. The site is designed for adults, but students can find useful information.

Name: Foundation for Teaching Economics (FTE)
Address: 260 Russell Boulevard, Suite B Davis, CA 95616–3839
Phone: (800) 383–4335
Web address: www.fte.org
Web site: The Foundation for Teaching Economics (FTE) is a nonprofit organization for educators as well as students. Program topics include the environment and the economy, economic forces in American history, and the economic demise of the Soviet Union. Lesson plans are available as well as simulations geared for all ages.

Name: Internal Revenue Service
Address: IRS, Department of the Treasury, 1500 Pennsylvania Ave., NW, Washington, DC 20220
Phone: (202) 622–2000
Web address: www.irs.ustreas.gov
Web site: This site contains everything from a section called Tax Information for You, to a learning lab where students can see how taxes impact the salaries of Music Girl and Pizza Dude. Also includes a teacher's tool kit and a section on frequently asked tax questions. This user-friendly site works for students and educators as well as adults who need tax information and forms.

Name: Office of Washington Attorney General, Consumer Protection Division
Address: 1220 Main Street, Suite 549, Vancouver, WA 98660–2964
Phone: (360) 759–2150
Web address: www.access.wa.gov
Web site: This consumer protection information is available through the Access Washington Home Page, the official Web site for Washington State's government. Includes consumer education, quick tips, and a consumer page for teens with topics; car buying, calling cards, return policies, fake product scams, music clubs, and more.

Name: Ohio Consumers' Counsel, Telephone Information
Address: 77 South High Street, 15th Floor, Columbus, OH 43266–0550
Phone: (877) 742–5622 (toll-free)
Web address: www.state.oh.us/cons/hardbook/3telephone.html
Web site: This site is provided by the state of Ohio's consumer office and contains abundant information on telephone scams, how to choose a long-distance provider, addresses for removing your name from national telemarketers' lists, and other consumer telephone rights. Information is geared toward an adult audience.

Name: Securities and Exchange Commission, SEC Investor Assistance and Complaints
Address: 450 Fifth Street, NW, Washington, DC 20549
Phone: (202) 942–7040
Web address: www.sec.gov/invkhome.htm
Web site: This site is provided by the SEC's Office of Investor Education and

Assistance to inform consumers about securities fraud abuse and to provide investment information. Includes a financial facts tool kit, Internet fraud brochures, tips for online investing, a mutual fund cost calculator, other financial information, plus links to other sites. This site is developed with the knowledgeable investor in mind.

Name: U.S. Consumer Gateway, Federal Trade Commission
Address: FTC, CRC-240, Washington, DC 20580
Phone: (202) 382–4357
Web address: www.consumer.gov
Web site: This is a link to a broad range of federal information resources available online. The Federal Trade Commission operates the gateway. Information ranges from product safety to health, money, and transportation and includes a children's page. The children's page has information ranging from scholarship scams to a national runaway switchboard. There are links to government agencies from the Department of Housing and Urban Development (HUD) to the Food and Drug Administration (FDA) as well as the White House. The majority of links are for adults, but some sites do include material developed for a student audience.

Name: U.S. Department of Education
Address: 400 Maryland Avenue, SW, Washington, DC 20202–0498
Phone: (800) USA–LEARN
Web address: www.ed.gov
Web site: This U.S. Department of Education Web site in conjunction with its Office of Post-Secondary Education offers information on student financial aid and how to apply for grants, loans, and work-study, as well as a student guide that details other facts and programs.

Name: U.S. Department of Justice, Telemarketing Fraud
Address: 950 Pennsylvania Ave., NW, Washington, DC 20530–0001
Phone: (202) 514–1888
Web address: www.usdoj.gov
Web site: The section on telemarketing fraud covers everything from charity schemes to credit card scams, credit repair schemes, and prize promotion schemes, and even has a section on what fraudulent telemarketers sound like. There is a section on the Justice Department's efforts against fraud and sections on public education and prevention. Information is adult-oriented. DOJ Home Page offers a KIDS Page divided into age-appropriate sections on a variety of consumer fraud topics.

Name: U.S. Department of the Treasury
Address: 1500 Pennsylvania Ave., NW, Washington, DC 20220
Phone: (202) 622–2000
Web address: www.ustreas.gov
Web site: The Treasury Department site has substantial education information, including a kids' page, a learning vault that provides the history of the de-

partment and its role in the federal government. The STAWRS Kids' page is available to provide information for students about starting a business and related taxes. Includes forms as well as an interactive "game" that allows the student to start a business, make money, hire employees, and pay taxes. All materials have been developed for use by teachers, parents, and/or students.

Name: U.S. Savings Bonds, Bureau of the Public Debt Online
Address: U.S. Department of the Treasury, 1500 Pennsylvania Ave., NW, Washington, DC 20220
Phone: (202) 622–2000
Web address: www.publicdebt.treas.gov
Web site: Information includes the history of the U.S. public debt, interest rates, bankruptcy, links to other Web sites, and details on specific bond series for investors as well as software for those who want to determine if their bonds have stopped earning interest. Includes a section on bonds for youngsters.

FINANCIAL RESOURCES AND WEB SITES

Name: America's Job Bank, Name: American Savings Education Council Retirement Confidence Survey
Address: Suite 600, 2121 K Street, NW, Washington, DC 20037–1896
Phone: (202) 775–6364
Web address: www.asec.org
Web site: The ASEC is a coalition of private and public sector institutions that work toward raising public awareness of the need for long-term personal financial independence. Information includes a retirement confidence survey plus savings tools, and a listing of programs and events. Sponsors and partners include the American Association of Retired Persons (AARP), American Express Company, and Metropolitan Life Insurance Company.

Name: Currencies of the World/Pacific Exchange Rate Service
Address: University of British Columbia, Prof. Werner Antweiler, Ph.D., 2053 Main Mall, Vancouver, BC V6T 1Z2, Canada
Phone: (604) 822–8484
Web address: http://pacific.commerce.ubc.ca/xr/
Web site: This database includes historic daily exchange rates for a large number of currencies and a few commodities. Pacific's exchange rates are updated daily, and the site also provides analyses and forecasts plus educational pages on the new euro and purchasing power parity. The site was created by Werner Antweiler as a teaching tool for college courses and was also designed as a free data repository for researchers seeking information on exchange rate economics.

Name: Insurance News Network
Address: 76 LaSalle Road, West Hartford, CT 06107
Phone: (860) 233–2800
Web address: www.Insure.com
Web site: This site contains information on home, auto, health, and business

insurance. It also links to a directory; users can search by specific state for information. It is comprehensive and user-friendly and, although developed for adults, students can navigate with little problem. Includes a complaint finder, lawsuit library, glossary, and reader forums as well as news-style articles concerning the insurance industry.

Name: International Monetary Fund
Address: 700 19th Street, NW, Washington, DC 20431
Phone: (202) 623–7000
Web address: www.imf.org
Web site: This site offers everything from a historical timeline on the formation of the IMF to information about the Asian financial crisis or debt relief. Also includes publications, such as *World Economic Outlook*. Designed for an adult audience, but information is appropriate for older students as well.

Name: Investment Company Institute Mutual Fund Connection
Address: 1401 H Street, NW, Washington, DC 20005
Phone: (202) 326–5800
Web address: www.ici.org
Web site: Sponsored by the Investment Company Institute, this site is designed to provide information on and understanding of the investment company industry as well as policy issues, legislation, and regulations. Not intended to address individual investments, it does provide retirement facts and figures free for personal use. The site also has a user survey for feedback. Designed for adults.

Name: Investorguide.com
Address: Investorguide.com Inc., 643 North Abingdon Street, Arlington, VA 22203
Phone: (703) 351–1495
Web address: www.investorguide.com
Web site: This site, created by recent college graduates, offers information young investors can use to manage their investments and personal finances. Users can sign up for a free subscription to a weekly e-mail newsletter. This also links to other investor sites: Investorwords.com and Investorville.com. The Investorwords site is a glossary with over 5,000 definitions and 15,000 links between related terms. Investorville is a free discussion community that is open to conversations on a wide range of investing subjects as well as specific stocks.

Name: Money 2000, Department of Agriculture
Address: USDA, 14th and Independence Avenue, SW, Washington, DC 20250
Phone: (202) 720–2791
Web address: www.money2000.org
Web site: This national Web site for the Money 2000 program is offered by state and county extension offices across the country. Program costs will vary by state, and the program package includes a quarterly newsletter, a home

study course, workshops and seminars, newspaper articles, and a video program designed to help adults improve their spending and saving habits.

Name: Stock Market Game 2000
Address: Securities Industry Foundation for Economic Education, 120 Broadway, 35th Floor, New York, NY 10271–0080
Phone: (212) 608–1500
Web address: www.smg2000.org
Web site: Stock Market Game 2000 is an electronic education simulation program designed to introduce students and adults to basic economics. This simulation of Wall Street trading is designed to help students and adults understand the stock market plus the costs and benefits involved in decision making, the sources and uses of capital, and other economic concepts. The site is sponsored by the Securities Industry Foundation for Economic Education (SIFEE) and was developed in partnership with Economics America, the National Council on Economic Education (NCEE), and special corporate sponsor IBM.

Name: The United Savings Bond Consultant, Savingsbonds.com, Inc.
Address: 1540 Route #138, Suite #307, Wall, NJ 07719
Phone: (732) 280–1440
Web address: www.savingsbonds.com
Web site: This site, named the Ultimate Savings Bonds Information Source, provides redemption value for any bond issued since 1941. For a fee bondholders can obtain total interest earned to date, current and lifetime interest rates, plus final maturity date when bonds no longer earn interest. The site also offers software for purchase, plus free information on bonds. The information is geared for adults.

Name: Urban Programs Resource Network, Is Your Financial Security at Risk?
Address: Chicago Extension Center, 216 W. Jackson, Suite 625, Chicago, IL 60606
Phone: (312) 578–9956
Web address: www.urban.ext.uiuc.edu/risk/
Web site: Developed by Karen Chan, Extension Educator, Consumer and Family Economics, this activity is designed to help individuals develop a personal risk management plan. To develop the plan, users will identify events that pose a financial risk; learn the four basic methods of managing risk; determine which methods are currently being used to manage risk; and identify gaps in current risk management strategies. The site uses technology called "cookies." While using the site a small file is placed on your computer to "remember" individual selections which are erased after leaving the site. The information is geared toward families and can be used by students.

Name: Women's Wire, Women.com Network
Address: 1820 Gateway Drive, Suite 100, San Mateo, CA 94404
Phone: (650) 378–6500

Web address: www.womenswire.com
Web site: The information and tools available are geared specifically toward
women and their financial concerns. Includes everything from tips on investing
with a group to a 401(k) calculator and U.S. tax forms.

Name: The World Bank
  Address: 1818 H Street, NW, Washington, DC 20433
  Phone: (202) 477–1234
  Web address: www.worldbank.org
  Web site: The World Bank is the largest provider of development assistance
  in the world, committing about $20 billion in new loans each year. The bank
  also provides technical assistance and advice to help world governments set
  long-term financial goals and policies. This site includes information on the
  bank, its mission, local offices, as well as its strategies and financial policies.
  Students can find information on international financial issues as well as history of the bank.

CONSUMER PROTECTION AND SERVICE RESOURCES
AND WEB SITES

Name: Adbusters
  Address: 1243 West 7th Avenue, Vancouver, BC, V6H 1B7 Canada
  Phone: (604) 736–9401 / (800) 663–1243
  Web address: www.adbusters.org
  Web site: The Adbusters Web site is operated by the Media Foundation, based
  in Vancouver, British Columbia. The foundation describes itself as a global
  network of artists, students, and educators, and publishes *Adbuster Magazine*.
  It also operates Powershift, an advertising agency. The site is geared toward
  student users. It focuses on the "mental environment of the planet" and carries
  a strong anti-consumerism message.

Name: Center for a New American Dream
  Address: 156 College Street, 2nd Floor, Burlington, VT 05401
  Phone: (802) 862–6762
  Web address: www.newdream.org
  Web site: This not-for-profit membership-based organization was created to
  promote national efforts to turn away from consumerism. The site provides
  an excellent list of resources, organizations, and links to other sites of interest.
  Includes information for parents and educators in "Kids and Commercialism,"
  a section on insulating children from today's consumerism. Also offers online
  discussions and a variety of publications for adults.

Name: Citizens for Tax Justice
  Address: 1311 L Street, NW, Washington, DC 20005
  Phone: (202) 626–3780 / (888) 626–2622
  Web address: www.ctj.org
  Web site: CTJ was founded in 1979 and is a public interest research and ad-

vocacy organization dedicated to fair taxation at the federal, state, and local levels. The organization focuses on issues such as fair taxes for middle-and low-income families; closing corporate tax loopholes; reducing the federal debt; and taxation that minimizes distortion of economic markets. This site links to a large number of national organizations, as well as state and federal government and economic development sources. Designed for the adult taxpayer.

Name: The Cohousing Network
Address: P.O. Box 2584, Berkeley, CA 94702
Phone: (510) 486–2656
Web address: www.cohousing.org
Web site: The Cohousing Network is an organization promoting the cohousing concept and works to support individuals and groups who want to create communities for those interested in cohousing. Cohousing communities are designed so families live collaboratively, in private dwellings but sharing public spaces such as a large dining room, recreation facilities, and child care. The site includes a library as well as resources geared toward developing or completing cohousing communities. Adult-oriented materials.

Name: Consumer Credit Counseling Service
Address: 4660 South Laburnum Avenue, Richmond, VA 23231
Phone: (800) 388–2227 / (804) 222–4660
Web address: www.cccsdc.org
Web site: Local, nonprofit organizations affiliated with the National Foundation for Consumer Credit (NFCC) provide education and financial counseling to individuals and families. CCCS provides information and services at no cost or for a small fee based on individual income levels.

Name: Consumers Union
Address: 101 Truman Avenue, Yonkers, NY 10703–1057
Phone: (914) 378–2000
Web address: www.consumersunion.org
Web site: Consumers Union, the publisher of *Consumer Reports*, is an independent, nonprofit testing and information organization for consumers. They provide advice about products, personal finance, health, food and nutrition, and other consumer issues. The site also includes consumer news, tips, and resources. This site is user friendly for students and adults.

Name: Context Institute
Address: P.O. Box 946, Langley, WA 98260
Phone: (360) 221–6044
Web address: www.context.org
Web site: The Context Institute is a nonprofit research organization, formed in 1979 to encourage a humane sustainable culture. The site provides information about humane sustainable culture—a culture that is meaningful, satisfying to its members, and does not need to destroy or deplete the environment in order to be that way. Publishes *In Context*, an online magazine devoted to sustain-

ability. The online library includes over 1,000 articles from the magazine as well as a section on global information.

Name: Council of Better Business Bureaus
  Address: 4200 Wilson Boulevard, Suite 800, Arlington, VA 22203–1804
  Phone: (703) 276–0100
  Web address: www.bbb.org
  Web site: The BBB was founded in 1912 to create consumer confidence and contribute to an ethical business environment. The bureaus are private, non-profit organizations funded by membership dues and other support. The Web site contains a directory of local BBB's, a resource library, plus alerts, news releases, and publications to educate and inform consumers and businesses. Users can also file a consumer complaint online.

Name: Debt Counselors of America
  Address: P.O. Box 8587, Gaithersburg, MD 20898–8587
  Phone: (800) 680–3328
  Web address: www.dca.org
  Web site: This nonprofit organization assists consumers with credit and debt problems and has a Java program on its Web site which allows consumers to determine how long it will take them to become debt free. The program also allows users to calculate the total interest they will pay to become debt free. The Web site offers free publications and free software programs for adults dealing with debt.

Name: Kelley Blue Book
  Address: 5 Oldfield, Irvine, CA 92618
  Phone: (800) BLUE–BOOK (258–3266)
  Web address: www.kbb.com
  Web site: This is the site for the tried and true guide to car prices, and also includes information on everything from new and used car values to quotes on financing and insurance plus reviews and car care tips. The information is designed for adults, but can be effectively used by students with adult assistance.

Name: Money Management International, Educational Resources
  Address: 4600 Gulf Freeway, Suite 400, Houston, TX 77023–3551
  Phone: (800) 762–2271
  Web address: www.mmintl.org
  Web site: This national nonprofit agency provides free professional credit counseling, debt management programs, and consumer education. Also presents financial resources for teachers, parents, and students.

Name: National Consumers League
  Address: 1701 K Street, NW, Suite 1200, Washington, DC 20006
  Phone: (202) 835–3323
  Web address: www.natlconsumersleague.org

Web site: The NCL was established to provide research, education, and advocacy for consumers. This site provides adult-oriented materials designed to fight telemarketing fraud and to improve air safety, fair labor standards, and food and drug safety. Information includes a calendar of upcoming NCL conferences. Archives include past speeches, testimony, and press releases. Pages on Internet fraud, slamming—the unauthorized switching of consumers' telephone carriers—and cramming—billing telephone consumers for services they never ordered—are available, as well as a complaint page for those who may be fraud victims. The NCL operates the National Fraud Information Center and the Alliance Against Fraud in Telemarketing. *See also* National Fraud Information Center.

Name: National Foundation for Consumer Credit
Address: 8611 Second Avenue, Suite 100, Silver Spring, MD 20910
Phone: (800) 388–2227
Web address: www.nfcc.org
Web site: The NFCC is a network of nonprofit agencies that provide money management education, confidential budget or credit or debt counseling, plus debt repayment plans for individuals or families. Site also contains information about credit reports and bankruptcy, along with an online test to check whether individuals are headed for money trouble. Affiliated with the Consumer Credit Counseling Service (CCCS).

Name: National Fraud Information Center
Address: 1701 K Street, NW, Suite 1201 Washington, DC 20006
Phone: (800) 876–7060
Web address: www.fraud.org
Web site: The National Fraud Information Center (NFIC) is funded and supported by the National Consumers League (NCL) to fight telemarketing fraud by improving prevention and enforcement. Consumers can get advice about telephone solicitations and report possible telemarketing fraud to law enforcement agencies. Articles from the site may be reprinted with permission of the NCL and attribution of to the NFIC. Links to federal Web sites plus all state attorneys general, plus Canadian and other international resources. Aimed at an adult audience. *See also* National Consumers League.

Name: New Road Map Foundation
Address: 5557 38th Avenue, N.E., Seattle, WA 98105
Web address: www.slnet.com/cip/nrm/
Web site: Founded by Joe Dominguez and Vicki Robin, authors of *Your Money or Your Life*, this site seeks to provide information about the impact of overconsumption on individuals and the economy. Educational information focuses on personal finances, health, and human relations. Resources include books and study guides for the adult programs offered.

Name: Northwest Environment Watch (NEW)
Address: 1402 Third Avenue, Suite 1127, Seattle, WA 98101–2118

Phone: (206) 447–1880 / (888) 643–9820 (outside Washington)
Web address: www.northwestwatch.org
Web site: A not-for-profit research center, based in Seattle, created by World-watch Institute. NEW works to foster a sustainable economy and way of life in the Pacific Northwest. Information focuses on the impact of over-consumption and on reconciling the economy and ecology in that geographic region. *See also* Worldwatch Institute.

Name: Privacy Rights Clearinghouse
Address: 1717 Kettner Ave., Suite 105, San Diego, CA 92101
Phone: (619) 298–3396
Web address: www.privacyrights.org
Web site: The PRC offers fact sheets and other resources that provide information on privacy issues as well as tips on safeguarding personal privacy. Contains links to other Web sites as a member of ConsumerNet, an online network of consumer organizations. Those links include the American Civil Liberties Union and *Privacy Journal*, plus links to legal resources and general consumer sites. Adult-oriented materials.

Name: Redefining Progress
Address: One Kearny Street, 4th Floor, San Francisco, CA 94108
Phone: (415) 781–1191
Fax: (415) 781–1198
Web address: www.rprogress.org
Web site: This group encourages use of the Genuine Progress Indicator (GPI) rather than gross domestic product (GDP) as an economic measurement. Includes curriculum materials on Footprints, which compares the ecological impact of 52 large nations and shows to what extent their consumption can be supported by their local ecological capacity. College students should note that job opportunities and internships are listed.

Name: The Simple Living Network
Address: P.O. Box 233, Trout Lake, WA 98650
Phone: (800) 318–5725
Customer service: (509) 395–2323
Web address: www.slnet.com/
Web site: A source for books, tapes, and other information about voluntary simplicity. Includes program called Web of Simplicity along with a step by step guide. Also offers support materials and a program to help users create their own path to simplicity.

Name: Tax Foundation
Address: 1250 H Street, NW, Suite 750, Washington, DC 20005
Phone: (202) 783–2760
Web address: www.taxfoundation.org
Web site: The Tax Foundation analyzes data from all levels of government; explores the effect of tax policy on businesses and individuals; and serves as

a national clearinghouse to help Americans better understand their tax system and the effects of tax policy. This organization announces the annual Tax Freedom Day, the number of days the average worker has to work just to meet his or her tax liability for the year. In 1999, this day was May 11. Offers information on its latest studies, plus general tax facts on its *Tax Bites* page. Annual publications include "Facts and Figures on Government Finance" and "A Taxpayer's Guide to Federal Spending." Material appropriate for older students and adults.

Name: United for a Fair Economy
Address: 37 Temple Place, 2nd Floor, Boston, MA 02111
Phone: (617) 423–2148
Fax: (617) 423–0191
Web address: www.stw.org
Web site: This national, independent, nonpartisan organization focuses on the disparity between wages and distribution of wealth in the United States. The site contains information about the group's educational efforts, including its Close the Wage Gap campaign. The group co-publishes *Too Much*, a quarterly membership newsletter. There is information about the group's Art for a Fair Economy, which uses theatrical performance to animate the struggle for economic justice. Geared for adults, but resources can be used by students.

Name: Worldwatch Institute
Address: 1776 Massachusetts Avenue, NW, Washington, DC 20036–1904
Phone: (202) 452–1999
Web address: www.worldwatch.org
Web site: The institute is a nonprofit public policy research organization dedicated to informing policymakers and the public about emerging global problems and trends and the complex links between the world economy and its environmental support system. The institute's outlook is global and focuses on issues from climate change to loss of biological diversity and population growth. Includes publications as well as a speaker's bureau. *See also* Northwest Environment Watch (NEW).

MAJOR NATIONAL CREDIT BUREAUS

Many lenders submit credit information on their loan holders to one of these three national credit bureaus. These are the same bureaus that lenders check with to see the credit history of potential borrowers. Under the Fair Credit Reporting Act, if you are rejected for a loan because of inaccurate information in a credit report, you have a right to get a free copy of that credit report and to have mistakes corrected. Catching and correcting any mistakes may have a positive effect on your credit score and could improve the chances that your loan will be approved.

What to do? Issuers that deny a person a credit card must supply the name, address, and telephone number of the credit bureau that produced negative in-

formation. You can contact the company within 60 days and receive a free copy
of the credit report.

Equifax
  PO Box 740241
  Atlanta, GA 30375–0241
  (800) 685–1111

Experian (formerly TRW)
  PO Box 949
  Allen, TX 75002
  (800) 682–7654

Trans Union
  PO Box 390
  Springfield, IL 19064
  (800) 888–4213

Appendix C: State Resources

STATE CONSUMER PROTECTION AND INSURANCE DIVISIONS

The following is a list of state consumer and insurance departments. Additionally, many larger counties and cities have their own consumer oversight agency, most often through the district attorney's office.

Alabama

Consumer Affairs Section
Office of the Attorney General
11 South Union Street
Montgomery, AL 36130
(334) 242–7334
Toll free in AL: (800) 392–5658
Fax: (334) 242–2433
Web site: e-pages.com/aag/cuspro.html
Department of Insurance
(334) 269–3550

Alaska

Consumer Protection Unit
Office of the Attorney General
1031 West 4th Avenue, Suite 200
Anchorage, Alaska 99501
(907) 269–5100
Fax: (907) 276–8554
Web site: www.law.state.ak.us

Arizona
Consumer Protection
Office of the Attorney General
1275 West Washington Street
Room 259
Phoenix, AZ 85007
(602) 542–3702
(602) 542–5763 (consumer information and complaints)
Toll free in AZ: (800) 352–8431
TDD: (602) 542–5002
Fax: (602) 542–4377
Department of Insurance
(602) 912–8400

Arkansas
Consumer Protection Division
Office of Attorney General
200 Catlett Prien
323 Center Street
Little Rock, AR 72201
(501) 682–2341
TDD toll free in AR: (800) 482–8982
TDD: (501) 682–2014
Web site: www.ag-state.ar.us
Department of Insurance
(501) 371–2600

California
California Department of Consumer Affairs
400 R Street, Suite 3000
Sacramento, CA 95814
(916) 445–4465
Toll free in CA: (800) 952–5210
TDD: (916) 322–1700
(510) 785–7554
Web site: caag.state.ca.us/piu
Department of Insurance
(916) 492–3500

Colorado
State Office
Consumer Protection Division
Office of Attorney General
1525 Sherman Street, 5th Floor
Denver, CO 80203–1760
(303) 866–5189

Toll free: (800) 332–2071
Fax: (303) 866–5691
Department of Regulatory Agencies,
Division of Insurance
(303) 894–7499

Connecticut
State Offices
Department of Consumer Protection
165 Capitol Avenue
Hartford, CT 06106
(860) 566–2534
Toll free in CT: (800) 842–2649
Fax: (860) 566–1531
Web site: www.state.ct.us/dcp/
Antitrust/Consumer Protection: www.cslnet.ctstateu.edu/attygenl
Department of Insurance
(860) 297–3800

Delaware
Consumer Protection Unit
Department of Justice
820 North French Street
Wilmington, DE 19801
(302) 577–8600
Fax: (302) 577–6499
Toll Free in DE: (800) 220–5424
Fraud and Consumer Protection Unit
Office of Attorney General
820 North French Street
Wilmington, DE 19801
(302) 577–8800
Toll free: (800) 220–5424
Fax: (302) 577–3090
Department of Insurance
(302) 739–4251

District of Columbia
Department of Consumer and Regulatory Affairs
614 H Street, NW, Room 1120
Washington, DC 20001
(202) 727–7120
TDD/TTY: (202) 727–7842
Fax: (202) 727–8073
Insurance Administration
(202) 727–8000 ext. 3007

Florida
Department of Agriculture and Consumer Services
Division of Consumer Services
407 South Calhoun Street
Mayo Building, 2nd Floor
Tallahassee, FL 32399–0800
Outside FL: (850) 488–2221
Toll free in FL: (800) 435–7352
Fax: (850) 487–4177
Web site: www.fl-ag.com
Department of Insurance
(904) 922–3100

Georgia
Governor's Office of Consumer Affairs
2 Martin Luther King, Jr. Drive, SE
Suite 356
Atlanta, GA 30334
(404) 656–3790
Toll free in GA (outside Atlanta area):
(800) 869–1123
Fax: (404) 651–9018
Department of Insurance
(404) 656–2056

Hawaii
Office of Consumer Protection
Department of Commerce and Consumer Affairs
235 S. Beretania Street (96813)
Room 801, P.O. Box 3767
Honolulu, HI 96812–3767
(808) 586–2636
Fax: (808) 586–2640
Commerce & Consumer Affairs Department, Insurance Division
(808) 586–2790

Idaho
Office of the Attorney General
Consumer Protection Unit
650 West State Street
Boise, ID 83720–0010
(208) 334–2424
Toll free in ID: (800) 432–3545
TDD/TTY: (208) 334–2424
Fax: (208) 334–2830
Web site: www.state.id.us/ag
Department of Insurance
(208) 334–4250

Illinois
Consumer Protection Division
Office of Attorney General
100 West Randolph
12th Floor
Chicago, IL 60601
(312) 814–3000
(or consumer hotline serving southern Illinois) (800) 243–0607
TDD: (312) 793–2852
Fax: (312) 814–2593
Department of Insurance
(217) 782–4515

Indiana
Consumer Protection Division
Office of Attorney General
Indiana Government Center South
402 West Washington Street, 5th Floor
Indianapolis, IN 46204
(317) 232–6330
Toll free in IN: (800) 382–5516
Fax: (317) 233–4393
E-mail: INATTGN@ATG.IN.US
Web site: www.al.org/hoosieradvocate
Department of Insurance and Planning
(317) 233–4448

Iowa
Assistant Attorney General
Consumer Protection Division
Office of the Attorney General
1300 East Walnut Street, 2nd Floor
Des Moines, IA 50319
(515) 281–5926
Fax: (515) 281–6771
E-mail: consumer@max.state.ia.us
Web site: www.state.ia.us/government/ag/consumer.html
Department of Commerce, Division of Insurance
(515) 281–5705

Kansas
Deputy Attorney General
Consumer Protection Division
Office of Attorney General
301 West 10th
Kansas Judicial Center
Topeka, KS 66612–1597

(913) 296–3751
Toll free in KS: (800) 432–2310
Fax: (913) 291–3699
Department of Insurance
(913) 296–7801 / (913) 296–3071

Kentucky
Consumer Protection Division
Office of the Attorney General
1024 Capital Center Drive
Frankfort, KY 40601–8204
(502) 696–5389
Toll free in KY: (888) 432–9257
Fax: (502) 573–8317
Web site: www.law.state.ky.us/cp/default.htm
E-mail: webmaster@mail.law.state.ky.us
Department of Insurance
(502) 564–6027 / (800) 595–6053

Louisiana
Consumer Protection Section
Office of the Attorney General
1 America Place
P.O. Box 94095
Baton Rouge, LA 70804–9095
(504) 342–9639
Toll free nationwide: (800) 351–4889
Fax: (504) 342–9637
Web site: www.laag.com
Department of Insurance
(504) 342–5900

Maine
Office of Consumer Credit Regulation
35 State House Station
Augusta, ME 04333–0035
(207) 624–8527
Toll free in ME: (800) 332–8529
Fax: (207) 582–7699
Public Protection Division
Office of Attorney General
6 State House Station
Augusta, ME 04333
(207) 626–8849
Bureau of Insurance
(207) 624–8475

Maryland
Consumer Protection Division
200 Saint Paul Place, 16th Floor
Baltimore, MD 21202–2021
(410) 528–8662 (consumer complaint hotline)
(410) 576–6550 (consumer information)
TDD: (410) 576–6372 (MD only)
Fax: (410) 576–6566 / (410) 576–7040
E-mail: consumer@oag.state.md.us
Web site: www.oag.state.md.us
Business Licensing & Consumer Service
Motor Vehicle Administration
6601 Ritchie Highway, N.E.
Glen Burnie, MD 21062
(410) 768–7248
Fax: (410) 768–7189
Insurance Administration
(410) 468–2000 / (800) 468–2000

Massachusetts
Office of the Attorney General
Consumer Protection and Antitrust Division
One Ashburton Place
Boston, MA 02108–1698
(617) 727–8400, The Consumer Hotline provides information and referral to local county and city government consumer offices that work in conjunction with the Department of the Attorney General
Fax: (617) 727–5765
Web site: www.magnet.state.ma.us/ag/ago.htm
Division of Insurance
(617) 521–7794 / (617) 521–7777

Michigan
Consumer Protection Division
Office of the Attorney General
P.O. Box 30212
Lansing, MI 48909
(517) 373–1140 (complaint information)
(517) 373–1110
Fax: (517) 335–1935
Bureau of Automotive Regulation
Michigan Department of State
Lansing, MI 48918–1200
(517) 373–4777
Toll free in MI: (800) 292–4204
Fax: (517) 373–0964

Department of Commerce, Insurance Bureau
(517) 373–9273

Minnesota
Director, Consumer Services Division
Minnesota Attorney General's Office
1400 NCL Tower
445 Minnesota Street
St. Paul, MN 55101
(612) 296–3353
Toll free: (800) 657–3787
TDD/TTY: (612) 297–7206;
TDD/TTY toll free: (800) 366–4812
Fax: (612) 282–5801
Web site: www.ag.state.mn.us/consumer
E-mail: consumer.ag@state.mn.us
Insurance Commission
(612) 296–7033

Mississippi
Consumer Protection Division
802 North State Street, 3rd Floor
P.O. Box 22947
Jackson, MS 39225–2947
(601) 359–4230
Toll free in MS: (800) 281–4418
Fax: (601) 359–4231
Web site: www.ago.state.ms.us/consprot.htm
Department of Insurance
(601) 359–3569

Missouri
Consumer Complaint Unit
Office of the Attorney General
P.O. Box 899
Jefferson City, MO 65102
(573) 751–3321
Toll free in MO: (800) 392–8222
TDD/TTY toll free in MO: (800) 729–8668
Fax: (314) 751–7948
Department of Insurance
(314) 751–4126

Montana
Consumer Affairs Unit
Department of Commerce
1424 Ninth Avenue

Box 200501
Helena, MT 59620–0501
(406) 444–4312
Fax: (406) 444–2903
Department of Insurance
(406) 444–2040

Nebraska
Assistant Attorney General
Department of Justice
2115 State Capitol
P.O. Box 98920
Lincoln, NE 68509
(402) 471–2682
Fax: (402) 471–3297
Department of Insurance
(402) 471–2201

Nevada
Commissioner of Consumer Affairs
Department of Business and Industry
1850 East Sahara, Suite 101
Las Vegas, NV 89104
(702) 486–7355
Toll free: (800) 326–5202
TDD: (702) 486–7901
Fax: (702) 486–7371
E-mail: consumer@govnail.state.nv.us
Web site: www.state.nv.us/fyiconsumer/
Division of Insurance
(702) 687–4270

New Hampshire
Consumer Protection/Antitrust Bureau
New Hampshire Attorney General's Office
33 Capitol Street
Concord, NH 03301–6397
(603) 271–3641
TDD toll free: (800) 735–2964
Fax: 603–271–2110
Web site: www.state.nh.us/oag/cpb.htm
Department of Insurance
(603) 271–2261

New Jersey
New Jersey Consumer Affairs Division
124 Halsey Street

Newark, NJ 07102
(973) 504–6200
Fax: (973) 648–3538
TDD: 973–504–6588
E-mail: askconsumeraffairs@oag.lps.state.nj.us
Web site: www.state.nj.us/lps/ca/home.htm
Department of Insurance
(609) 292–5363

New Mexico
Consumer Protection Division
Office of Attorney General
P.O. Drawer 1508
Santa Fe, NM 87504
(505) 827–6060
Toll free in NM: (800) 678–1508
Department of Insurance
(505) 827–4601

New York
Bureau of Consumer Frauds and Protection
Office of Attorney General
State Capitol
Albany, NY 12224
(518) 474–5481
Toll free in NY: (800) 771–7755
TDD toll free: (800) 788–9898
Fax: (518) 474–3618
Web site: www.oag.state.ny.us
New York State Consumer Protection Board
5 Empire State Plaza, Suite 2101
Albany, NY 12223–1556
(518) 474–8583
Toll free in NY: (800) 697–1220
Fax: (518) 474–2474
Web site: www.consumer.state.ny.us
Department of Insurance
(518) 474–6600 / (518) 474–4556

North Carolina
Special Deputy Attorney General
Consumer Protection Section
Office of Attorney General
P.O. Box 629
Raleigh, NC 27602
(919) 716–6000
Fax: (919) 716–6050

Web site: www.jus.state.nc.us/cpsmain/cpsmain.htm
Department of Insurance
(919) 733–7349 / (919) 733–7343

North Dakota
Attorney General
The State Capitol Building
600 East Boulevard Avenue
Bismarck, ND 58505–0040
(701) 328–2210
TDD:(701) 328–3409
Fax:(701) 328–2226
Web site: www.state.nd.us/ndag/cpat/cpat.htm
or for the Consumer Protection and Antitrust Division
www.state.nd.us/cpat/cpat.html
Department of Insurance
(701) 328–2440

Ohio
Consumer Protection Section
Office of the Attorney General
State Office Tower, 25th Floor
30 East Broad Street
Columbus, OH 43215–3428
(614) 466–4986 (complaints)
Toll free in OH: (800) 282–0515
TDD: (614) 466–1393
E-mail:consumer@ag.ohio.gov
Office of Consumers' Counsel
77 South High Street, 15th Floor
Columbus, OH 43266–0550
(614) 466–9605 (outside OH)
Toll free in OH: (877) PICKOCC (1742–5622)
E-mail: occ@occ.state.oh.us
Web site: www.state.oh.us/cons/
Department of Insurance
(614) 644–2658

Oklahoma
Department of Consumer Credit
4545 N. Lincoln Blvd., Suite 260
Oklahoma City, OK 73105
(405) 521–3653
Fax: (405) 521–6740
Office of Attorney General
Consumer Protection Unit
4545 N. Lincoln Blvd., Suite 260

Oklahoma City, OK 73105
(405) 521–2029 (consumer hotline)
Fax: (405) 528–1867
Web site: www.oag.state.ok.us
Department of Insurance
(405) 521–2828

Oregon
Financial Fraud Section
Department of Justice
1162 Court St. NE
Salem, OR 97310
(503) 378–4732
(503) 378–4320 (hotline)
(503) 229–5576 (in Portland only)
Fax: (503) 378–5017
E-mail: boj@state.or.us
Web site: www.doj.state.or.us/FinFraud/welcome3.htm
Department of Consumer and Business Services, Insurance Division
(503) 378–4271
Department of Insurance
(503) 521–2828/(800) 542–3104

Pennsylvania
Bureau of Consumer Protection
Office of Attorney General
Strawberry Square, 14th Floor
Harrisburg, PA 17120
(717) 787–9707
Toll free in PA: (800) 441–2555
Fax: (717) 787–1190
Web site: www.attorneygeneral.gov
E-mail: consumers@attorneygeneral.gov
Office of Consumer Advocate
Office of Attorney General
Forum Place, 5th Floor
555 Walnut Street
Harrisburg, PA 17101–1921
(717) 783–5048 (for utilities only)
Fax: (717) 783–7152
E-mail: paoca@ptd.net
Web site: www.oca.state.pa.us
Department of Insurance
(717) 787–5173

Rhode Island
Consumer Unit

Department of the Attorney General
72 Pine Street
Providence, RI 02903
(401) 274–4400
Toll free in RI: (800) 852–7776
TDD: (401) 453–0410
Fax: (401) 277–1331
Insurance Division
(401) 277–2223

South Carolina
Office of the Attorney General
P.O. Box 11549
Columbia, SC 29211
(803) 734–3970
Fax: (803) 734–3677
Web site: www.scattorneygeneral.org
Consumer Advocate
Department of Consumer Affairs
2801 Devine Street
P.O. Box 5757
Columbia, SC 29250–5757
(803) 734–9452
Toll free in SC: (800) 922–1594
Fax: (803) 734–9365
Web site: www.state.sc.us/consumer
Department of Insurance
(803) 737–6160

South Dakota
Director of Consumer Affairs
Office of the Attorney General
500 East Capitol
State Capitol Building
Pierre, SD 57501–5070
(605) 773–4400
Toll free in SD: (800) 300–1986
TDD: (605) 773–6585
Fax: (605) 773–7163
Department of Commerce and Regulation, Division of Insurance
(605) 773–4104

Tennessee
Division of Consumer Affairs
Fifth Floor
500 James Robertson Parkway
Nashville, TN 37243–0600

(615) 741–4737
Toll free in TN: (800) 342–8385
Fax: (615) 532–4994
Web site: www.state.tn.us/consumer
Division of Consumer Protection
Office of Attorney General
425 Fifth Ave N., 2nd Floor
Nashville, TN 37243–0491
(615) 741–1671
Fax: (615) 532–2910
Department of Commerce and Insurance
(615) 741–2241

Texas
Consumer Protection Division
Office of Attorney General
P.O. Box 12548
Austin, TX 78711–2548
(512) 463–2070
Fax: (512) 463–8301
Department of Insurance
(512) 463–6464

Utah
Division of Consumer Protection
Department of Commerce
160 East 300 South
Box 146704
Salt Lake City, UT 84114–6704
(801) 530–6601
Toll free in UT: (800) 721–7233
Fax: (801) 530–6001
Department of Insurance, Consumer Service Division
(801) 538–3805 / (800) 439–3805 within the state
http://www.ins-Departmentstate.ut.us/welcome.htm

Vermont
Consumer Assistance Program
104 Morrill Hall
University of Vermont
Burlington, VT 05405
(802) 656–3183
Toll free in VT: (800) 649–2424
Public Protection Division
Office of the Attorney General
109 State Street
Montpelier, VT 05609–1001

(802) 828–5507
Fax: (802) 828–2154
Web site: www.state.vt.us/atg
Department of Banking, Insurance and Securities
(802) 828–3301

Virginia
Antitrust and Consumer Litigation Section
Office of the Attorney General
900 East Main Street
Richmond, VA 23219
(804) 786–2116
(804) 371–2086 / 2087
Office of Consumer Affairs
Department of Agriculture and Consumer Services
Washington Building, Suite 100
P.O. Box 1163
Richmond, VA 23219
(804) 786–2042
Toll free in VA: (800) 552–9963
TDD: (804) 371–6344
Fax: (804) 371–7479
State Corporation Commission, Bureau of Insurance
(804) 371–9694 / (800) 371–9694

Washington
Office of the Attorney General
Consumer Resource Center
900 Fourth Avenue, Suite 2000
Seattle, WA 98164–1012
(206) 464–6684
Office of the Attorney General, Consumer Protection Division
Toll free in Washington: (800) 551–4636 (Consumer Resource Centers)
Toll free in Washington: (800) 692–5082 (ConsumerLine tapes)
Toll free in Washington: (800) 541–8898 (Lemon Law)
Toll free in Washington: (800) 276–9883 (TDD)
Web site: www.wa.gov/ago
Insurance Department
(360) 753–7301

West Virginia
Deputy Attorney General
Consumer Protection Division
Office of the Attorney General
812 Quarrier Street, 6th Floor
P.O. Box 1789
Charleston, WV 25326–1789

(304) 558–8986
Toll free in WV: (800) 368–8808
Fax: (304) 558–0184
Department of Insurance
(304) 558–3386 / (304) 558–3394

Wisconsin
Division of Trade and Consumer Protection
Department of Agriculture, Trade and Consumer Protection
2811 Agriculture Dr., P.O. Box 8911
Madison, WI 53708
(608) 224–4976
Toll free in WI: (800) 422–7128
Fax: 608–224–4939
Insurance Commission
(608) 224–0102

Wyoming
Assistant Attorney General
Office of the Attorney General
123 State Capitol Building
Cheyenne, WY 82002
(307) 777–7874
Fax: (307) 777–6869
Department of Insurance
(307) 777–7401

STATE COUNCILS ON ECONOMIC EDUCATION

The following is a list of councils on economic education. Many states have several university-based councils. To see the full listing, visit the National Council on Economic Education Web site. http://www.economicsamerica.org/directory/brings you to the additional listings of state councils.

Alabama
Alabama Council on Economic Education
University of Alabama
Culverhouse College of Commerce & Bus. Admin.
P.O. Box 870321, 127 Bidgood Hall
Tuscaloosa, AL 35487–0321
Telephone: (205) 348–5794
Fax: (205) 348–5768
Web site: http://bos.business.uab.edu/acee

Alaska
Alaska Council on Economic Education
University of Alaska, Anchorage

3211 Providence Drive
Anchorage, AK 99508
Telephone: (907) 786–1901
Fax: (907) 786–4059

Arizona
Arizona Council on Economic Education
7975 North Hayden Road, Suite B-128
Scottsdale, AZ 85258
Telephone: (480) 368–8020
Fax: (480) 368–8011
E-mail: EconZone@aol.com

Arkansas
Arkansas Council on Economic Education
#4 State Capitol Mall, Room 404A
Little Rock, AR 72201
Mailing Address:
PO Box 3447
Little Rock, AR 72203–3447
Telephone: (501) 682–4230
Fax: (501) 682–4987

California
Economics America of California
California State University San Bernardino
5500 University Parkway
San Bernardino, CA 92407
Telephone: (909) 880–5553
Fax: (909) 880–7025

Colorado
Colorado Council on Economic Education
225 E. 16th Avenue
Suite 740
Denver, CO 80203
Telephone: (303) 832–8480
Fax: (303) 832–8474
E-mail: ccee@csn.net

Connecticut
Connecticut Council on Economic Education
Assistant Dean
Division of Extended and Continuing Education
U14E Bishop Center
Storrs, CT 06269–4014

Telephone: (860) 486–1059
Fax: (860) 486–5221

Delaware

Delaware Council on Economic Education
University of Delaware
103 MBNA America Hall
Newark, DE 19716
Telephone: (302) 831–2559
Fax: (302) 831–6659

Florida

Florida Council on Economic Education
1211 N. Westshore Blvd., Suite 300
Tampa, FL 33607–4615
Telephone: (813) 289–8489
Fax: (813) 286–7090
Web site: http://www.fcee.org

Georgia

Georgia Council on Economic Education
Georgia State University
35 Broad Street, Room 425
Atlanta, GA 30303
Or: P.O. Box 1619
Atlanta, GA 30301–1619
Telephone: (404) 651–3280
Fax: (404) 651–4306
Web site: http://www.gcedunet.peachnet.edu/talk/org/edu/gcee

Hawaii

Hawaii Council on Economic Education
University of Hawaii–Manoa
Porteus Hall 540
2424 Maile Way
Honolulu, HI 96822
Telephone: (808) 956–7009
Fax: (808) 956–9564
Web site: http://www2.hawaii.edu/hcee/

Idaho

Idaho Council on Economic Education
Boise State University
E-228
1910 University Drive
Boise, ID 83725–1640
Telephone: (208) 385–1360

Fax: (208) 385–4006
E-mail: jrucker@cobfac.idbsu.edu

Illinois
Illinois Council on Economic Education
Northern Illinois University
DeKalb, IL 60115
Telephone: (815) 753–0356
Fax: (815) 753–0355
Web site: http://www.economicsamerica.org/econed

Indiana
Indiana Council for Economic Education
Purdue University
1310 KCTR 221
West Lafayette, IN 47907–1310
Telephone: (765) 494–8544
Fax: (765) 496–1505
Web site: http://www.mgmt.purdue.edu/icee

Iowa
Iowa Council on Economic Education
Iowa State University
Dept. of Economics
260 Heady Hall
Ames, IA 50011–1070
Telephone: (515) 294–4038
Fax: (515) 294–0221
E-mail: talex@iastate.edu

Kansas
Kansas Council on Economic Education
Wichita State University
Devlin Hall, Box 147
Wichita, KS 67260–0147
Telephone: (316) 978–5183
Fax: (316) 978–3687
Web site: http://www.kcee.twsu.edu

Kentucky
Kentucky Council on Economic Education
University of Louisville
Dept. of Secondary Education
Louisville, KY 40292
Telephone: (502) 852–0592
Fax: (502) 852–0726
Web site: http://www.econ.org

Louisiana
Louisiana State University
201 Lakeshore House
Baton Rouge, LA 70803
Louisiana Council for Economic Education
Telephone: (504) 388–8611
Fax: (504) 388–3860
Web site: http://www.economicsamerica.org/La/

Maine
Maine Council on Economic Education
P.O. Box 9715–159
Portland, ME 04104
or
120 Bedford St., 1st Floor
Portland, ME 04104
Telephone: (207) 780–5926
Fax: (207) 780–5282
E-mail: econmaine@aol.com
Web site: http://www.economicsamerica.org/maine/index.html

Maryland
Council on Economic Education Council in Maryland
Towson University
8000 York Road
Towson, MD 21252–0001
Telephone: (410) 830–2137
Fax: (410) 830–3796

Massachusetts
Economics Education Council of Massachusetts
Bridgewater State College
Bridgewater, MA 02325
Telephone: (508) 279–6125

Michigan
Economics America of Michigan
37000 Grand River Drive, Suite 365
Farmington Hills, MI 48335
Telephone: (248) 888–1075
Fax: (248) 888–1076

Minnesota
Minnesota Council on Economic Education
University of Minnesota
Dept. of Applied Economics
1994 Buford Ave.

St. Paul, MN 55108–6040
Telephone: (612) 625–5733
Fax: (612) 625–6245
Web address: http://mcee.coafes.umn.edu/

Mississippi
Mississippi Council on Economic Education
University of Mississippi
School of Business Administration
212 Conner Hall
Oxford, MS 38677
State Council presently restructuring. For information, please contact National
Office.

Gatlin Center for Economic Education
Telephone: (601) 232–5835
Fax: (601) 232–5821

Missouri
Missouri Council on Economic Education
Room 104H, Geosciences Bldg.
5100 Rockhill Road
Kansas City, MO 64110–2499
Telephone: (816) 235–2654 or 2655
Fax: (816) 235–2651
E-mail: mengels@umkc.edu

Montana
Montana Council on Economic Education
Montana State University
College of Business
Bozeman, MT 59717
Telephone: (406) 994–4874
Fax: (406) 994–6206
E-mail: zdb7017@montana.edu

Nebraska
Nebraska Council on Economic Education
University of Nebraska–Lincoln
College of Business Admin.
Lincoln, NE 68588–0404
Telephone: (402) 472–2333
Fax: (402) 472–9700
E-mail: ratwood@unl.edu

Nevada
Nevada Council for Economic Education

P.O. Box 71042
Las Vegas, NV 89170–1042
Telephone: (702) 895–3608
Fax: (702) 895–3632

New Hampshire
New Hampshire Council on Economic Education
State Council presently restructuring. For information, contact the National
Office.

New Jersey
New Jersey Council on Economic Education
Kean College
East Campus—Room 219
Union, NJ 07083
Telephone: (908) 629–7256 / (908) 527–2238

New Mexico
New Mexico Council on Economic Education
Center for Entrepreneurship and Economic Development
1009 Bradbury Drive S.E.
Albuquerque, NM 87106
Telephone: (505) 272–7677
Fax: (505) 842–8018

New York
New York State Council on Economic Education
State University of New York College at Purchase
735 Anderson Hill Road
Purchase, NY 10577
Telephone: (914) 251–6664
Fax: (914) 251–6629
Web site: http://www.purchase.edu/departments/econed/nyscee

North Carolina
North Carolina Council on Economic Education
P.O. Box 10289
Greensboro, NC 27404–0289
or:
University of North Carolina at Greensboro
301-N Bryan School of Bus. & Econ.
1000 Spring Garden Street
Greensboro, NC 27412–5001
Telephone: (336) 334–5056 / (919) 839–8052
Fax: (336) 334–4272

North Dakota
North Dakota Council on Economic Education
Minot State University
500 University Avenue, West
Minot, ND 58707
Telephone: (701) 858–3135
Fax: (701) 839–6933

Ohio
Ohio Council on Economic Education
The Ohio State University
1900 Kenny Road
Columbus, OH 43210
Telephone: (614) 292–1178
Fax: (614) 688–4667

Oklahoma
Oklahoma Council on Economic Education
University of Central Oklahoma
100 N. University
Department of Economics
Edmond, OK 73034
Telephone: (405) 974–5627
Fax: (405) 974–3853

Oregon
Oregon Council on Economic Education
Portland State University
PO Box D
Portland, OR 97439
Telephone: (503) 725–3169
Fax: (541) 997–8507

Pennsylvania
Pennsylvania Partnership for Economic Education
417 Walnut Street
Harrisburg, PA
Telephone: (717) 232–5581
Fax: (717) 232–5908
Web site: www.economicsamerica.org/pa/

Rhode Island
Rhode Island Council on Economic Education
Rhode Island College
Providence, RI 02908
Telephone: (401) 456–8037

Fax: (401) 456–8851
Web site: http://www.ric.edu/eced/

South Carolina
South Carolina Council on Economic Education
University of South Carolina
College of Bus. Adm., Rm. 651
1705 College Street
Columbia, SC 29208
Additional address:
PO Box 11789, Columbia, SC 29211
Telephone: (803) 777–8676 or
(888) 861–6345
Fax: (803) 777–8328

South Dakota
South Dakota Council on Economic Education
University of South Dakota
Department of Economics
210 Patterson Hall, 414 E. Clark
Vermillion, SD 57069
Telephone: (605) 677–5455

Tennessee
Tennessee Center for Economic Education
The University of Tennessee at Chattanooga
Suite 313 Fletcher Hall, 615 McCallie Ave.
Chattanooga, TN 37403–2598
Telephone: (615) 755–4118
Fax: (615) 755–5218

Texas
Texas Council on Economic Education
PO Box 56187
Houston, TX 77256
Telephone: (713) 655–1650
Fax: (713) 655–1655

Utah
Utah Council on Economic Education
Telephone: (801) 538–7859
Fax: (801) 538–7868

Vermont
Vermont State Council presently restructuring. For information, please contact
National Office.

Virginia
Virginia Council on Economic Education
Virginia Commonwealth University
School of Business Building
1015 Floyd Ave., PO Box 844000
Richmond, VA 23284–4000
Web site: www.vcu.edu/busweb/vcee/
Telephone: (804) 828–1627
Fax: (804) 828–7215

Washington
Washington Council on Economic Education
1305 Fourth Avenue
Suite 1000
Seattle, WA 98101–2401
Telephone: (206) 622–0965
Fax: (206) 622–6525

West Virginia
West Virginia Council on Economic Education
Marshall University
213 Harris Hall
Huntington, WV 25755
Telephone: (304) 696–2958
Fax: (304) 696–6565

Wisconsin
Wisconsin Council on Economic Education
P.O. Box 2005
Milwaukee, WI 53201
For shipping: 161 West Wisconsin Ave.
Suite 3150
Milwaukee, WI 53203
Telephone: (414) 221–9400
Web site: http://www.uwsp.edu/WisEcon.

Wyoming
Wyoming Council on Economic Education
3718 Dover Road
Cheyenne, WY 82001
Telephone: (307) 632–8388

Appendix D: School Curricula on Financial Management/ Lesson Plans and Worksheets

This appendix contains a compilation of lesson plans available from a variety of sources. Many of these lesson plans are available on the Internet, but the following compilation covers many of the major teaching points and may serve to inspire teachers, parents, and students themselves to study the issues of money management in greater depth. The lesson plans in this section were developed by Kim Sigler for use in BankUSA, described in Chapter 2.

BANK USA GUIDELINE SHEET

(Everything you need to know about Bank USA on one sheet)

1. Each Monday will be payday. You will receive wages for the *previous* week's attendance. You will earn $10 each day with 2 days of sick pay each month. Payday activities will take place in your homeroom class during the USA period (2nd period).

2. All checks/deposits will be recorded on a transaction sheet. This guideline sheet and all transaction sheets will be kept in the Bank section of your math notebook.

3. To receive a full day's pay you must be at school by the USA period (2nd period). This policy makes it easier for your homeroom teacher to keep track of your paycheck.

4. You will pay $15 each week to USA Properties for the use of your desk/ table and locker.

5. You will pay $10 each week to UPU (USA Power and Utilities) for use of electricity and water.

6. You may earn $20 for the A honor roll or $10 for the A/B honor roll at the conclusion of the six weeks. This payment may come to you in check or cash form on the next payday following report cards.

7. Each payday will also feature bonus checks/cash awards for exceptional work by USA students for class/homework efforts, responsible choices or respectful behavior shown in class or on campus. You may keep the cash or deposit it into your account using a Bank USA deposit ticket.

8. The last Friday of each month will be USA Mart. This will be held 2nd period and allows students to spend some or all of their money on merchandise in the store.

9. If you report to class without necessary supplies, you will purchase a pencil for $5 or three sheets of notebook paper for $5 from the teacher. You must write a check to the teacher and she will forward it to your homeroom teacher.

10. Your checks/deposit tickets will be kept on file with your homeroom teacher and may be checked out to verify your account balance. Your account will be balanced each Monday morning.

11. Some team activities may require an admission ticket for entrance. Prices and dates will be announced in advance so you may plan for upcoming activities. Event tickets will be purchased prior to the team activity.

12. If you become bankrupt, you are still responsible for paying all bills. Teachers can assign extra jobs in the classroom for extra pay, but they will not come to you if your account is in trouble. It is your responsibility to plan ahead and ask for such class jobs to pay for your bills each Monday. If you are unable to pay your rent and utility bills, the amounts will be increased by $5 for a late fee.

The End of USA Inc.: A Company Report

Company Name:_____

Product:_____

Assets:

Current company balance (from Getting Ready sheet)   _____

Earnings from USA Market Day   +_____

Total assets: _____

Expenses:

Inventory loss (surplus items × price per item)   _____

Sales tax on supply purchases from USA Mart (4.5% ×
total purchases from Getting Ready sheet)   +_____

Total expenses: _____

Account Balance:

Total Assets: _____

Total Expenses   −_____

Account balance: _____

Account balance_____ × Income tax_____   =_____

Income tax schedule:

Less than $100	5%	$301–$400	9%
$101–$200	7%	$401–$500	11%
$201–$300	8%	more than $500	14%

Net Income:

Account balance_____ − Income tax_____   =_____*

Corporations:

Net income_____divided by number of stocks sold_____(From Getting Ready sheet) = _____dividend earnings p/share

Name	Profit
_____	_____
_____	_____
_____	_____
_____	_____
_____	_____

*Be sure to write a dividend check to each stockholder and give to the teacher for distribution.

Getting Ready for USA Market Day

Company Summary:

Current balance:_____

    (Checked by teacher)
    Total purchases from

USA Mart for supplies:_____

    (Checked by teacher)
    Number of stocks sold:_____
    Total inventory:_____

    Expected earnings from Market Day:_____
    (If all inventory items sell)

Has your company

    Created a sign for your table at USA Market Day?
    Labeled all prices clearly on each item or signs for the table?
    Arranged a schedule for selling times among company members?

    Arranged a schedule for buying times among company members?

        2:00–2:10 Set up
        2:10–2:15 Browsing time I
        2:15–2:20 Browsing time II
        2:20–2:28 Buying time I

2:29–2:37 Buying time II
2:37–2:45 Clean up; Complete Money Report
2:45 Return to homeroom

Arranged for a cleanup procedure? A bag for unsold merchandise? Discarded signs or trash accumulated by your company?

Designated one company member to complete Money Report?

Designated one company member to be responsible for company earnings until Monday for deposit?

Raw Materials List for USA Inc.

The following raw materials may be purchased from USA Mart for the listed prices. Plan your purchases carefully. Remember, *No refunds!* All receipts must be hole-punched and kept in the company notebook.

White letter size paper	.50 per sheet
Colored letter size paper	.75 per sheet
Construction paper	1.00 per sheet
Legal size construction paper	1.50 per sheet
Manila folder	.75**
Colored folder	1.50
Craft sticks	1.00 for 2
Pipe cleaners	.20 each
Drinking straws	1.00 for 3
Colored drinking straws	1.50 for 2
Foil stars	.50 for 10
String	1.00 for 6 inches
Yarn	.50 for 6 inches
Eyes	3.00 for 4
Scotch tape	.50 for 3 inches
Masking tape	.50 for 3 inches
Paper clips (small)	1.00 for 10
Paper clips (large)	1.00 for 5
Glue stick (one time rental)	5.00
Clothes pins	1.00 for 3
Scissors (one time rental)	1.00 pair

**Each company needs a manila folder for collecting homework and company related materials. You may purchase one here or supply your own.

You may request items for USA Mart if they are important for production. You can supply the items and then purchase them from USA Mart. Outside materials are not allowed.

Each company may want to bring a large grocery bag to store raw materials until the next production day. The bag should be clearly labeled with the company name in marker and stored on the shelves next to the closet. USA Inc. is not responsible for lost items and will not replace misplaced items. Replacements must be purchased from USA Mart.

Welcome to USA Inc.

You are about to become your own company! You will create, produce and sell a product designed by your company. It is very important that you carefully follow all requirements to ensure a great team activity and the success of your company. These rules must be followed:

1. Each company may have no more than 5 members.

2. Each company will start with $200 in their company account with the option of expanding their individual members' personal accounts. These deposits may be made only on the team payday!!

3. Each company has the option of selling stock to increase capital. A company may have no more than 200 shares of stock and must retain 100 shares among its own members. The decision to incorporate must be made only on paydays if the company chooses not to begin selling stock on the first Stock Exchange Day.

4. You may purchase from any company on the team with your personal accounts on the designated Stock Exchange periods. If a company or individual wishes to sell stock, they must register their sale prior to the Stock Exchange Day. Only registered stock will be sold on this day.

5. Your company may borrow money from Bank USA at these interest rates:

$100–$300	20% interest
$301–$500	15% interest
$501–$800	10% interest
$801–above	10% interest

Note: All loans must be paid in full on December 15th.

6. You may use only materials from USA Mart for the creation of your product. If you need to use items that are not available, you may supply the items (upon approval) and then purchase them from USA Mart for your company's use only. Any company found violating this policy will be fined $250.

7. You must apply for a business license. Cost: $20.

8. You may apply for a patent to protect your product. Cost: $25.

9. You may apply for a trademark for your product. Cost: $20.

10. All companies will produce a marketing plan for their product. You must select one of the following:

Television commercial	$75
Billboard	$50
Radio	$50

Note: Your company may select more than one marketing technique if the company funds allow it.

11. Each company will keep a 3-ring notebook of all transactions, receipts, approved documents and other company paperwork. This notebook (on sale at USA Mart) *must* stay in the classroom in the appropriate color box with the company name clearly labeled. The team notebook should not leave Tyler-3 for *any* reason.

12. Companies will submit all paperwork (official/homework) in a company folder (available at USA Mart). No papers will be accepted if they are not in this folder. (This helps keep the massive amounts of paper needed to run this organization at a minimum!)

Good luck manufacturing your product!! Class days will alternate with production days, so assignments will need to be completed at home. Any company member not completing assignments to the utmost of his/her ability will be charged $10 from the company's account and will complete the assignment in class, thereby missing a production day of the product.

Your individual needs must be set aside; you are now a member of a company. Think about how your actions will impact the success of your company!

Happy Manufacturing!!!

Paperwork needed in company notebook (must be present at all times!):

1. "Welcome to USA Inc." sheet
2. Raw Materials list
3.
4.
5.
6.
7.
8.
9.
10.

Other company reminders:

SUPPLY AND DEMAND

This lesson plan originated with Columbia Education Center, Portland, OR.

Description

This lesson allows for personal involvement in the concept of supply and demand, which helps the students see how it relates to their everyday life.

Objectives

Students will be able to:
1. Define the terms supply and demand.
2. Identify what happens when demand exceeds supply.
3. Identify what happens when supply exceeds demand.
4. Explain how supply and demand affect choices such as careers, types of cars made, etc.
5. Give recent examples of instances where demand exceeded supply and the results.
6. Explain how economic stability or affluence affects supply and demand.

Materials

Teacher materials: tokens, prize for each student in class (it can be something as simple as chocolate kisses). Student materials: pencil, three index cards.

Procedure

1. Students will be given a box of tokens with at least two different colors in it and asked to select any number of them from one to a handful.
2. Place a value on the tokens. (Make certain this is done *after* students have already selected their tokens.)
3. Pull out an object students would desire to own and let the students know that they will receive an "A" on this lesson only if they own this selected item, of which you happen to have *exactly* one. You will announce the bidding to be open at 10, and they may use their tokens to purchase the item.
4. Continue auction until a student has paid a high price for this item and received it. Then pull out a large supply of the very same item just sold while announcing that you do just happen to have a few more of these items and you're willing to open the bidding at 1. *Wait and watch reaction!*
5. Write "supply" and "demand" on board. Ask the individual who bought the overpriced item to define what these terms mean to him in light of the experience he just had, explain why he was motivated to pay such a high price for it, and let us know if he would have paid so much had he known there were enough items to go around.
6. Guide students in a discussion which covers all objectives. (I found that an effective lead-in to objective #6 is to ask the following: "What if these tokens represented money and this was all the money you had available for two months?")

Tying It All Together

1. Ask students to think of three items in their desks and to secretly set a price for each one of them on an index card which is folded so that it can stand upright on the desk.
2. Instruct students to then take out the items and place them by the appropriate "price tag" on their desks.

3. Invite students to go "shopping" and check out all the prices in the "store."

4. Lead the students in the discussion which will naturally follow with questions such as: "Now that you know how other merchants priced their items, how will it affect your pricing of the same items?" "Were there some items that would be in high demand because of their low supply? How might that affect pricing?"

5. Students may want to stock their "shelves" differently after doing some comparison shopping and seeing the availability of certain items. You may then choose to give them another opportunity to price three items of their choice and discuss their changes and why they were made.

CONSUMER BORROWING AND SAVING

This lesson plan was developed by Chris E. Parill.
Grade Level/Subject: 11–12, economics

Overview

The use of credit has long been a part of the American economy; it fuels the nation's economic growth. Using credit to buy consumer goods benefits the economy by stimulating production. Increased production creates more jobs, and lenders profit by charging interest.

The overuse of credit, however, hurts the individual and the national economy. Savings are necessary if the economy is to grow. Too much consumer credit puts a drain on personal savings. Banks use these savings to finance loans to business and agriculture.

Many economists, business people, and private citizens believe that Americans are using too much credit. Total personal debt in the United States has doubled since 1975. In 1982, the amount of debt per person was calculated at more than $7,000. At the same time, many people who once considered themselves well off were filing for bankruptcy. Personal bankruptcies rose from 224,354 in 1975 to 449,389 in 1982 to over 850,000 in 1990.

Purpose

To give students the needed background in the positive and negative aspects of credit, its impact upon individuals and the nation, and practical knowledge and understanding of the wise use of credit.

Objectives

This unit emphasizes the following concepts:

1. The opportunity cost of using credit is a reduction of future spending power.

2. The opportunity cost of saving is the reduction of current spending power,

which means the loss of the "best" alternative for which you could use the money.

Resources/Materials

economics book—will have a section explaining the introductory concepts

magazines—*Consumer Lifestyles* often has articles and activities related to the use/misuse of credit and is geared toward high school students; *Money* magazine; *Fortune*

newspaper—often has stories related to consumer rights

credit card applications—have several kinds available for students to fill out

a credit report—to discuss what's on one

loan applications—student loans, car loans, home loans

calculators

guest speaker—banks will usually provide someone to come in and talk about credit with students. How to apply, what loan officers look for before giving credit, what are some alternative ways of establishing credit.

Activities and Procedures

1. Students should read about the use of credit and the many types of credit available, reasons for borrowing, when to pay cash, when to use credit, the costs associated with credit, and sources of loans/credit.

2. Compare making a credit purchase and taking out a loan.

3. Contrast the advantages and disadvantages of repaying a loan over a longer period of time.

4. Identify two reasons people use credit.

5. Explain how borrowing or using credit is basically a question of comparing costs and benefits.

6. Contrast the major sources of loans (student loans for college should also be included).

7. Compare and contrast the different kinds of charge accounts.

8. Describe the costs of using credit cards.

9. Be able to fill out credit applications and know by what criteria applicants are judged as to whether they will receive a credit card.

10. Explain the importance of knowing annual percentage rates and the various methods used to calculate finance charges.

11. Determine the purposes of regulations governing the credit industry. (What happens when you are denied credit due to felonious credit history.)

12. Typical exercises include a group working on a specific topic and presenting it to the class (no lectures allowed); students participating in role-playing various aspects of the credit process; asking for firsthand information from students who have used credit; having students interview other teachers, parents,

older friends/family who have credit; having students bring in articles from the newspaper about credit and its effect on the economy.

Tying It All Together

Students will have been exposed to current economic conditions relating to credit and how it affects the individual, the family, the city in which they live, the section of the country where they live, the nation, and the world.

A culminating activity that I have used is to break students into groups of three or four. They must use their understanding of credit to state how they view credit, how this unit has changed their view of credit, if it has, or why it has not changed anything, if that is the case. Give them a card with a possible scenario on it, or ask the students to come up with possible scenarios where the credit choice they have made might not be the best answer and how they would handle the given situation. Example:

Student A: "After hearing how bad the credit situation is in this country, I don't think I want to use credit. I'll just save my money until I can buy whatever it is that I want."

Student X: "So you are saying that you won't ever get a credit card? How are you ever going to establish a credit history to buy a house or a new car?"

Student A: "I'll save up for the car and can always rent a place to live."

Student X: "Oh right. You're gonna get married, have three kids and be able to save enough to buy a nice car for your family or a nice house."

Student Y: "So, what are your alternatives, A? Is credit always bad?"

Other possible situations:

They have their own business and know that if they expand, they will make more money. First they need to have capital.

They are away at school and their car breaks down in some small town. All they have is the $50 in their pocket and another $125 in the bank.

They need to buy books at school and their student loan has not come in yet.

I also like to bring up the idea of the 900 phone numbers which guarantee people a "gold" card. What are the different scams associated with these types of gimmicks? How can one be sure that the card offered is a legitimate credit card? What are the real costs involved?

How credit promotes economic growth

1. Credit increases private sector demand.
2. Businesses increase production to meet new demand.
3. Businesses increase R&D to improve competitiveness.
4. Businesses expand.

5. New businesses form to compete for expanded markets.

6. Businesses hire workers for new plants, which creates new demand.

7. Return to number 1.

BUY A CAR

The following lesson plan was developed by Karlys Wells.
Grade Level: 9–12

Description

A project requiring research, critical thinking, and complex decision-making about an expensive consumer item—a car.

Question

What general factors enter into a decision about buying a vehicle? How can resources and a decision grid be used to make choices about a specific set of vehicles?

Action

Research phase

1. With the class, brainstorm all the factors to consider when buying a car. Divide the ideas into logical categories—for example, body styles, frequency of repair, safety rating, condition, and fuel efficiency.

2. Assign individual students or teams to research each category. Internet sites to suggest:

http://www.webfoot.com/cgi-bin/loan.pl

http://edmunds.com

http://www.kbb.com

http://www.consumereports.com

Decision-making phase

1. Students create a decision grid on a spreadsheet. The spreadsheet will list possible vehicle choices vertically along the left side. Criteria to apply to choosing the vehicle are listed horizontally along the top.

2. Students search newspaper ads for new or used cars that might meet their criteria and select three or four. These vehicles are listed along the left side of the decision grid.

3. Then each vehicle is compared to the criteria that were selected for the horizontal axis of the grid. For example, students might use low mileage, pow-

erful motor, and fuel-efficient. In the grid they record pluses or minuses according to their rating of the vehicle.

4. Students consult with each other in the area of their expertise (which was developed during the research phase).

Sharing phase

Each student writes a summary of his or her research findings and how they were used in the comparison of actual cars.

Tools: Internet, newspaper, spreadsheet, and desktop publisher

Analysis: Students will justify their choice of vehicle to their classmates, citing how well the vehicle meets the criteria selected and how they used the knowledge gained from their consultation with a classmate "expert."

Publication: Students create a collaborative list of buying principles using word processing or desktop publishing to share with each other and to be placed in the library for other students to take. A cooperative car sales business might allow the list to be placed in its dealership.

MICRO ECONOMICS: PERSONAL BUDGETING

This plan was also developed by Chris E. Parrill.

Grade Level: Appropriate for grades 9–12.

Description

How many people can do their own income tax? Know about life, health, or property insurance? Wills? How many shop wisely for an automobile? What about raising children? Adoption? Infertility? How many people compare interest rates? Is it better, financially, to withdraw money from your savings account to pay for a large purchase, or should you charge it? How do you figure compound interest? All these questions and more are discussed in a class entitled "Modern Problems."

Goal

The purpose of the class is to show students that life in the "real world" away from the secure confines of home is drastically different. Decisions must be made with your spouse or, if you're single, by yourself. The outlook changes when the money comes out of your pocket and not someone else's.

Objectives

Students will be able to make their own "real world" decisions based on information presented by expert lecturers from the insurance, banking, law, real estate, and tax professions.

Materials

Teacher creativity.

Procedures

1. Invite experts to the classroom and discuss the importance of their fields and how young adults can use them. Topics will include catastrophic insurance, bankruptcy, and income tax forms.
2. The students are "married," with children, jobs, bills, and a weekly budget. The budget is due every week. The couple must pay their bills and present a signed grocery receipt. Single people are single parents. They have the same responsibilities and assignments as the "married" couples.

Once a week each couple and each single parent draws a paper from a large container. This paper could represent a bill, money received, or even pregnancy. The money that comes in or has to be spent must be shown in the weekly budget.

The budget must show a savings account that earns compound interest (that the student must compute weekly).

Income tax statements are due April 15, and a check must accompany the form if money is owed. If there is a refund, it cannot be added to the budget for six weeks.

All single parents and married couples must take out a loan ($1,000) at 12% simple interest.

To make it more authentic, the students must carry dolls to represent their children while at school. If they don't have the child they must pay for babysitting. This teaches them responsibility. If they neglect or forget their "children," "Social Services" will take them away.

3. Write a reaction paper about the above activity. This gives the students insight into what has happened to them over the past several months.

Tying It All Together

The ongoing activity must be kept organized, and students are encouraged to suggest topics for discussion, which continues through the activity segment. It is hoped that this activity will make the students' step into the "real world" somewhat easier by providing them with answers to their questions, having experts explain various facets of life, and giving them hands-on experience with life's little surprises.

HOW WOULD YOU SPEND A MILLION DOLLARS?

This lesson plan was developed at River Oaks Baptist School in Houston, Texas.

Purpose

To encourage students in grades 5 and up to learn about the Internet while planning and organizing a theme under which to spend one million dollars.

Materials

A computer with Internet and World Wide Web (WWW) access and word processing and spreadsheet software.

Prior Knowledge

Students should know how to use a Windows graphical interface, be able to create formulas in a spreadsheet, and know how to use a word processing application. (The project can be done without the use of word processing and spreadsheet software if Internet use only is desired.)

Description

Students will decide on a theme in which they will try to spend one million dollars. All expenses must be related to the theme. They may not just randomly make purchases. If they can creatively incorporate them into their theme, great!

They will use the Internet and the WWW to research prices on items required by their theme. All expenditures must be accounted for. For example, if a student chooses to hire a limousine to take friends on a tour of the country, then accommodation, food, gasoline, mileage, driver's tip, etc., must all be accounted for.

Once their expenses have been researched, they will organize the information into a spreadsheet showing major category totals and itemizations within each category.

Students will then create a final project from their data including an introductory paragraph explaining their plan and the major categories required. They will present these to the class and turn in all spreadsheets and the paragraph explaining their project to the teacher.

Time

This project could take from one to two weeks depending on how much in-class time is allowed for research, data organization, writing, etc.

Procedure

Research

Decide on a theme in which to spend your million dollars. This could be a trip around the world with your family or friends, or something you build or create, like a pet shelter, a bike racing track, etc.

Search for information related to your theme. As you search, be thinking about large categories of items needed for your theme. For example, if you are taking a trip, one of your large categories should be Transportation; another would be Accommodation, etc. Under these categories will be smaller itemized expenses, such as airline tickets, gasoline, taxis, etc.

Collect names of companies and prices of items needed from sources on the Internet. For some items, you may need to call the company's toll-free number to obtain price information. You should be able to find these numbers on the Internet.

As you search, keep track of your totals for each category. As these approach one million dollars, your project should be nearing the research completion stage.

Organizing Data

Organize your expenses according to major categories. For example, put all transportation-related expenses in a category called Transportation.

Create a spreadsheet to organize each major category and to sum, or add up, all of the expenses in each category.

Create a spreadsheet to sum, or add up, all major categories. This total should equal $1,000,000. Each spreadsheet should have itemized expenses in major categories.

Write a paragraph summarizing your theme. Explain why you chose your theme and everything that you did within that theme. Concentrate on the most exciting things. Don't overwhelm us with every little purchase. Make it sound like the great adventure that it could be!

Presenting Results

Think of a way to present your results to the class. Make it interesting! You could dress up in clothes native to the area you traveled to, or create a model of your creation.

Organize your spreadsheets and paragraph into a packet with a cover sheet. Turn this in to your teacher after you present to the class.

Extension.   Make the theme a charitable one or a specific one, such as a family vacation, carnival, etc. Encourage a visual aid of some sort. Many of my students made models of their ideas (e.g., a BMX bike track, a pet shelter, etc).

Gender Issues.   Once all students have presented, brainstorm and discuss the different ways the money was spent. Did boys and girls tend to buy similar items, or were there vast differences in their purchases?

WHAT IS A STOCK, OR, WHO OWNS MCDONALD'S?

This lesson was adapted from the Stock Market Game Guide, published in 1990 by the Securities Industry Foundation for Economic Education, Inc.

Introduction

Private ownership is fundamental to the operation of a market economy. This lesson introduces the idea that individuals can become owners of a business by purchasing stock.

Economics Background

People who buy stock in corporations are owners of that corporation. They risk their money (personal wealth) on the success of the business. Any business is risky because the future is uncertain. The owners of the business bear that risk. If the business succeeds, the owners benefit.

Language of Economics

Economize
To base decisions on an assessment of costs and benefits, choosing the best combination of costs and benefits from among the alternatives.
Ownership
The right to use something and enjoy its benefits.
Profit
The difference between revenues and the costs entailed in producing or selling a good or service; it is a return for risk-taking.
Risk
The chance of losing money. Risk is the opposite of safety.
Stock
A share of ownership in a company. Owners of stock receive part of the company's profits—or bear some of its losses—up to the amount of money they put into the stock.

Cross curriculum skills

Students develop skills in reading, listening, group participation, and writing.

Objectives

1. Students explain that a stock is a share of ownership in a business.
2. Students explain that a company's risk is assumed by those who own it.
3. Students explain that owners of stock are entitled to a share of a company's profits.
4. Students describe the risk that a company's owners assume when the business introduces a new product.
5. Students make decisions regarding stock ownership, weighing expected benefits against expected costs.

Materials

Activities 1, 2, and 3 (see below).

Time Required

One class period.

Procedure

A. Explain to students that today they will learn what a stock is and how stock ownership provides limited risks and potential rewards to investors.

B. Ask the students if they know anyone who owns something. (Everyone owns something: clothes, books, cars, business.) Have students provide examples of ownership they are familiar with. Find out whether any students know people who own businesses.

C. Why do people like to own things? (Private ownership is a powerful incentive. It allows people to enjoy the benefits of what they own.)

D. Ask: Can people legally do anything they want with items they own? To prompt discussion, provide a few problematic examples—e.g.,

1. Can you drive on the left side of the road with your car?

2. Can you use your clothes to tie up a student and lock him or her in a locker?

3. Can you use your books to start a fire in someone's living room?

4. Can you use your makeup to color over the computer monitor screen in school?

(The answer is no to each question. Each of these activities is illegal.)

E. Ask: What does ownership mean? (It establishes who gets the benefits associated with the items and who bears the responsibility for what happens with them. You get to drive your car—no one else may without your permission—but you are responsible for driving legally and answering for any harm you cause when you use the car. Ownership means that privileges and responsibilities are clearly defined.)

F. Distribute Activity 1, Stock Ownership: A Delicious Topic, to the class. Ask students to read it individually. Their purpose is to identify the costs and benefits of stock ownership. Ask:

1. How many people own McDonald's? (226,656)

2. Why would people wish to buy McDonald's stock? (They hope to share in the profits and increase their wealth.)

3. How do you become an owner of McDonald's? (Buy McDonald's stock.)

4. What are the benefits of stock ownership? (Owners may share in the profits in the company.)

5. What are the risks of stock ownership? (Owners may lose some or all the money used to buy stock.)

6. Will McDonald's accept Toad's suggested menu? (McDonald's is not ready for ants, mosquitoes, or earthworm parts—even if they are dipped in chocolate.)

7. How do profits help McDonald's? (Profits help by increasing dividends paid to stockholders and expanding the number of restaurants.)

G. Divide the class into groups of three. Distribute Activity 2, Happy Birthday, Cookie. Ask students to use the information in Activity 1 as they answer the questions in Activity 2. Discuss the answers in class.

1. When Nabisco introduced its new cookies in 1912, Nabisco stockholders assumed a risk that was similar to Toad's risk in wanting to sell chocolate insects. What was that risk? (They risked losing money when the company introduced the new cookies. Neither Toad nor Nabisco knew that customers would buy enough of their products.)

2. Why were stockholders willing to assume this risk? (They thought they could earn a profit.)

3. Did the risk-taking turn out to be worthwhile for Nabisco's stockholders? Why or why not? (Yes and no. Stockholders have earned profits from the Oreo cookie, but they lost money on the other two cookies.)

4. Did the risk-taking by Nabisco's stockholders benefit the company's customers and employees? Why or why not? (Customers have benefited by obtaining products they enjoy, and the company's employees have benefited by having a place to work and earn income.)

5. If you owned stock in the company, would you be entitled to take a package of Oreos from the supermarket whenever you wanted? Why or why not? (No. I would own only a tiny fraction of each cookie, building, or machine belonging to the company.)

H. Distribute copies of Activity 3, Thank-You Note. Remind the students that every economic choice involves weighing expected costs against expected benefits. For homework, ask students to read the directions and write Aunt Elizabeth a thank-you note that demonstrates that they understand the answers to the questions in Activity 2.

Closure

Review the main points of the lesson:
1. A stock is a fractional share of ownership of a business.
2. Stock owners are entitled to a share of a company's profits.
3. There is risk in owning any company, and stockholders share that risk.
4. Introducing a new product is a risky venture for companies.

Assessment

Multiple Choice Questions

1. What benefits do you receive from owning a share of a company's stock?

    a. You may vote for members of the board of directors.

    b. You receive a share of profits if the company does well.

    c. You might lose your home or car.

    *d. Answers "a" and "b" are correct.

2. Who decides what products will be produced by a company with many stockholders?

    a. The owners

    *b. The managers

    c. The customers

    d. The employees

Essay

Most of us are aware of successful products that companies make—Coke, hamburgers, headlights, and personal computers, for example. But not all ideas succeed in the market. What would happen if a company decided to sell a soft drink that tasted like baking soda? Discuss this question in a short essay. (Customers tend to prefer soft drinks that are sweet and thirst-quenching. A baking soda taste would not taste sweet or quench anybody's thirst, so customers would probably choose not to buy it. The company would not make money selling it. Employees would lose their jobs making it. Managers would discontinue production of the beverage and use the resources to produce something different. Owners would share in the loss the company suffered in making the product.)

Letter

Think of one company whose shares you would be willing to purchase. Spend a few minutes writing descriptive notes to yourself about two popular products made by that company. Then write a letter to Maria explaining under what conditions stock in this company might be a smart buy.

Activity 1: Stock Ownership—A Delicious Topic

Name_____   Date_____

Toad is Maria's best friend, but sometimes his impractical schemes are a bit much, even for Maria.

Yesterday was a good example. He embarrassed her at McDonald's just because he was ignorant about stock ownership and insects.

Stock ownership and insects? Yes. It all started when Toad stopped by Maria's house and asked her to go to lunch at McDonald's. "Nothing like fries and a burger and something special for lunch," he said, as they walked over to the local Golden Arches.

"Something special?" she asked. But he just ignored her as he hopped along, carrying a carefully folded brown bag.

At the restaurant, Toad offered to buy lunch. He asked Maria to find a table and to guard his brown bag. "Don't look inside, it's a surprise," he said. That should have been enough warning, Toad buying lunch and asking her to guard a brown bag; but she just went along with everything because her brain was temporarily locked in the numb position.

Shortly he joined her at the table with the food and a sour mood. "What is the matter?" she asked. "Didn't they give you good service?"

"Oh, yes," Toad grumped, "but apart from the service she was so uncooperative! I said I wanted to see the owner about this great idea of mine, but she said she was the local franchise owner. I said, 'so you own all the McDonald's in the world?' And she said, 'No, it is impossible to talk to those owners.' Then she started waiting on the next customers. She's so rude!" Toad moaned.

"Actually," Maria replied, "she is right. There are 226,656 owners of McDonald's. Maybe you should become an owner."

"That's a great idea," Toad replied. "Then I could have the restaurants serve my favorite foods and I could eat free. If I own the business, then I get to run it my way, right?"

"Not exactly," Maria replied. "I learned a lot about ownership and business by surfing the Internet. If you want to become a part owner of McDonald's, all you have to do is buy stock in that company. You become a part owner of the company, but many other people will also have bought stock in the company. So you are only one of many people who share its ownership. That's why stocks are called shares."

"But I could only eat a tiny share of all the food McDonald's cooks each day," said Toad. "As a part owner, couldn't I eat part of their food?"

"No, you couldn't. McDonald's has close to 694 million shares of stock. That means that the ownership of every hamburger McDonald's produces is really divided into 694 million parts. If you buy one share of stock then you would own one of 694 million parts of each hamburger."

"That's hard to imagine," said Toad. "That little bit wouldn't fill me up."

"And the same would be true for the company's buildings, stoves, and furniture. You would own only one 1/694 millionth of each thing."

"Well, maybe I could decide what food to put on the menu if I were an owner of McDonald's stock," Toad said. "They are really missing a sure bet by not offering a more varied menu."

"Actually, you can't do that either," Maria replied. "For each share of stock, you get one vote for the company's top managers, or directors. With so many owners or stockholders, you by yourself would not have a big influence on what the company offers as its menu. Actually, managers run the company for you and the other stockholders."

"So what would I get for buying a share of stock in the company?" asked Toad. "It doesn't sound like much of a deal to me."

"Each share of ownership entitles you to some of the profits the company earns," she explained. "But profit is not a sure thing. If people don't like the food, the company wouldn't earn enough money to cover the costs and earn a profit. Any business is risky because the future is uncertain. A company could spend lots of money for buildings, equipment, or developing a new product. But if customers don't like the product or if prices are too high or products of other restaurants are more attractive, business income will be too low. Success is never a sure thing, so there is always a chance of losing your money. Any business is risky and someone has to bear that risk. That's what stockholders do as owners of a business."

"Sounds exciting," said Toad. "So why buy a stock and risk losing money?"

"Because you can make a gain also. You think the business will earn a profit on the product, so you take the risk. The possibility of earning a profit gives the owners and managers of a business an incentive to produce something consumers want to buy at a price they are willing to pay. If the business succeeds, its owners will earn a profit. That is the reward stockholders get for risking their money. Customers also benefit because they get something they like. Employees of the business benefit because they have a place to work and earn income. It's like they're all on one big team with the same goal. But owners are the only ones who risk their own money on whether the goal is accomplished."

"So by buying a stock," Toad said, "I become a business owner who takes part of the risk that the company might fail. But if the company succeeds, I may get some of the company's profit. I'd like to do this, because I know McDonald's could make a profit from my new menu idea. It's tasty, inexpensive to produce, and everyone in my family likes it."

Then Maria asked the fatal question. "Toad," she said, "what is the food you think McDonald's should have on its menu?"

"Look at this great stuff!" Toad shouted as he opened the bag and dumped the contents onto their plates. "Over at Windy Willows Community Center where all my relatives live, this is our favorite food. Try some. It's got chocolate on it. I know you will like it."

The food was very small—bite sized—and very tasty. The chocolate taste dominated, but Maria noticed an unusual aftertaste that was not unpleasant. Other people sitting nearby were interested, so Toad also shared it with them. Even the franchise owner came over to see what the fuss was about and tried some. Everything was going great until someone asked, "What is this food?"

On the way home Maria was mad enough to spit. "How could you embarrass me that way? You know most people do not like to eat ants, flies, mosquitoes, and earthworm parts. Now we can never go back to that McDonald's Restaurant! I know for sure McDonald's will never hire you to decide on their food menu. Can you imagine what would happen to their sales if they served your food?"

"I'm sorry," Toad replied. "I just thought that the chocolate flavor would take care of the problem."

Questions for Discussion:

How many people own McDonald's?

Why would people wish to buy McDonald's stock?

How do you become an owner of McDonald's?

What are the benefits of stock ownership?

What are the risks of stock ownership?

Will McDonald's accept Toad's suggested menu?

How do profits help McDonald's?

Activity 2: Happy Birthday, Cookie

Name_____   Date_____

Directions: Read the following story and answer the questions that follow.

When April 2 rolls around again, why don't you celebrate the birthday of an old friend? On that day in 1912, the Nabisco company announced "three entirely new varieties of the highest class biscuit packed in a new style." The company described the new cookies—or biscuits, as they were then called—in the following way: The Mother Goose biscuit was "a rich, high class biscuit bearing impressions of the Mother Goose legends"; the Veronese biscuit was "a delicious, hard sweet biscuit of beautiful design and high quality"; and, finally, the Oreo was "two beautifully embossed, chocolate-flavored wafers with a rich cream filling."

The Oreo has become a familiar friend to all of us, but the other two "biscuits" were never popular. So Nabisco stopped producing them after a few years. It was not the Mother Goose or the Veronese cookie that rose to fame and is now dunked in milk, crumbled in ice cream, or rolled into hungry mouths.

Because people like Oreos so much, the company sells more than five billion of these little sweeties every year. But where did the unusual name Oreo come from? Maybe it came from the first chairman of the National Biscuit Company, Adolphus Green. He knew that *oreo* was the Greek word for mountain and that in early testing the cookie actually looked like a little mountain. Or perhaps the name came from the word *or*, which means gold, an important color on the original label.

We don't know where the name came from, but we do know that Nabisco was one smart cookie when it came up with the Oreo. But being top cookie is tough. Who knows what might happen? Consumers could start eating fewer sweets, and the company's production costs could push prices out of reach for many buyers. The business is also very competitive, for there is always another tough cookie ready to take Oreo's place in our hearts and stomachs. But, so far, Oreo hasn't crumbled.

Questions for Discussion:

When Nabisco introduced its new cookies in 1912, Nabisco stockholders assumed a risk that was similar to Toad's risk in wanting to sell chocolate insects. What was the risk?

Why were stockholders willing to assume this risk?

Did the risk-taking turn out to be worthwhile for Nabisco's stockholders? Why or why not?

Did the risk-taking by Nabisco's stockholders benefit the company's customers and employees? Why or why not?

If you owned stock in the company, would you be entitled to take a package of Oreos from the supermarket whenever you wanted? Why or why not?

Activity 3: Thank-You Note

Name_____   Date_____

After talking with Toad, Maria thought some more about stocks, profits, and risk. She thought about the $500.00 her Aunt Elizabeth had given her as a gift for making the school honor roll. She talked to her parents about what to do with the money and then she decided to invest it in stock.

Pretend that you are Maria. Write a letter to your Aunt Elizabeth and thank her for her gift. Explain that you have decided to use the money to help buy shares of stock in a business. Aunt Elizabeth might be made uneasy by the news of your decision to buy stock. She keeps all her extra money in a savings account. Anticipate Aunt Elizabeth's concerns. Explain why you think you are making good use of the money, even though stock ownership involves risks.

Appendix E: 66 Ways to Save Money

The information in this appendix is courtesy of Consumer Literacy Consortium, Washington, DC.

TRANSPORTATION

Airline Fares

1. You may lower the price of a roundtrip air fare by as much as two-thirds by making certain your trip includes a Saturday evening stayover, and by purchasing the ticket in advance.

2. To make certain you have a cheap fare, even if you use a travel agent, contact all the airlines that fly where you want to go and ask what the lowest fare to your destination is.

3. Be flexible, if possible. Consider using low-fare carriers or alternative airports and keep an eye out for fare wars.

Car Rental

1. Since car rental rates can vary greatly, shop around for the best basic rates. Ask about any additional charges (extra driver, gas, drop-off fees) and special offers.

2. Rental car companies offer various insurance and waiver options. Check with your automobile insurance agent and credit card company in advance to avoid duplicating any coverage you may already have.

New Cars

1. You can save thousands of dollars over the lifetime of a car by selecting a model that combines a low purchase price with low financing, insurance, gasoline, maintenance, and repair costs. Ask your local librarian for new car guides that contain this information.

2. Having selected a model, you can save hundreds of dollars by comparison shopping. Call at least five dealers for price quotes and let each know that you are calling others.

3. Remember there is no "cooling off" period on new car sales. Once you have signed a contract, you are obligated to buy the car.

Used Cars

1. Before buying any used car:

a. Compare the seller's asking price with the average retail price in a "bluebook" or other guide to car prices, found at many libraries, banks, and credit unions.

b. Have a mechanic you trust check the car, especially if the car is sold "as is."

2. Consider purchasing a used car from someone you know and trust. They are more likely than other sellers to charge a lower price and point out any problems with the car.

Auto Leasing

1. Don't decide to lease a car just because the payments are lower than on a traditional auto loan. The leasing payments may be lower because you don't own the car at the end of the lease.

2. Leasing a car is very complicated. When shopping, consider the price of the car (known as the capitalized cost), your trade-in allowance, any down payment, monthly payments, various fees (excess mileage, excess "wear and tear," end-of-lease), and the cost of buying the car at the end of the lease. "Keys to Vehicle Leasing: A Consumer Guide," published by the Federal Reserve Board and Federal Trade Commission, is a valuable source of information about auto leasing.

Gasoline

1. You can save hundreds of dollars a year by comparing prices at different stations, pumping gas yourself, and using the lowest octane called for in your owner's manual.

2. You can save up to $100 a year on gas by keeping your engine tuned and your tires inflated to their proper pressure.

Car Repairs

1. Consumers lose billions of dollars each year on unneeded or poorly done car repairs. The most important step that you can take to save money on these repairs is to find a skilled, honest mechanic. Before you need repairs, look for a mechanic who is certified and well established; has done good work for someone you know; and communicates well about repair options and costs.

INSURANCE

Auto Insurance

1. You can save several hundred dollars a year by purchasing auto insurance from a licensed, low-price insurer. Call your state insurance department for a publication showing typical prices charged by different companies. Then call at least four of the lowest-priced, licensed insurers to learn what they would charge you for the same coverage.

2. Talk to your agent or insurer about raising your deductibles on collision and comprehensive coverages to at least $500 or, if you have an old car, dropping these coverages altogether. Taking these steps can save you hundreds of dollars a year.

3. Make certain that your new policy is in effect before dropping your old one.

Homeowner/Renter Insurance

1. You can save several hundred dollars a year on homeowner insurance and up to $50 a year on renter insurance by purchasing insurance from a low-price, licensed insurer. Ask your state insurance department for a publication showing typical prices charged by different licensed companies. Then call at least four of the lowest priced insurers to learn what they would charge you. If such a publication is not available, it is even more important to call at least four insurers for price quotes.

2. [When buying homeowner's insurance] make certain you purchase enough coverage to replace the house and its contents. "Replacement" on the house means rebuilding to its current condition.

3. Make certain your new policy is in effect before dropping your old one.

Life Insurance

1. If you want insurance protection only, and not a savings and investment product, buy a term life insurance policy.

2. If you want to buy a whole life, universal life, or other cash value policy, plan to hold it for at least 15 years. Canceling these policies after only a few years can more than double your life insurance costs.

3. Check your public library for information about the financial soundness of insurance companies and the prices they charge. The July 1998 issue of *Consumer Reports* is a valuable source of information about a number of insurers.

BANKING/CREDIT

Checking

1. You can save more than $100 a year in fees by selecting a checking account with a low (or no) minimum balance requirement that you can, and do, meet. Request a list of these and other fees that are charged on these accounts.
2. Banking institutions often will drop or lower checking fees if paychecks are directly deposited by your employer. Direct deposit offers the additional advantages of convenience, security, and immediate access to your money.

Savings and Investment Products

1. Before opening a savings or investment account with a bank or other financial institution, find out whether the account is insured by the federal government (FDIC or NCUA). An increasing number of products offered by these institutions, including mutual stock funds and annuities, are not insured.
2. To earn the highest return on savings (annual percentage yield) with little or no risk, consider certificates of deposit (CDs) and treasury bills or notes.
3. Once you select a type of savings or investment product, compare rates and fees offered by different institutions. These rates can vary a lot and, over time, can significantly affect interest earnings.

Credit Cards

1. You can save as much as a thousand dollars or more each year in lower credit card interest charges by paying off your entire bill each month.
2. If you are unable to pay off a large balance, pay as much as you can and switch to a credit card with a low annual percentage rate (APR). For a modest fee, RAM Research Corp. (800–344–7714) will send you a list of low-rate cards. You can obtain a list of low-rate cards by accessing www.ramresearch.com. cardtrack on the Internet.
3. You can reduce credit card fees, which may add up to more than $100 a year, by getting rid of all but one or two cards, and by avoiding late payment and over-the-credit-limit fees.

Auto Loans

1. If you have significant savings earning a low interest rate, consider making a large down payment or even paying for the car in cash. This could save you as much as several thousand dollars in finance charges.
2. You can save as much as hundreds of dollars in finance charges by shopping

for the cheapest loan. Contact several banks, your credit union, and the auto manufacturer's own finance company.

First Mortgage Loans

1. Although your monthly payment may be higher, you can save tens of thousands of dollars in interest charges by shopping for the shortest-term mortgage you can afford. On a $100,000 fixed-rate loan at an 8% annual percentage rate (APR), for example, you will pay $90,000 less in interest on a 15-year mortgage than on a 30-year mortgage.

2. You can save thousands of dollars in interest charges by shopping for the lowest-rate mortgage with the fewest points. On a 15-year, $100,000 fixed-rate mortgage, just lowering the APR from 8.5% to 8.0% can save you more than $5,000 in interest charges. On this mortgage, paying two points instead of three would save you an additional $1,000.

3. If your local newspaper does not periodically run mortgage rate surveys, call at least six lenders for information about their rates (APRs), points, and fees. Then ask an accountant to compute precisely how much each mortgage option will cost and its tax implications.

4. Be aware that the interest rate on most adjustable rate mortgage loans (ARMs) can vary a great deal over the lifetime of the mortgage. An increase of several percentage points might raise payments by hundreds of dollars per month.

Mortgage Refinancing

1. Consider refinancing your mortgage if you can get a rate that is at least one percentage point lower than your existing mortgage rate and plan to keep the new mortgage for several years or more. Ask an accountant to calculate precisely how much your new mortgage (including upfront fees) will cost and whether, in the long run, it will cost less than your current mortgage.

Home Equity Loans

1. Be cautious in taking out home equity loans. These loans reduce the equity that you have built up in your home. If you are unable to make payments, you could lose your home.

2. Compare home equity loans offered by at least four banking institutions. In comparing these loans, consider not only the annual percentage rate (APR) but also points, closing costs, other fees, and the index for any variable rate changes.

HOUSING

Home Purchase

1. You can often negotiate a lower sale price by employing a buyer broker who works for you, not the seller. If the buyer broker or the broker's firm also

lists properties, there may be a conflict of interest, so ask them to tell you if they are showing you a property that they have listed.

2. Do not purchase any house until it has been examined by a home inspector that you selected.

Renting a Place to Live

1. Do not limit your rental housing search to classified ads or referrals from friends and acquaintances. Select buildings where you would like to live and contact their building manager or owner to see if anything is available.

2. Remember that signing a lease probably obligates you to make all monthly payments for the term of the agreement.

Home Improvement

1. Home repairs often cost thousands of dollars and are the subject of frequent complaints. Select from among several well established, licensed contractors who have submitted written, fixed-price bids for the work.

2. Do not sign any contract that requires full payment before satisfactory completion of the work.

Major Appliances

1. Consult *Consumer Reports*, available in most public libraries, for information about specific brands and how to evaluate them, including energy use. There are often great price and quality differences among brands.

2. Once you've selected a brand, check the phone book to learn what stores carry this brand, then call at least four of these stores for the prices of specific models. After each store has given you a quote, ask if that's the lowest price they can offer you. This comparison shopping can save you as much as $100 or more.

UTILITIES

Electricity

1. To save as much as hundreds of dollars a year on electricity, make certain that any new appliances you purchase, especially air conditioners and furnaces, are energy-efficient. Information on the energy efficiency of major appliances is found on Energy Guide Labels required by federal law.

2. Enrolling in load management programs and off-hour rate programs offered by your electric utility may save you up to $100 a year in electricity costs. Call your electric utility for information about these cost-saving programs.

Home Heating

1. A home energy audit can identify ways to save up to hundreds of dollars a year on home heating (and air conditioning). Ask your electric or gas utility if they can do this audit for free or for a reasonable charge. If they cannot, ask them to refer you to a qualified professional.

Local Telephone Service

1. Check with your phone company to see whether a flat rate or measured service plan will save you the most money.
2. You will usually save money by buying your phones instead of leasing them.
3. Check you local phone bill to see if you have optional services that you don't really need or use. Each option you drop could save you $40 or more each year.

Long Distance Telephone Service

1. Long distance calls made during evenings, at night, or on weekends can cost significantly less than weekday calls.
2. If you make more than a few long distance calls each month, consider subscribing to a calling plan. Call several long distance companies to see which one has the least expensive plan for the calls you make.
3. Whenever possible, dial your long distance calls directly. Using the operator to complete a call can cost you an extra $6.

OTHER

Food Purchased at Markets

1. You can save hundreds of dollars a year by shopping at the lower-priced food stores. Convenience stores often charge the highest prices.
2. You will spend less on food if you shop with a list.
3. You can save hundreds of dollars a year by comparing price-per-ounce or other unit prices on shelf labels. Stock up on those items with low per-unit costs.

Prescription Drugs

1. Since brand name drugs are usually much more expensive than their generic equivalents, ask your physician and pharmacist for generic drugs whenever appropriate.
2. Since pharmacies may charge widely different prices for the same medicine, call several. When taking a drug for a long time, also consider calling mail-order pharmacies, which often charge lower prices.

Funeral Arrangements

1. Make your wishes known about your funeral, memorial, or burial arrangements in writing. Be cautious about prepaying because there may be risks involved.

2. For information about the least costly options, which could save you several thousand dollars, contact a local memorial society, which is usually listed in the Yellow Pages under funeral services.

3. Before selecting a funeral home, call several and ask for prices of specific goods and services, or visit them to obtain an itemized price list. You are entitled to this information by law and, by using it to comparison shop, you can save hundreds of dollars.

Appendix F: Important Forms

The following tax forms are typically available from your local library, Post office or local government office.

a Control number	OMB No. 1545-0008	This information is being furnished to the Internal Revenue Service. If you are required to file a tax return, a negligence penalty or other sanction may be imposed on you if this income is taxable and you fail to report it.

b Employer identification number	1 Wages, tips, other compensation	2 Federal income tax withheld

c Employer's name, address, and ZIP code	3 Social security wages	4 Social security tax withheld
	5 Medicare wages and tips	6 Medicare tax withheld
	7 Social security tips	8 Allocated tips

d Employee's social security number	9 Advance EIC payment	10 Dependent care benefits

e Employee's name, address, and ZIP code	11 Nonqualified plans	12 Benefits included in box 1
	13 See instrs. for box 13	14 Other

15 Statutory employee ☐	Deceased ☐	Pension plan ☐	Legal rep. ☐	Deferred compensation ☐

16 State	Employer's state I.D. no.	17 State wages, tips, etc.	18 State income tax	19 Locality name	20 Local wages, tips, etc.	21 Local income tax

Form **W-2** Wage and Tax Statement **1999**

(O)

Department of the Treasury—Internal Revenue Service

Copy C For EMPLOYEE'S RECORDS (See Notice to Employee on back of Copy B.)

250

Instructions *(Also see Notice to Employee on back of Copy B)*

Box 1. Enter this amount on the wages line of your tax return.

Box 2. Enter this amount on the Federal income tax withheld line of your tax return.

Box 8. This amount is not included in boxes 1, 3, 5, or 7. For information on how to report tips on your tax return, see your Form 1040 instructions.

Box 9. Enter this amount on the advance earned income credit payments line of your Form 1040 or 1040A.

Box 10. This amount is the total dependent care benefits your employer paid to you or incurred on your behalf (including amounts from a section 125 (cafeteria) plan). Any amount over $5,000 also is included in box 1. You must complete Schedule 2 (Form 1040A) or Form 2441, Child and Dependent Care Expenses, to compute any taxable and nontaxable amounts.

Box 11. This amount is (a) reported in box 1 if it is a distribution made to you from a nonqualified deferred compensation or section 457 plan or (b) included in box 3 and/or 5 if it is a prior year deferral under a nonqualified or section 457 plan that became taxable for social security and Medicare taxes this year because there is no longer a substantial risk of forfeiture of your right to the deferred amount.

Box 12. This amount is the taxable fringe benefits included in box 1. You may be able to deduct expenses that are related to fringe benefits; see the Form 1040 instructions.

Box 13. The following list explains the codes shown in box 13. You may need this information to complete your tax return.

Note: If a year follows code D, E, F, G, H, or S, you made a make-up pension contribution for a prior year(s) when you were in military service. To figure whether you made excess deferrals, consider these amounts for the year shown, not the current year. If no year is shown, the contributions are for the current year.

A—Uncollected social security or RRTA tax on tips (include this tax on Form 1040. See "Total Tax" in Form 1040 instructions.)

B—Uncollected Medicare tax on tips (include this tax on Form 1040. See "Total Tax" in Form 1040 instructions.)

C—Cost of group-term life insurance over $50,000 (included in box 1)

D—Elective deferrals to a section 401(k) cash or deferred arrangement. Also includes deferrals under a SIMPLE retirement account that is part of a section 401(k) arrangement.

E—Elective deferrals under a section 403(b) salary reduction agreement

F—Elective deferrals to a section 408(k)(6) salary reduction SEP

G—Elective and nonelective deferrals to a section 457(b) deferred compensation plan

H—Elective deferrals to a section 501(c)(18)(D) tax-exempt organization plan (see "Adjusted Gross Income" in Form 1040 instructions for how to deduct)

J—Nontaxable sick pay (not includible as income)

K—20% excise tax on excess golden parachute payments (see "Total Tax" in Form 1040 instructions)

L—Substantiated employee business expense reimbursements (nontaxable)

M—Uncollected social security or RRTA tax on cost of group-term life insurance coverage over $50,000 (former employees only) (see "Total Tax" in Form 1040 instructions)

N—Uncollected Medicare tax on cost of group-term life insurance coverage over $50,000 (former employees only) (see "Total Tax" in Form 1040 instructions)

P—Excludable moving expense reimbursements paid directly to employee (not included in box 1)

Q—Military employee basic housing, subsistence, and combat zone compensation (use this amount if you qualify for EIC)

R—Employer contributions to your medical savings account (MSA) (see Form 8853, Medical Savings Accounts and Long-Term Care Insurance Contracts)

S—Employee salary reduction contributions to a section 408(p) SIMPLE (not included in box 1)

T—Adoption benefits (not included in box 1). You must complete Form 8839, Qualified Adoption Expenses, to compute any taxable and nontaxable amounts.

Box 15. If the "Pension plan" box is checked, special limits may apply to the amount of traditional IRA contributions you may deduct. If the "Deferred compensation" box is checked, the elective deferrals in box 13 (codes D, E, F, G, H, and S) (for all employers, and for all such plans to which you belong) are generally limited to $10,000. Elective deferrals for section 403(b) contracts are limited to $10,000 ($13,000 in some cases; see Pub. 571). The limit for section 457(b) plans is $8,000. Amounts over these limits must be included in income. See "Wages, Salaries, Tips, etc." in the Form 1040 instructions.

Note: Keep Copy C of Form W-2 for at least 3 years after the due date for filing your income tax return. However, to help protect your social security benefits, keep Copy C until you begin receiving social security benefits, just in case there is a question about your work record and/or earnings in a particular year. SSA suggests you confirm your work record with them from time to time.

Form W-4 (2000)

Purpose. Complete Form W-4 so your employer can withhold the correct Federal income tax from your pay. Because your tax situation may change, you may want to refigure your withholding each year.

Exemption from withholding. If you are exempt, complete only lines 1, 2, 3, 4, and 7, and sign the form to validate it. Your exemption for 2000 expires February 16, 2001.

Note: *You cannot claim exemption from withholding if (1) your income exceeds $700 and includes more than $250 of unearned income (e.g., interest and dividends) and (2) another person can claim you as a dependent on their tax return.*

Basic Instructions. If you are not exempt, complete the **Personal Allowances Worksheet** below. The worksheets on page 2 adjust your withholding allowances based on itemized deductions, adjustments to income, or two-earner/two-job situations. Complete all worksheets that apply. They will help you figure the number of withholding allowances you are entitled to claim. However, you may claim fewer (or zero) allowances.

Child tax and higher education credits. For details on adjusting withholding for these and other credits, see Pub. 919, How Do I Adjust My Tax Withholding?

Head of household. Generally, you may claim head of household filing status on your tax return only if you are unmarried and pay more than 50% of the costs of keeping up a home for yourself and your dependent(s) or other qualifying individuals. See line E below.

Nonwage income. If you have a large amount of nonwage income, such as interest or dividends, you should consider making estimated tax payments using Form 1040-ES, Estimated Tax for Individuals. Otherwise, you may owe additional tax.

Two earners/two jobs. If you have a working spouse or more than one job, figure the total number of allowances you are entitled to claim on all jobs using worksheets from only one Form W-4. Your withholding usually will be most accurate when all allowances are claimed on the Form W-4 prepared for the highest paying job and zero allowances are claimed for the others.

Check your withholding. After your Form W-4 takes effect, use Pub. 919 to see how the dollar amount you are having withheld compares to your projected total tax for 2000. Get Pub. 919 especially if you used the Two-Earner/Two-Job Worksheet on page 2 and your earnings exceed $150,000 (Single) or $200,000 (Married).

Recent name change? If your name on line 1 differs from that shown on your social security card, call 1-800-772-1213 for a new social security card.

Personal Allowances Worksheet (Keep for your records.)

A Enter "1" for yourself if no one else can claim you as a dependent . . . . **A** _____

B Enter "1" if:
- You are single and have only one job; or
- You are married, have only one job, and your spouse does not work; or
- Your wages from a second job or your spouse's wages (or the total of both) are $1,000 or less.

. . **B** _____

C Enter "1" for your spouse. But, you may choose to enter -0- if you are married and have either a working spouse or more than one job. (Entering -0- may help you avoid having too little tax withheld.) . . . . **C** _____

D Enter number of dependents (other than your spouse or yourself) you will claim on your tax return . . . . **D** _____

E Enter "1" if you will file as head of household on your tax return (see conditions under Head of household above) . **E** _____

F Enter "1" if you have at least $1,500 of child or dependent care expenses for which you plan to claim a credit . . **F** _____

G Child Tax Credit:
- If your total income will be between $18,000 and $50,000 ($23,000 and $63,000 if married), enter "1" for each eligible child.
- If your total income will be between $50,000 and $80,000 ($63,000 and $115,000 if married), enter "1" if you have two eligible children, enter "2" if you have three or four eligible children, or enter "3" if you have five or more eligible children. **G** _____

H Add lines A through G and enter total here. Note: *This may be different from the number of exemptions you claim on your tax return.* ▶ **H** _____

For accuracy, complete all worksheets that apply.
- If you plan to itemize or claim adjustments to income and want to reduce your withholding, see the **Deductions and Adjustments Worksheet** on page 2.
- If you are **single, have more than one job and your combined earnings from all jobs exceed $34,000, OR** if you **are married and have a working spouse or more than one job and the combined earnings from all jobs exceed $60,000,** see the **Two-Earner/Two-Job Worksheet** on page 2 to avoid having too little tax withheld.
- If neither of the above situations applies, stop here and enter the number from line H on line 5 of Form W-4 below.

---------------------- Cut here and give Form W-4 to your employer. Keep the top part for your records. ----------------------

Form **W-4**	**Employee's Withholding Allowance Certificate**	OMB No. 1545-0010
Department of the Treasury Internal Revenue Service	▶ For Privacy Act and Paperwork Reduction Act Notice, see page 2.	**2000**

1 Type or print your first name and middle initial	Last name	2 Your social security number

Home address (number and street or rural route)	3 ☐ Single ☐ Married ☐ Married, but withhold at higher Single rate. Note: *If married, but legally separated, or spouse is a nonresident alien, check the Single box.*
City or town, state, and ZIP code	4 If your last name differs from that on your social security card, check here. You must call 1-800-772-1213 for a new card . . . ▶ ☐

5 Total number of allowances you are claiming (from line H above OR from the applicable worksheet on page 2) | **5** _____

6 Additional amount, if any, you want withheld from each paycheck . . . . | **6** $ _____

7 I claim exemption from withholding for 2000, and I certify that I meet BOTH of the following conditions for exemption:
- Last year I had a right to a refund of ALL Federal income tax withheld because I had NO tax liability AND
- This year I expect a refund of ALL Federal income tax withheld because I expect to have NO tax liability.

If you meet both conditions, write "EXEMPT" here . . . . ▶ | **7** ___

Under penalties of perjury, I certify that I am entitled to the number of withholding allowances claimed on this certificate, or I am entitled to claim exempt status.

Employee's signature (Form is not valid unless you sign it) ▶ _____ Date ▶ _____

8 Employer's name and address (Employer: Complete lines 8 and 10 only if sending to the IRS.)	9 Office code (optional)	10 Employer identification number

Cat. No. 10220Q

252

Deductions and Adjustments Worksheet

Note: Use this worksheet only if you plan to itemize deductions or claim adjustments to income on your 2000 tax return.

1	Enter an estimate of your 2000 itemized deductions. These include qualifying home mortgage interest, charitable contributions, state and local taxes, medical expenses in excess of 7.5% of your income, and miscellaneous deductions. (For 2000, you may have to reduce your itemized deductions if your income is over $128,950 ($64,475 if married filing separately). See **Worksheet 3** in Pub. 919 for details.) . . . **1** $_____

2 Enter: { $7,350 if married filing jointly or qualifying widow(er)
$6,450 if head of household
$4,400 if single
$3,675 if married filing separately } . . . . **2** $_____

3 Subtract line 2 from line 1. If line 2 is greater than line 1, enter -0- . . . . **3** $_____

4 Enter an estimate of your 2000 adjustments to income, including alimony, deductible IRA contributions, and student loan interest **4** $_____

5 Add lines 3 and 4 and enter the total (include any amount for credits from **Worksheet 7** in Pub. 919.) . **5** $_____

6 Enter an estimate of your 2000 nonwage income (such as dividends or interest) . . . . **6** $_____

7 Subtract line 6 from line 5. Enter the result, but not less than -0- . . . . **7** $_____

8 Divide the amount on line 7 by $3,000 and enter the result here. Drop any fraction . . . . . . **8** _____

9 Enter the number from the **Personal Allowances Worksheet**, line H, page 1 . . . . **9** _____

10 Add lines 8 and 9 and enter the total here. If you plan to use the **Two-Earner/Two-Job Worksheet**, also enter this total on line 1 below. Otherwise, **stop here** and enter this total on Form W-4, line 5, page 1 . **10** _____

Two-Earner/Two-Job Worksheet

Note: Use this worksheet only if the instructions under line H on page 1 direct you here.

1 Enter the number from line H, page 1 (or from line 10 above if you used the **Deductions and Adjustments Worksheet**) **1** _____

2 Find the number in **Table 1** below that applies to the **LOWEST** paying job and enter it here . . . . **2** _____

3 If line 1 is **MORE THAN OR EQUAL TO** line 2, subtract line 2 from line 1. Enter the result here (if zero, enter -0-) and on Form W-4, line 5, page 1. **Do not** use the rest of this worksheet . . . . **3** _____

Note: If line 1 is **LESS THAN** line 2, enter -0- on Form W-4, line 5, page 1. Complete lines 4–9 below to calculate the additional withholding amount necessary to avoid a year end tax bill.

4 Enter the number from line 2 of this worksheet . . . . **4** _____

5 Enter the number from line 1 of this worksheet . . . . **5** _____

6 Subtract line 5 from line 4 . . . . **6** _____

7 Find the amount in **Table 2** below that applies to the **HIGHEST** paying job and enter it here . . . . **7** $_____

8 Multiply line 7 by line 6 and enter the result here. This is the additional annual withholding needed . . **8** $_____

9 Divide line 8 by the number of pay periods remaining in 2000. For example, divide by 26 if you are paid every other week and you complete this form in December 1999. Enter the result here and on Form W-4, line 6, page 1. This is the additional amount to be withheld from each paycheck . . . . **9** $_____

Table 1: Two-Earner/Two-Job Worksheet

Married Filing Jointly				All Others			
If wages from LOWEST paying job are—	Enter on line 2 above	If wages from LOWEST paying job are—	Enter on line 2 above	If wages from LOWEST paying job are—	Enter on line 2 above	If wages from LOWEST paying job are—	Enter on line 2 above
$0 - $4,000	0	41,001 - 45,000	8	$0 - $5,000	0	65,001 - 80,000	8
4,001 - 7,000	1	45,001 - 55,000	9	5,001 - 11,000	1	80,001 - 100,000	9
7,001 - 13,000	2	55,001 - 63,000	10	11,001 - 17,000	2	100,001 and over	10
13,001 - 19,000	3	63,001 - 70,000	11	17,001 - 22,000	3		
19,001 - 25,000	4	70,001 - 85,000	12	22,001 - 27,000	4		
25,001 - 31,000	5	85,001 - 100,000	13	27,001 - 40,000	5		
31,001 - 37,000	6	100,001 - 110,000	14	40,001 - 50,000	6		
37,001 - 41,000	7	110,001 and over	15	50,001 - 65,000	7		

Table 2: Two-Earner/Two-Job Worksheet

Married Filing Jointly		All Others	
If wages from HIGHEST paying job are—	Enter on line 7 above	If wages from HIGHEST paying job are—	Enter on line 7 above
$0 - $50,000	$420	$0 - $30,000	$420
50,000 - 100,000	780	30,001 - 60,000	780
100,001 - 130,000	870	60,001 - 120,000	870
130,001 - 250,000	1,000	120,001 - 270,000	1,000
250,001 and over.	1,100	270,001 and over.	1,100

Privacy Act and Paperwork Reduction Act Notice. We ask for the information on this form to carry out the Internal Revenue laws of the United States. The Internal Revenue Code requires this information under sections 3402(f)(2)(A) and 6109 and their regulations. Failure to provide a properly completed form will result in your being treated as a single person who claims no withholding allowances; providing fraudulent information may also subject you to penalties. Routine uses of this information include giving it to the Department of Justice for civil and criminal litigation, to cities, states, and the District of Columbia for use in administering their tax laws, and for use in the National Directory of New Hires.

You are not required to provide the information requested on a form that is subject to the Paperwork Reduction Act unless the form displays a valid OMB control number. Books or records relating to a form or its instructions must be retained as long as their contents may become material in the administration of any Internal Revenue law. Generally, tax returns and return information are confidential, as required by Code section 6103.

The time needed to complete this form will vary depending on individual circumstances. The estimated average time is: **Recordkeeping** 46 min., **Learning about the law or the form** 13 min., **Preparing the form** 59 min. If you have comments concerning the accuracy of these time estimates or suggestions for making this form simpler, we would be happy to hear from you. You can write to the Tax Forms Committee, Western Area Distribution Center, Rancho Cordova, CA 95743-0001. DO NOT send the tax form to this address. Instead, give it to your employer.

Printed on recycled paper

*U.S. GPO: 1999-456-128

Department of the Treasury—Internal Revenue Service

Form 1040EZ

Income Tax Return for Single and Joint Filers With No Dependents (L) **1999**

OMB No. 1545-0675

Use the IRS label here

Your first name and initial | Last name | **Your social security number**

If a joint return, spouse's first name and initial | Last name

Home address (number and street). If you have a P.O. box, see page 12. | Apt. no. | **Spouse's social security number**

City, town or post office, state, and ZIP code. If you have a foreign address, see page 12.

Presidential Election Campaign (See page 12.)

Note. *Checking "Yes" will not change your tax or reduce your refund.*

Do you want $3 to go to this fund? ▶

If a joint return, does your spouse want $3 to go to this fund? ▶

Income

Attach Copy B of Form(s) W-2 here. Enclose, but do not staple, any payment.

1 Total wages, salaries, and tips. This should be shown in box 1 of your W-2 form(s). Attach your W-2 form(s). **1**

2 Taxable interest. If the total is over $400, you cannot use Form 1040EZ. **2**

3 Unemployment compensation, qualified state tuition program earnings, and Alaska Permanent Fund dividends (see page 14). **3**

4 Add lines 1, 2, and 3. This is your **adjusted gross income.** **4**

Note. You must check Yes or No.

5 Can your parents (or someone else) claim you on their return?

Yes. Enter amount from worksheet on back.

No. If **single,** enter 7,050.00. If **married,** enter 12,700.00. See back for explanation. **5**

6 Subtract line 5 from line 4. If line 5 is larger than line 4, enter 0. This is your **taxable income.** ▶ **6**

Payments and tax

7 Enter your Federal income tax withheld from box 2 of your W-2 form(s). **7**

8a Earned income credit (see page 15).
b Nontaxable earned income: enter type and amount below.

Type $ **8a**

9 Add lines 7 and 8a. These are your **total payments.** **9**

10 **Tax.** Use the amount on **line 6 above** to find your tax in the tax table on pages 24–28 of the booklet. Then, enter the tax from the table on this line. **10**

Refund

Have it directly deposited! See page 20 and fill in 11b, 11c, and 11d.

11a If line 9 is larger than line 10, subtract line 10 from line 9. This is your **refund.** **11a**

▶ **b** Routing number
▶ **c** Type: Checking Savings **d** Account number

Amount you owe

12 If line 10 is larger than line 9, subtract line 9 from line 10. This is the **amount you owe.** See page 21 for details on how to pay. **12**

Sign here

Keep copy for your records.

Your signature | Spouse's signature if joint return. See page 11.

Date | Your occupation | Date | Spouse's occupation

Cat. No. 12617R   1999 Form 1040EZ

Use this form if

- Your filing status is single or married filing jointly.
- You do not claim any dependents.
- You (and your spouse if married) were under 65 on January 1, 2000, and not blind at the end of 1999.
- Your taxable income (line 6) is less than $50,000.
- You do not claim a student loan interest deduction (see page 8) or an education credit.
- You had **only** wages, salaries, tips, taxable scholarship or fellowship grants, unemployment compensation, qualified state tuition program earnings, or Alaska Permanent Fund dividends, and your taxable interest was not over $400. **But** if you earned tips, including allocated tips, that are not included in box 5 and box 7 of your W-2, you may not be able to use Form 1040EZ. See page 13. If you are planning to use Form 1040EZ for a child who received Alaska Permanent Fund dividends, see page 14.
- You did not receive any advance earned income credit payments.

If you are not sure about your filing status, see page 11. If you have questions about dependents, use TeleTax topic 354 (see page 6). If you **cannot** use this form, use TeleTax topic 352 (see page 6).

Filling in your return

For tips on how to avoid common mistakes, see page 29.

Enter your (and your spouse's if married) social security number on the front. Because this form is read by a machine, please print your numbers inside the boxes like this:

9 8 7 6 5 4 3 2 1 0   Do not type your numbers. Do not use dollar signs.

If you received a scholarship or fellowship grant or tax-exempt interest income, such as on municipal bonds, see the booklet before filling in the form. Also, see the booklet if you received a Form 1099-INT showing Federal income tax withheld or if Federal income tax was withheld from your unemployment compensation or Alaska Permanent Fund dividends.

Remember, you must report all wages, salaries, and tips even if you do not get a W-2 form from your employer. You must also report all your taxable interest, including interest from banks, savings and loans, credit unions, etc., even if you do not get a Form 1099-INT.

Worksheet for dependents who checked "Yes" on line 5

(keep a copy for your records)

Use this worksheet to figure the amount to enter on line 5 if someone can claim you (or your spouse if married) as a dependent, even if that person chooses not to do so. To find out if someone can claim you as a dependent, use TeleTax topic 354 (see page 6).

A. Amount, if any, from line 1 on front _____

+ 250.00   Enter total ▶ **A.** _____

B. Minimum standard deduction . . . . **B.** _____700.00

C. Enter the LARGER of line A or line B here . . . . **C.** _____

D. Maximum standard deduction. If **single,** enter 4,300.00; if **married,** enter 7,200.00 . . . . **D.** _____

E. Enter the SMALLER of line C or line D here. This is your standard deduction . . . . **E.** _____

F. Exemption amount.
- If single, enter 0.
- If married and—
  —both you and your spouse can be claimed as dependents, enter 0.
  —only one of you can be claimed as a dependent, enter 2,750.00.   **F.** _____

G. Add lines E and F. Enter the total here and on line 5 on the front . . **G.** _____

If you checked "No" on line 5 because no one can claim you (or your spouse if married) as a dependent, enter on line 5 the amount shown below that applies to you.

- Single, enter 7,050.00. This is the total of your standard deduction (4,300.00) and your exemption (2,750.00).
- Married, enter 12,700.00. This is the total of your standard deduction (7,200.00), your exemption (2,750.00), and your spouse's exemption (2,750.00).

Mailing return

Mail your return by **April 17, 2000.** Use the envelope that came with your booklet. If you do not have that envelope, see page 32 for the address to use.

Paid preparer's use only

See page 21.

Under penalties of perjury, I declare that I have examined this return, and to the best of my knowledge and belief, it is true, correct, and accurately lists all amounts and sources of income received during the tax year. This declaration is based on all information of which I have any knowledge.

Preparer's signature ▶	Date	Check if self-employed ☐	Preparer's SSN or PTIN
Firm's name (or yours if self-employed) and address ▶		EIN	
		ZIP code	

♲ *Printed on recycled paper*   Form **1040EZ** (1999)

☆ U.S GPO 1999 456-058

Department of the Treasury—Internal Revenue Service

U.S. Individual Income Tax Return (L) **1999**   IRS Use Only— Do not write or staple in this space.

OMB No. 1545-0085

Label
(See page 19.)

Use the IRS label.
Otherwise, please print or type.

L A B E L   H E R E

Your first name and initial	Last name		Your social security number
If a joint return, spouse's first name and initial	Last name		Spouse's social security number
Home address (number and street). If you have a P.O. box, see page 20		Apt. no.	
City, town or post office, state, and ZIP code. If you have a foreign address, see page 20			

▲ IMPORTANT! ▲
You **must** enter your SSN(s) above.

Presidential Election Campaign Fund (See page 20.)
Do you want $3 to go to this fund? . . . .
If a joint return, does your spouse want $3 to go to this fund?

Yes | No

Note. Checking "Yes" will not change your tax or reduce your refund.

Filing status

Check only one box

1 ☐ Single
2 ☐ Married filing joint return (even if only one had income)
3 ☐ Married filing separate return. Enter spouse's social security number above and full name here. ▶
4 ☐ Head of household (with qualifying person). (See page 21.) If the qualifying person is a child but not your dependent, enter this child's name here. ▶
5 ☐ Qualifying widow(er) with dependent child (year spouse died ▶ 19   ). (See page 22.)

Exemptions

If more than seven dependents, see page 22.

6a ☐ **Yourself.** If your parent (or someone else) can claim you as a dependent on his or her tax return, do not check box 6a.

b ☐ **Spouse**

c **Dependents:**

(1) First name Last name	(2) Dependent's social security number	(3) Dependent's relationship to you	(4) ✓ if qualifying child for child tax credit (see page 23)
			☐
			☐
			☐
			☐
			☐
			☐
			☐

No. of boxes checked on 6a and 6b ____

No. of your children on 6c who:
• lived with you ____
• did not live with you due to divorce or separation (see page 24) ____
Dependents on 6c not entered above ____

d Total number of exemptions claimed.

Add numbers entered on lines above

Income

Attach Copy B of your Form(s) W-2 here. Also attach Form(s) 1099-R if tax was withheld.

If you did not get a W-2, see page 25.

Enclose, but do not staple, any payment.

7 Wages, salaries, tips, etc. Attach Form(s) W-2. | 7

8a **Taxable interest.** Attach Schedule 1 if required. | 8a
  b **Tax-exempt** interest. DO NOT include on line 8a.   8b

9 Ordinary dividends. Attach Schedule 1 if required. | 9

10a Total IRA distributions.   10a | 10b Taxable amount (see page 25).   10b

11a Total pensions and annuities.   11a | 11b Taxable amount (see page 26).   11b

12 Unemployment compensation, qualified state tuition program earnings, and Alaska Permanent Fund dividends. | 12

13a Social security benefits.   13a | 13b Taxable amount (see page 28).   13b

14 Add lines 7 through 13b (far right column). This is your **total income.** ▶   14

Adjusted gross income

15 IRA deduction (see page 30).   15

16 Student loan interest deduction (see page 30).   16
17 Add lines 15 and 16. These are your **total adjustments.** | 17

18 Subtract line 17 from line 14. This is your **adjusted gross income.** ▶   18

For Disclosure, Privacy Act, and Paperwork Reduction Act Notice, see page 53.   Cat. No. 12601H   Form **1040A** (1999)

Taxable income	19	Enter the amount from line 18.	19

20a Check ⎰ ☐ **You** were 65 or older ☐ Blind ⎱ **Enter number of**
if: ⎱ ☐ **Spouse** was 65 or older ☐ Blind ⎰ **boxes checked ▶** 20a ☐

b If you are married filing separately and your spouse itemizes
deductions, see page 32 and check here . . . . ▶ 20b ☐

21 Enter the **standard deduction** for your filing status. **But see page 33** if
you checked any box on line 20a or 20b **OR** if someone can claim you
as a dependent.
• Single—$4,300   • Married filing jointly or Qualifying widow(er)—$7,200
• Head of household—$6,350   • Married filing separately—$3,600   21

22 Subtract line 21 from line 19. If line 21 is more than line 19, enter -0-.   22

23 Multiply $2,750 by the total number of exemptions claimed on line 6d.   23

24 Subtract line 23 from line 22. If line 23 is more than line 22, enter -0-.
This is your **taxable income**.   ▶ 24

Tax, credits, and payments	25	Find the tax on the amount on line 24 (see page 34).	25

26 Credit for child and dependent care expenses.
Attach Schedule 2.   26

27 Credit for the elderly or the disabled. Attach
Schedule 3.   27

28 Child tax credit (see page 35).   28

29 Education credits. Attach Form 8863.   29

30 Adoption credit. Attach Form 8839.   30

31 Add lines 26 through 30. These are your **total credits.**   31

32 Subtract line 31 from line 25. If line 31 is more than line 25, enter -0-.   32

33 Advance earned income credit payments from Form(s) W-2.   33

34 Add lines 32 and 33. This is your **total tax.**   ▶ 34

35 Total Federal income tax withheld from
Forms W-2 and 1099.   35

36 1999 estimated tax payments and amount
applied from 1998 return.   36

37a Earned income credit. Attach
Schedule EIC if you have a qualifying child.   37a

b Nontaxable earned income:
amount ▶   and type ▶

38 Additional child tax credit. Attach Form 8812.   38

39 Add lines 35, 36, 37a, and 38. These are your **total payments.**   ▶ 39

Refund	40	If line 39 is more than line 34, subtract line 34 from line 39. This is the amount you **overpaid.**	40
Have it directly deposited! See page 47 and fill in 41b, 41c, and 41d.	41a	Amount of line 40 you want **refunded** to you.	41a

▶ b Routing
number   **▶ c** Type: ☐ Checking ☐ Savings

▶ d Account
number

42 Amount of line 40 you want **applied** to your
2000 estimated tax.   42

Amount you owe	43	If line 34 is more than line 39, subtract line 39 from line 34. This is the **amount you owe.** For details on how to pay, see page 48.	43
	44	Estimated tax penalty (see page 48). 44	

Sign here	Under penalties of perjury, I declare that I have examined this return and accompanying schedules and statements, and to the best of my knowledge and belief, they are true, correct, and accurately list all amounts and sources of income I received during the tax year. Declaration of preparer (other than the taxpayer) is based on all information of which the preparer has any knowledge.

Joint return?
See page 20.
Keep a copy for
your records.

Your signature	Date	Your occupation	Daytime telephone number (optional) ( )
Spouse's signature. If joint return, BOTH must sign	Date	Spouse's occupation	

Paid preparer's use only	Preparer's signature ▶

	Date	Check if self-employed ☐	Preparer's SSN or PTIN
Firm's name (or yours if self employed) and address ▶			EIN
			ZIP code

Form **1040A** (1999)

U.S. GPO 1999 456-058   ⊕ Printed on recycled paper

257

Free Application for Federal Student Aid

OMB 1845-0001   **July 1, 2000 — June 30, 2001 school year**

Use this form to apply for federal and state* student grants, work-study, and loans.

You can also apply over the Internet at **http://www.fafsa.ed.gov** instead of using this paper form. In addition to federal student aid, you may also be eligible for a Hope or a Lifetime Learning income tax credit, both of which you claim when you file your taxes. For more information on these tax credits, this application, and the U.S. Department of Education's student aid programs, look on the Internet at **http://www.ed.gov/studentaid** You can also call 1-800-4FED-AID (1-800-433-3243) Monday through Friday between 8:00am and 8:00pm eastern time. TTY users may call 1-800-730-8913.

Your answers on this form will be read by a machine. Therefore,

- use black ink or #2 pencil and fill in ovals completely, like this: ●

- print clearly in CAPITAL letters and skip a box between words: | I | 5 | | E | L | M | | S | T |

- report dollar amounts (such as $12,356.00) like this: $ | 1 | 2 | , | 3 | 5 | 6 | **(no cents)**

- write numbers less than 10 with a zero (0) first: | 0 | 7 |

Pink is for students and purple is for parents.

- If you are filing a **1999 income tax return**, we recommend that you fill it out before completing this form. However, you do not need to file your income tax return with the IRS before you fill out this form.
- After you complete this application, make a copy of it. Then send the original of pages 3 through 6 in the attached envelope or send it to Federal Student Aid Programs, P.O. Box 4015, Mt. Vernon, IL. 62864-8615.
- We must receive your application—pages 3 through 6— no earlier than **January 1, 2000, and no later than July 2, 2001.**
- You should hear from us within four weeks. If you do not, please call 1-800-433-3243.
- If you or your family has **unusual circumstances** (such as loss of employment) that might affect your need for student financial aid, submit this form and consult with the financial aid office at the college you plan to attend.
- You may also use this form to apply for **aid from other sources, such as your state or college.** The deadlines for states (see below) or colleges may be as early as January 2000 and may differ. You may be required to complete additional forms.

Now go to page 3 and begin filling out this form. Refer to the notes as needed.

Deadline dates for state aid. Generally, state aid comes from your state of legal residence. **Check with your high school guidance counselor** or the financial aid administrator at your college about state and college sources of student financial aid. State deadlines are below.

AZ June 30, 2001 *(date received)*
*^CA March 2, 2000 *(date postmarked)*
DE April 15, 2000 *(date received)*
* DC June 24, 2000 *(date received by state)*
FL May 15, 2000 *(date processed)*
HI March 1, 2000
IL First-time applicants – September 30, 2000
   Continuing applicants – June 30, 2000
   (date received)
^ IN For priority consideration – March 1, 2000
   (date postmarked)
^ IA June 1, 2000 *(date received)*
* KS For priority consideration – April 1, 2000
   (date received)
KY For priority consideration – March 15, 2000
   (date received)
^ LA For priority consideration April 15, 2000
   Final deadline – June 30, 2000
   (date received)

ME May 1, 2000 *(date received)*
MD March 1, 2000 *(date postmarked)*
^ MA For priority consideration - May 1, 2000
   (date received)
MI High school seniors - February 21, 2000
   College students – March 21, 2000
   (date received)
MN June 30, 2001 *(date received)*
MO April 1, 2000 *(date received)*
MT For priority consideration – March 1, 2000
   (date received)
NH May 1, 2000 *(date received)*
^ NJ June 1, 2000 if you received a
   Tuition Aid Grant in 1999-2000
   All other applicants
   – October 1, 2000, for fall and spring terms
   – March 1, 2001, for spring term only
   (date received)
*^NY May 1, 2001 *(date postmarked)*

NC March 15, 2000 *(date received)*
ND April 15, 2000 *(date processed)*
OH October 1, 2000 *(date received)*
OK April 30, 2000 *(date received)*
OR May 1, 2001 *(date received)*
* PA All 1999-2000 State grant recipients and all
   non-1999-2000 State grant recipients in
   degree programs - May 1, 2000
   All other applicants - August 1, 2000
   (date received)
PR May 2, 2001 *(date application signed)*
RI March 1, 2000 *(date received)*
SC June 30, 2000 *(date received)*
TN May 1, 2000 *(date processed)*
*^WV March 1, 2000 *(date received)*

Check with your financial aid administrator for these states: AL, AK, *AS, AR, CO, *CT, *FM, GA, *GU, ID, *MP, *MH, MS, *NE, *NV, *NM, *PW, *SD, *TX, UT, *VT, *VI, *VA, WA, WI, and *WY.

* *Additional form may be required*   ^ *Applicants encouraged to obtain proof of mailing*

258

Notes for questions 14–15 (page 3)

If you are an eligible noncitizen, write in your eight or nine digit Alien Registration Number. Generally, you are an eligible noncitizen if you are: (1) a U.S. permanent resident and you have an Alien Registration Receipt Card (I-551); (2) a conditional permanent resident (I-551C); or (3) an other eligible noncitizen with an Arrival-Departure Record (I-94) from the U.S. Immigration and Naturalization Service showing any one of the following designations: "Refugee," "Asylum Granted," "Indefinite Parole," "Humanitarian Parole," or "Cuban-Haitian Entrant." If you are in the U.S. on only an F1 or F2 student visa, or only a J1 or J2 exchange visitor visa, or a G series visa (pertaining to international organizations), you must fill in oval c. If you are neither a citizen nor eligible noncitizen, you are not eligible for federal student aid. However, you may be eligible for state or college aid. You should check with your financial aid administrator at your school before completing this form.

Notes for questions 18–22 (page 3)

For undergraduates, full time generally means taking at least 12 credit hours in a term or 24 clock hours per week. 3/4 time generally means taking at least 9 credit hours in a term or 18 clock hours per week. Half time generally means taking at least 6 credit hours in a term or 12 clock hours per week. Provide this information about the college you plan to attend.

Notes for question 31 (page 3) — Enter the correct number in the box in question 31.

Enter 1 for 1ˢᵗ bachelor's degree
Enter 2 for 2ⁿᵈ bachelor's degree
Enter 3 for associate degree (occupational or technical program)
Enter 4 for associate degree (general education or transfer program)
Enter 5 for certificate or diploma for completing an occupational, technical, or educational program of less than two years

Enter 6 for certificate or diploma for completing an occupational, technical, or educational program of at least two years
Enter 7 for teaching credential program (nondegree program)
Enter 8 for graduate or professional degree
Enter 9 for other/undecided

Notes for question 32 (page 3) — Enter the correct number in the box in question 32.

Enter 1 for 1st year undergraduate/never attended college
Enter 2 for 1st year undergraduate/attended college before
Enter 3 for 2nd year undergraduate/sophomore
Enter 4 for 3rd year undergraduate/junior

Enter 5 for 4th year undergraduate/senior
Enter 6 for 5th year/other undergraduate
Enter 7 for graduate/professional or beyond

Notes for questions 38 c. and d. (page 4) and 72 c. and d. (page 5)

If you filed or will file a foreign tax return, use the information from your foreign tax return to fill out this form. Convert all figures to U.S. dollars, using the exchange rate that is in effect today.

If you filed or will file a tax return with Puerto Rico, Guam, American Samoa, the Virgin Islands, the Marshall Islands, the Federated States of Micronesia, or Palau, use the information from these tax returns to fill out this form.

Notes for questions 39 (page 4) and 73 (page 5)

In general, a person is eligible to file a 1040A or 1040EZ if he or she makes less than $50,000, does not itemize deductions, does not receive income from his or her own business or farm, and does not receive alimony or capital gains. The person is not eligible if he or she itemizes deductions or receives self-employment income, alimony, or capital gains.

Notes for questions 42 (page 4) and 76 (page 5) — only for people who filed a 1040EZ or Telefile

On the 1040EZ, if a person answered "Yes" on line 5, use EZ worksheet line F to determine the number of exemptions ($2750 equals one exemption). If a person answered "No" on line 5, enter 01 if he or she is single, or 02 if he or she is married.

On the Telefile, use line J to determine the number of exemptions ($2750 equals one exemption).

Notes for questions 49–51 (page 4) and 83–85 (page 5)

Net worth means current value minus debt.

Investments include real estate (other than the home you live in), trust funds, money market funds, mutual funds, certificates of deposit, stocks, bonds, other securities, Education IRAs, installment and land sale contracts (including mortgages held), commodities, etc. Investment value includes the market value of these investments. Do not include the value of life insurance and retirement plans (pension funds, annuities, non-Education IRAs, Keogh plans, etc.) or the value of prepaid tuition plans. Investment debt means only those debts that are related to the investments.

Business value includes the market value of land, buildings, machinery, equipment, and inventory. Business debt means only those debts for which the business was used as collateral.

Notes for question 59 (page 4)

Answer "Yes" (you are a veteran) if (1) you have engaged in active service in the U.S. Armed Forces (Army, Navy, Air Force, Marines, and Coast Guard), or were a cadet or midshipman at one of the service academies, and (2) you were released under a condition other than dishonorable. Also answer "Yes" if you are not a veteran now but will be one by June 30, 2001.

Answer "No" (you are not a veteran) if (1) you have never served in the U.S. Armed Forces, or (2) you are currently an ROTC student, a cadet or midshipman at a service academy, or a National Guard or Reserves enlistee (and were not activated for duty). Also answer "No" if you are currently serving in the U.S. Armed Forces and will continue to serve through June 30, 2001.

Page 2

259

Free Application for Federal Student Aid

OMB 1845-0001

July 1, 2000 — June 30, 2001 school year

Step One: For questions 1-36, leave blank any questions that do not apply to you (the student).

1-3. Your full name (as it appears on your Social Security card)

1. LAST NAME	2. FIRST NAME	3. M.I.

4-7. Your permanent mailing address

4. NUMBER AND STREET (INCLUDE APARTMENT NUMBER)

5. CITY (AND COUNTRY, IF NOT U.S.)   6. STATE   7. ZIP CODE

8. Your Social Security Number — AREA CODE

9. Your date of birth   MONTH / DAY / YEAR   1 9

10. Your permanent telephone number   AREA CODE

11. Do you have a driver's license?   Yes ○ 1   No ○ 2

12-13. Driver's license number and state   12. LICENSE NUMBER   13. STATE

14. Are you a U.S. citizen? Pick one. See Page 2.

   a. Yes, I am a U.S. citizen. .... ○ 1

   b. No, but I am an *eligible noncitizen*. Fill in question 15. ○ 2   **15.** ALIEN REGISTRATION NUMBER   A

   c. No, I am not a citizen or *eligible noncitizen*. .... ○ 3

16. Marital status as of today

   I am single, divorced, or widowed. ○ 1

   I am married. ○ 2

   I am separated. ○ 3

17. Month and year you were married, separated, divorced, or widowed   MONTH / YEAR

For each question (18 - 22), please mark whether you will be <u>full time</u>, <u>3/4 time</u>, <u>half time</u>, less than half time, or not attending. Mark "Full time" if you are not sure. See page 2.

18. Summer 2000	Full time ○ 1	3/4 time ○ 2	Half time ○ 3	Less than half time ○ 4	Not attending ○ 5
19. Fall semester or quarter 2000	Full time ○ 1	3/4 time ○ 2	Half time ○ 3	Less than half time ○ 4	Not attending ○ 5
20. Winter quarter 2000-2001	Full time ○ 1	3/4 time ○ 2	Half time ○ 3	Less than half time ○ 4	Not attending ○ 5
21. Spring semester or quarter 2001	Full time ○ 1	3/4 time ○ 2	Half time ○ 3	Less than half time ○ 4	Not attending ○ 5
22. Summer 2001	Full time ○ 1	3/4 time ○ 2	Half time ○ 3	Less than half time ○ 4	Not attending ○ 5
23. Highest school your father completed	Middle school/Jr. High ○ 1	High school ○ 2	College or beyond ○ 3	Other/unknown ○ 4	
24. Highest school your mother completed	Middle school/Jr. High ○ 1	High school ○ 2	College or beyond ○ 3	Other/unknown ○ 4	

25. What is your state of legal residence?   STATE

26. Did you become a legal resident of this state before January 1, 1995?   Yes ○ 1   No ○ 2

27. If the answer to question 26 is "No," give month and year you became a legal resident.   MONTH / YEAR

28. If you have **never** been convicted of any illegal drug offense, enter "1" in the box and go to question 29. A drug-related conviction does not necessarily make you ineligible for aid; call 1-800-433-3243 or go to http://www.fafsa.cd.gov/q28 to find out how to fill out this question.

29. Most male students must register with Selective Service to get federal aid. Are you male?   Yes ○ 1   No ○ 2

30. If you are male (age 18-25) and not registered, do you want Selective Service to register you?   Yes ○ 1   No ○ 2

31. What degree or certificate will you be working towards during 2000-2001? See page 2 and enter the correct number in the box.

32. What will be your grade level when you begin the 2000-2001 school year? See page 2 and enter the correct number in the box.

33. Will you have a high school diploma or GED before you enroll?   Yes ○ 1   No ○ 2

34. Will you have your first bachelor's degree before July 1, 2000?   Yes ○ 1   No ○ 2

35. In addition to grants, are you interested in student loans (which you must pay back)?   Yes ○ 1   No ○ 2

36. In addition to grants, are you interested in "work-study" (which you earn through work)?   Yes ○ 1   No ○ 2

Page 3

Step Two: For 37-51, if you (the student) are now married (even if you were not married in 1999), report both your and your spouse's income and assets. Ignore references to "spouse" if you are currently single, separated, divorced, or widowed.

37. For 1999, have you filed your IRS income tax return or another tax return listed in question 38?

   a. I have already filed. ○ 1   **b.** I will file, but I have not yet filed. ○ 2   **c.** I'm not going to file. (Skip to question 44.) ○ 3

38. What income tax return did you file or will you file for 1999?

   a. IRS 1040 .... ○ 1   **c.** A foreign tax return. See Page 2. .... ○ 3

   b. IRS 1040A, 1040EZ, 1040Telefile ...... ○ 2   **d.** A tax return for Puerto Rico, Guam, American Samoa, the Virgin Islands, the Marshall Islands, the Federated States of Micronesia, or Palau. See Page 2. ...... ○ 4

39. If you have filed or will file a 1040, were you eligible to file a 1040A or 1040EZ? See page 2.   Yes ○ 1   No/don't know ○ 2

For questions 40-53, if the answer is zero or the question does not apply to you, enter 0.

40. What was your (and spouse's) adjusted gross income for 1999? Adjusted gross income is on IRS Form 1040–line 33; 1040A–line 18; 1040EZ–line 4; or Telefile–line I.

41. Enter the total amount of your (and spouse's) income tax for 1999. Income tax amount is on IRS Form 1040–line 49 plus 51; 1040A–line 32; 1040EZ–line 10; or Telefile–line K.

42. Enter your (and spouse's) exemptions. Exemptions are on IRS Form 1040–line 6d, or on Form 1040A–line 6d. For Form 1040EZ or Telefile, see page 2.

43. Enter your Earned Income Credit from IRS Form 1040–line 59a; 1040A–line 37a; 1040EZ–line 8a; or Telefile–line L.

44-45. How much did you (and spouse) earn from working in 1999? Answer this question whether or not you filed a tax return. This information may be on your W-2 forms, or on IRS Form 1040–lines 7, 12, and 18; 1040A–line 7; or 1040EZ–line 1. Telefilers should use their W-2's.   You (44) $ Your Spouse (45) $

46. Go to page 8 of this form; complete the column on the left of **Worksheet A**, enter student total here. $

47. Go to page 8 of this form; complete the column on the left of **Worksheet B**, enter student total here. $

48. Total current balance of cash, savings, and checking accounts $

For 49-51, if net worth is one million or more, enter $999,999. If net worth is negative, enter 0.

49. Current net worth of investments (investment value minus investment debt) See page 2. $

50. Current net worth of business (business value minus business debt) See page 2. $

51. Current net worth of investment farm (Don't include a farm that you live on and operate.) $

52-53. If you receive veterans education benefits, for **how many months** from July 1, 2000 through June 30, 2001 will you receive these benefits, and **what amount** will you receive per month? Do not include your spouse's veterans education benefits.   Months (52)   Amount (53) $

Step Three: Answer all six questions in this step.

54. Were you born before January 1, 1977? .... Yes ○ 1   No ○ 2

55. Will you be working on a degree beyond a bachelor's degree in school year 2000-2001? .... Yes ○ 1   No ○ 2

56. As of today, are you married? (Answer yes if you are separated, but not divorced.) .... Yes ○ 1   No ○ 2

57. Answer "Yes" if: (1) You have children who receive more than half of their support from you; **or** (2) You have dependents (other than your children or spouse) who live with you and receive more than half of their support from you, now and through June 30, 2001.... Yes ○ 1   No ○ 2

58. Are you an orphan or ward of the court or were you a ward of the court until age 18? .... Yes ○ 1   No ○ 2

59. Are you a veteran of the U.S. Armed Forces? See page 2. .... Yes ○ 1   No ○ 2

If you (the student) answer "No" to every question in Step Three, go to Step Four.

If you answer "Yes" to any question in Step Three, skip Step Four and go to Step Five.

(If you are a graduate health profession student, you may be required to complete Step Four even if you answered "Yes" to any question in Step Three.)   Page 4

Step Four: Complete this step if you (the student) answered "No" to all questions in Step Three. Please tell us about your parents. **See page 7 for who is considered a parent.**

60. Parents' marital status as of today? (Pick one.) Married ○ ₁ Single ○ ₂ Divorced/Separated ○ ₃ Widowed ○ ₄

61-62. Your father's Social Security Number and last name
61. FATHER'S/STEPFATHER'S SSN ☐☐☐-☐☐-☐☐☐☐   **62. FATHER'S/STEPFATHER'S LAST NAME** ☐☐☐☐☐☐☐☐☐☐☐☐☐☐☐☐

63-64. Your mother's Social Security Number and last name
63. MOTHER'S/STEPMOTHER'S SSN ☐☐☐-☐☐-☐☐☐☐   **64. MOTHER'S/STEPMOTHER'S LAST NAME** ☐☐☐☐☐☐☐☐☐☐☐☐☐☐☐☐

65. How many people are in your parents' household? See page 7.

66. How many in question 65 (**exclude your parents**) will be college students between July 1, 2000, and June 30, 2001? See page 7.

STATE

67. What is your parents' state of legal residence?

68. Did your parents become legal residents of the state in question 67 before January 1, 1995?   Yes ○ ₁   No ○ ₂

69. If the answer to question 68 is "No," give the month and year legal residency began for the parent who has lived in the state the longest.   **MONTH YEAR** ☐☐ / ☐☐☐☐

70. What is the age of your older parent?

71. For 1999, have your parents filed their IRS income tax return or another tax return listed in **question 72?**
   a. My parents have already filed. ○ ₁   b. My parents will file, but they have not yet filed. ○ ₂   c. My parents are not going to file. **(Skip to question 78.)** ○ ₃

72. What income tax return did your parents file or will they file for 1999?
   a. IRS 1040 .... ○ ₁   c. A foreign tax return. **See Page 2.** .... ○ ₃
   b. IRS 1040A, 1040EZ, 1040Telefile ..... ○ ₂   d. A tax return for Puerto Rico, Guam, American Samoa, the Virgin Islands, the Marshall Islands, the Federated States of Micronesia, or Palau. **See Page 2.** ...... ○ ₄

73. If your parents have filed or will file a 1040, were they eligible to file a 1040A or 1040EZ? See page 2.   Yes ○ ₁ No/ don't know ○ ₂

For 74 - 85, if the answer is zero or the question does not apply, enter 0.

74. What was your parents' adjusted gross income for 1999? Adjusted gross income is on IRS Form 1040–line 33; 1040A–line 18; 1040EZ–line 4; or Telefile–line I. $☐☐☐,☐☐☐

75. Enter the total amount of your parents' income tax for 1999. Income tax amount is on IRS Form 1040–line 49 plus 51; 1040A–line 32; 1040EZ–line 10; or Telefile–line K. $☐☐☐,☐☐☐

76. Enter your parents' exemptions. Exemptions are on IRS Form 1040–line 6d or on Form 1040A–line 6d. For Form 1040EZ or Telefile, see page 2.   ☐☐

77. Enter your parents' Earned Income Credit from IRS Form 1040–line 59a; 1040A–line 37a; 1040EZ–line 8a; or Telefile–line L. $☐☐☐,☐☐☐

78-79. How much did your parents earn from working in 1999? Answer this question whether or not your parents filed a tax return. This information may be on their W-2 forms, or on IRS Form 1040–lines 7, 12, and 18; 1040A–line 7; or 1040EZ–line 1. Telefilers should use their W-2's.
   Father/ Stepfather (78) $☐☐☐,☐☐☐
   Mother/ Stepmother (79) $☐☐☐,☐☐☐

80. Go to page 8 of this form; complete the column on the right of **Worksheet A**; enter parent total here. $☐☐☐,☐☐☐

81. Go to page 8 of this form; complete the column on the right of **Worksheet B**; enter parent total here. $☐☐☐,☐☐☐

82. Total current balance of cash, savings, and checking accounts $☐☐☐,☐☐☐

For 83–85, if net worth is one million or more, enter $999,999. If net worth is negative, enter 0.

83. Current **net worth** of investments (investment value minus investment debt) See page 2. $☐☐☐,☐☐☐

84. Current **net worth** of business (business value minus business debt) See page 2. $☐☐☐,☐☐☐

85. Current **net worth** of investment farm (Don't include a farm that your parents live on and operate.) $☐☐☐,☐☐☐

Now go to Step Six.   **Page 5**

Step Five: Complete this step only if you (the student) answered "Yes" to any question in Step Three.

86. How many people are in your (and your spouse's) household? See page 7.

87. How many in question 86 will be college students between July 1, 2000, and June 30, 2001? Do not include your parents. See page 7.

Step Six: Please tell us which schools should receive your information.

For each school (up to six), please provide the federal school code and your housing plans (enter "1" for on campus, "2" for off campus, and "3" for with parents). Look for the federal school codes on the Internet at http://www.ed.gov/studentaid, at your college financial aid office, at your public library, or by asking your high school guidance counselor. If you cannot get the federal school code, write in the complete name, address, city, and state of the college.

Federal school code	OR Name of college	College street address and city	State	Housing Plans
FIRST SCHOOL CODE				89.
88.				
SECOND SCHOOL CODE				91.
90.				
THIRD SCHOOL CODE				93.
92.				
FOURTH SCHOOL CODE				95.
94.				
FIFTH SCHOOL CODE				97.
96.				
SIXTH SCHOOL CODE				99.
98.				

Step Seven: Please read, sign, and date.

By signing this application, you agree, if asked, to provide information that will verify the accuracy of your completed form. This information may include a copy of your U.S. or state income tax form. Also, you certify that you (1) will use federal and/or state student financial aid only to pay the cost of attending an institution of higher education, (2) are not in default on a federal student loan or have made satisfactory arrangements to repay it, (3) do not owe money back on a federal student grant or have made satisfactory arrangements to repay it, (4) will notify your school if you default on a federal student loan, and (5) understand that the Secretary of Education has the authority to verify income reported on this application with the Internal Revenue Service. If you purposely give false or misleading information, you may be fined $10,000, sent to prison, or both.

100. Date this form was completed.

MONTH   DAY   / 2000 ○ or 2001 ○

101. Student signature   (Sign in box)

Parent signature (one parent whose information is provided in Step Four.)   (Sign in box)

If this form was filled out by someone other than you, your spouse, or your parent(s), that person must complete this part.

Preparer's Name and Firm _____

Address _____

102. Social Security #

OR

103. Employer ID #

SCHOOL USE ONLY
D/O   Federal School Code

FAA SIGNATURE

104. Signature and Date

MDE USE ONLY
Special Handle

Page 6

263

Notes for questions 60–85 (page 5) **Step Four:** Who is considered a <u>parent</u> in this Step?

If your parents are both living and married to each other, answer the questions about them. (You will be providing information about two people.)

If your parent is widowed or single, answer the questions about that parent. (You will be providing information about one person.) If your widowed parent has remarried as of today, answer the questions about that parent and the person whom your parent married. (You will be providing information about two people.)

If your parents have divorced or separated, answer the questions about the parent you lived with more during the past 12 months. If you did not live with one parent more than the other, give answers about the parent who provided more financial support during the last 12 months, or during the most recent year that you actually were supported by a parent. (You will be providing information about one person.) If this parent has remarried as of today, answer the questions on the rest of this form about that parent and the person whom your parent married. (You will be providing information about two people.)

Notes for question 65 (page 5)

Include in your <u>parents' household</u>:

- yourself and your parents, and
- your parents' other children if (a) your parents will provide more than half of their support from July 1, 2000 through June 30, 2001 or (b) the children could answer "No" to every question in Step Three, and
- other people if they now live with your parents, your parents provide more than half of their support and will continue to provide more than half of their support from July 1, 2000 through June 30, 2001.

Notes for questions 66 (page 5) and 87 (page 6)

Count yourself as a <u>college student</u> even if you will attend college less than half time in 2000-2001. **Do not include your parents.** Include others only if they will attend at least half time in 2000-2001 in a program that leads to a college degree or certificate.

Notes for question 86 (page 6)

Include in your (and your spouse's) <u>household</u>:

- yourself (and your spouse, if you have one), and
- your children, if you will provide more than half of their support from July 1, 2000 through June 30, 2001, and
- other people if they now live with you, and you provide more than half of their support and will continue to provide more than half of their support from July 1, 2000 through June 30, 2001.

Information on the Privacy Act and use of your Social Security Number.

We use the information that you provide on this form to determine if you are eligible to receive federal student financial aid and the amount that you are eligible to receive. Section 483 of the Higher Education Act of 1965, as amended, gives us the authority to ask you and your parents these questions, and to collect the social security numbers of you and your parents.

State and institutional student financial aid programs may also use the information that you provide on this form to determine if you are eligible to receive state and institutional aid and the need that you have for such aid. Therefore, we will disclose the information that you provide on this form to each institution you list in questions 88–99, state agencies in your state of legal residence, and the state agencies of the states in which the colleges that you list in questions 88–99 are located.

If you are applying solely for federal aid, you must answer all of the following questions that apply to you: 1–9, 14–16, 25, 28–30, 33–34, 37–41, 43–51, 54–60, 65–67, 70–75, 77-87, and 100–101. If you do not answer these questions, you will not receive federal aid.

Without your consent, we may disclose information that you provide to entities under a published "routine use." Under such a routine use, we may disclose information to third parties that we have authorized to assist us in administering the above programs; to other federal agencies under computer matching programs, such as those with the Internal Revenue Service, Social Security Administration, Selective Service System, Immigration and Naturalization Service, and Veterans Administration; to your parents or spouse; and to members of Congress if you ask them to help you with student aid questions.

If the federal government, the U.S. Department of Education, or an employee of the U.S. Department of Education is involved in litigation, we may send information to the Department of Justice, or a court or adjudicative body, if the disclosure is related to financial aid and certain conditions are met. In addition, we may send your information to a foreign, federal, state, or local enforcement agency if the information that you submitted indicates a violation or potential violation of law, for which that agency has jurisdiction for investigation or prosecution. Finally, we may send information regarding a claim that is determined to be valid and overdue to a consumer reporting agency. This information includes identifiers from the record; the amount, status, and history of the claim; and the program under which the claim arose.

State Certification.

By submitting this application, you are giving your state financial aid agency permission to verify any statement on this form and to obtain income tax information for all persons required to report income on this form.

The Paperwork Reduction Act of 1995

The Paperwork Reduction Act of 1995 says that no one is required to respond to a collection of information unless it displays a valid OMB control number, which for this form is 1845-0001. The time required to complete this form is estimated to be one hour, including time to review instructions, search data resources, gather the data needed, and complete and review the information collection. If you have comments about this estimate or suggestions for improving this form, please write to: U.S. Department of Education, Washington DC 20202-4651.

Page 7

Worksheets — Even though you may have few of these items, check carefully.

Do not mail these worksheets in with your application. Keep these worksheets with a copy of your application.

_____ Worksheet A _____

For question 46: Enter and add together all of the following that apply to you (and your spouse) in the column on the left. Enter the total amount in question 46 on page 4.

For question 80: Enter and add together all of the following that apply to your parents in the column on the right (if you are required to complete Step 4 of the application). Enter the total amount in question 80 on page 5.

For question 46 Student (and spouse)	Calendar Year 1999	For question 80 Parent(s)
$_____	Payments to tax-deferred pension and savings plans (paid directly or withheld from earnings), including amounts reported on the W-2 Form in Box 13, codes D, E, F, G, H, and S. Include untaxed portions of 401(k) and 403(b) plans.	$_____
$_____	Deductible IRA and/or Keogh payments: IRS Form 1040-total of lines 23 and 29; or 1040A-line 15	$_____
$_____	Child support received for all children. Don't include foster care or adoption payments.	$_____
$_____	Welfare benefits, including Temporary Assistance for Needy Families (TANF). Don't include food stamps.	$_____
$_____	Tax exempt interest income from IRS Form 1040-line 8b; or 1040A-line 8b	$_____
$_____	Foreign income exclusion from IRS Form 2555-line 43; or 2555EZ-line 18	$_____
$_____	Untaxed portions of pensions from IRS Form 1040-(line 15a minus 15b) plus (16a minus 16b); or 1040A (line 10a minus 10b) plus (11a minus 11b) excluding rollovers	$_____
$_____	Credit for federal fuels on special fuels from IRS Form 4136-line 9 - nonfarmers only	$_____
$_____	Social Security benefits received that were not taxed	$_____
$_____	Housing, food, and other living allowances paid to members of the military, clergy, and others (including cash payments and cash value of benefits)	$_____
$_____	Workers' Compensation	$_____
$_____	Veterans noneducation benefits, such as Death Pension or Dependency & Indemnity Compensation (DIC)	$_____
$_____	Any other untaxed income and benefits, such as VA Educational Work-Study allowances, untaxed portions of Railroad Retirement Benefits, Black Lung Benefits, Refugee Assistance, etc. Don't include student aid, educational WIA (formerly JTPA) benefits, or benefits from flexible spending arrangements, e.g., cafeteria plans.	$_____
$_____	Cash received, or any money paid on your behalf, not reported elsewhere on this form	XXXXXXXXX
$_____ (Enter this amount in question 46.)		(Enter this amount in question 80.) $_____
Student (and spouse) total		**Parent(s) total**

_____ Worksheet B _____

For question 47: Enter and add together all of the following that apply to you (and your spouse) in the column on the left. Enter the total amount in question 47 on page 4.

For question 81: Enter and add together all of the following that apply to your parents in the column on the right (if you are required to complete Step 4 of the application). Enter the total amount in question 81 on page 5.

For question 47 Student (and spouse)	Calendar Year 1999	For question 81 Parent(s)
$_____	Education credits (Hope and Lifetime Learning Tax Credits) from IRS Form 1040-line 44; or 1040A-line 29.	$_____
$_____	Child support paid because of divorce or separation. Do not include support for children in your (or your parents') household, as reported in question 86 (or question 65 for your parents).	$_____
$_____	Taxable earnings from Federal Work-Study or other need-based work programs	$_____
$_____	AmeriCorps awards — living allowances only	$_____
$_____	Student grant and scholarship aid (in excess of the tuition, fees, books, and supplies) that was reported to the IRS in question 40 for students and 74 for parents	$_____
$_____ (Enter this amount in question 47.)		(Enter this amount in question 81.) $_____
Student (and spouse) total		**Parent(s) total**

Page 8

265

Index

About the Authors

MARJOLIJN BIJLEFELD is an author and editor. She is the author of *The Gun Control Debate: A Documentary History* (Greenwood Press, 1997) and *People For and Against Gun Control* (Greenwood Press, 1999).

SHARON K. ZOUMBARIS is a professional librarian, freelance writer, and storyteller.